by George

The Wit and Wisdom
of George Davis

AuthorHouse™
1663 Liberty Drive
Bloomington, IN 47403
www.authorhouse.com
Phone: 1-800-839-8640
© 2009 George H. Davis. All rights reserved.

No part of this book may be reproduced, stored in a retrieval system, or transmitted by any means without the written permission of the author.

First published by AuthorHouse 6/17/2009
Printed in the United States of America
Bloomington, Indiana

This book is printed on acid-free paper.

ISBN: 978-1-4389-8942-6 (e)
ISBN: 978-1-4389-8941-9 (sc)
ISBN: 978-1-4389-8943-3 (hc)

To George

He's a good man, a wise man -- I call him my friend
When the going gets tough -- He will not break or bend
He'll just size up an issue, decide what is right
Then guard and defend it -- with all of his might.

He's a preacher, a teacher, but no Holy Joe
And if you have a problem -- To him you can go.
Then "By George" he will help you. His judgment is sound
His head may be in the air, but his feet on the ground.

He has a great sense of humor - gets a bang out of life
With three sons and Jane and Leona, his wife
We know that his life has been fruitful and full
Maybe sometimes quite hectic, but it's never been dull

I've known him in pleasure, I've seen him in pain
I've shared in his loss - I've rejoiced in his gain
As he walks down life's highway - you know that you can
Say with every assurance, Friend, there goes a man

One of life's greatest blessing, Is to have such a friend
May his seed multiply, may his tribe never end
For Heaven alone will be able to save us
If we run out of men of the stripe of George Davis

by David Dickey

The Tie
Mt. Erie/Greater Wabash Baptist Association
April 1973 – August 1980

A New Era

It hardly seems possible, but I've just completed one month as missionary of the Mt. Erie Baptist Association. My doesn't time fly when you're having fun!

These have been busy days. I have been getting settled, finding churches, attending meetings, meeting people, and preaching. I have preached ten times this month. I have visited three churches in revival.

I have discovered that one could almost keep busy simply visiting revivals. There seems to be one or more going on all the time. Next week there are five in our Association. (I'm afraid I won't make all of them.)

Work on the additional bedroom at the missionary's home is progressing nicely. The room is closed in now. The walls will be paneled and the floor carpeted. A large closet and a small bath are being fixed along the North side.

I don't know when my family has received a warmer welcome than we did here in Fairfield. Men were ready to help us move in. Meals were brought to our home. It has been a real joy meeting new people and making new friends.

A special word of appreciation is due Norris Price. During this time without a missionary, he has served as Director of the Baptist Hour. He is also chairman of the committee to turn the carport into a bedroom. He has spent a good deal of time and I know you join me in saying, "Thank you, Norris."

I also appreciate the work of the committee to secure a missionary. I suppose it would be immodest of me to call attention to their wisdom in recommending me. But seriously, they have been most kind and considerate of me and of the church I was serving.

Brother Kelley has also carried extra responsibility during this period of adjustment. He has seen that the work of the Association and planning for camp progressed.

Now, a word about the paper. I have had to compile a mailing list from hither and yon. I want to include the associational officers, pastors, church officers, and board members. If you are getting two copies please let me know. If you are not getting any . . . how did you get this? Let me know about others who should be included.

The First Baptist church in Fairfield has provided an office. Come in the back door (on the South) and go down the hall until you come to the first room on the right. I plan to visit on the field each morning and be in the office in the afternoon. I haven't kept that schedule very well so far, but that is still my plan.

My phone-number here is 847-3041. The home phone is still 842-2744.

April 1973

by George

What is a Baptist association?

I doubt that many of us have thought through the purpose of our association. We assume that Baptists have always had associations and always will.

District associations do go way back in Baptist life. Within thirty years of the establishment of Baptist churches in England, they were forming associations. In this country, it took sixty-three years.

Some would look on associations as a carryover from a bygone era — an appendage to the body of Christ which has outlived its usefulness.

I believe the association exists for the sake of the churches. The churches come first, not only in time but in function as well. It is the job of the association to strengthen the churches.

This is reflected in the constitution of our state convention. "The purpose of this Convention is to assist in establishing and developing Baptist churches...."

A group of leaders in Williamson Association drew up a statement of their objectives a few years ago:

(1) To afford and promote a larger fellowship of Christians in the work of Christ.
(2) To discover needs which cannot be met effectively by churches individually, and to coordinate the use of resources in meeting these needs.
(3) To provide programs and projects to strengthen the churches and to assist them in achieving their objectives and goals.
(4) To encourage every church to support the missionary, educational, and benevolent causes of the Association, the Illinois Baptist State Association, and the Southern Baptist Convention.
(5) To discuss such subjects as biblical doctrines, polity, and ethical standards and to interpret the Baptist position.

If the association exists to help the churches, then our talk about how cooperative or uncooperative a pastor or church is may be out of place. Maybe we should ask instead how we can help that pastor and church to do the work God expects them to do.

Meetings and projects need to be seen, not as something we have to drum up attendance for but, as a means to meeting the needs of churches for assistance in special areas.

Our need for fellowship certainly has not diminished. We shall surely be poorer if we see ourselves only as isolated congregations in a hostile world. We need not only the presence of God's Holy Spirit — we need each other!

May 1973

Nominating Committees

This is the time when some very important decisions are being made by churches. Nominating committees are meeting or will be soon. Workers are being selected to serve this coming year. They will set the pattern for the church for years to come.

George H. Davis

I have found it helpful at times to elect the nominating committee by ballot at a Sunday morning service. Members could be instructed to write down three or five names of persons they feel should serve. When these have been tabulated, the top three or five are contacted to see if they will serve. If not, you simply go to the next person on the list.

It is also helpful for the committee to have a complete list of the resident membership of the church. Ideally every church member should have a place of service suited to his talents and abilities. Perhaps not everyone should teach, but all can use God-given gifts.

Some will serve through the church organizations. Others may serve as effectively through other organizations in the community. Both are sharing their faith in Christ and bearing witness to his salvation.

As the nominating committee considers a person for a job they should ask, "Could this person do the job?" and "Would they be acceptable to the church?" The committee has no right to try to answer the question of whether the person will take the job or not. Only the person may answer that.

One person should be selected for the job and someone should be chosen to contact them. This contact should be made personally. Do not stop a person in the hall at church and ask them to teach. If the job is really important it deserves a visit in the home. Don't try to enlist workers over the phone — it's awfully easy to say "no" there.

On the other hand, I don't feel we should beg people to work. They should be told what the job is and what they can expect to work with. Materials should probably be taken and shown to the prospective worker. I would try to get a decision then. Most people will know when first contacted if they will serve.

If we leave people without asking them to give us their decision, they may doubt our earnestness. Some may ask for time to consider the decision and this should be granted. Set a time (soon) to get an answer.

June 1973

Busy! Busy!

Phew!!!

I didn't know one person could be so busy!

I just finished a one week revival with Dan Zoeller at Barnhill. Enjoyed getting to know the folks there.

This week and next I'm getting the paper out and getting Camp materials out. I'm also meeting on Tuesday nights with a group of Young Adults from North Side Church to study Revelation (among other things).

On July 13-15 the family will be returning to Charleston for a Baptist Student Union Retreat in Forest Gregg's pasture. We were there last summer and had a great time. I don't know whether they liked my preaching or my wife's cooking.

On Monday, July 16 I begin helping the Ten Post Oak Church with a Vacation Bible School

by George

After that I think I'll be ready for a vacation.

We plan to take off the last week of July and into August. We'll be back a week and catch up before Youth Camp.

Folks continue to ask how I like the work and how we are getting along in the house. I keep saying, "Fine, Fine." And I really mean it on both counts.

So often we use "fine" as a by-word when we don't really want to get involved in a detailed answer. But I am enjoying my experience as an associational missionary. Individuals and churches continue to respond and request assistance. In some cases I can provide help. In others I can refer them to someone who can help.

I value my years as a pastor highly and feel I know something of the joys and disappointments of churches. I am resolved to try to help pastors and churches to do the work God wants us to do.

We had a good response to the Preacher's Family Picnic, June 30. There were nine families present with 30 people eating, hiking, and visiting. We're going to do it again soon.

The enclosure of the carport to make another bedroom has made the house quite comfortable. We really appreciate your provision for us. You have been most considerate of our needs.

Let's continue to remember Allen England, pastor at Olive Branch. He has suffered a heart attack and will be off work and out of his pulpit for about two months.

Let's also remember Grayville First and Wayne City as they seek a pastor and Carmi First as they seek a music and education worker.

July 1973

My First Youth Camp

I'm looking forward to my first Youth Camp.

My whole camp experience to date is spending one night as a watchman two years ago.

As I recall, Homer Short and I spent the night listening to a ball game, talking about fishing, squirrel hunting, and farming.

I believe we admitted one car to the grounds – parents bringing a camper something or another.

I'm glad to have an experienced hand like Dewitt Kelley directing the Camp. He has been working in Camp for about as long as he's been around – going on 7 years now.

I have sensed a great deal of excitement about Camp. Almost everywhere I have gone, folks have asked about Camp.

Young people have been planning for some time to attend. Their enthusiasm is rubbing off – others are deciding to come.

New registrations are coming in every day. It's not too late! If campers show up Monday (with parent's permission) we'll take them.

George H. Davis

Camp can mean a great deal to youth. Not only for the initial conversion experience, but for growth and maturity as a Christian.

They need each other for fellowship and encouragement. Spending five days with other youth and growing adults can be a great experience.

Pray that the Holy Spirit will bathe all of us with His presence and power.

August 1973

What's Next?

Well, Camp is over and the Association is coming!
What is it about out of the frying pan into the fire?
Busy days! Busy days!
Camp is over but not forgotten. How could you forget the kids? I guess I have never been so aware of the tremendous importance of the family.

Broken homes certainly have their effect on the children. They can be hurt spiritually as well as socially and emotionally.

I am impressed with the great need for churches to minister to families in distress.

Before the Association, I plan to attend an orientation session for new missionaries at the Home Mission Board in Atlanta.

I'll be there September 17-19. 32 of us will be considering concepts of associational work under the leadership of men with wide experience.

Almost daily I realize anew how big a job you have given me. I continue to rejoice in it and I am also more than ever aware of my need of your prayers and God's help.

September 1973

It was a *Great Day!*

The churches in Mt. Erie Association experienced a 15% increase in Sunday School attendance last Sunday, October 28 over a week ago. It was a Great Day!

15 churches that set attendance goals for the Day had an 18% increase. They were up 24% over a year ago! It *was* a Great Day!

This tells me that anytime we want to increase our Sunday School attendance by 15%, we can do it. If we are willing to contact people and invite them to Sunday School, we can reach them for Christ.

I don't want to minimize other factors — good teachers, adequate space, appropriate organization, and challenging literature. But I believe the primary factor in Sunday School growth is our concern for people. Without this all our other provisions are wasted.

If you want to reach more people for Christ, let them know you care about them! It may surprise them!

by George

Speaking of surprises – I remember taking my car to a garage for some work. All the mechanics were busy so the shop foreman worked on my car. When he had finished, I asked him what I owed him. "You probably couldn't pay me what I'm worth," he laughingly replied. I laughingly agreed with him, thanked him, and drove off. But I haven't forgotten him.

You probably can't pay your pastor what he's worth! The thing that really disturbs me though is that many churches go out to "hire" a preacher for as little as they can get him.

The joke maybe on them though. They may get about what they pay for! Churches that pay their pastor as little as they can get by with may find they have little preacher.

If your pastor has to worry about how he's going to pay his bills he's not going to be his best in studying and sharing God's word and in ministering in the community. All of us have some concern over our finances and preachers need to be careful in managing their money. But churches should attempt to pay their pastor a livable salary.

Your pastor likely won't ask for more money, but he probably should have it!

November 1973

Energy Crisis

The energy crisis is not new to Baptist churches.

For years we have tried to lead people to serve Christ wholeheartedly and have gotten a halfhearted response. Only about half our resident members are actively involved in the life of our churches.

Many of our churches are not finding it hard to raise the money needed to finance their work. But, they are having difficulty reaching people for Christ.

Perhaps the real crisis is we too often depend on our own plans and ingenuity to get the job done. We attempt to do spiritual tasks with physical power. We forget the word of the Lord to Zerubbabel, "Not by might, nor by power, but by my Spirit." (Zechariah 4:6)

We certainly ought to use the best intelligence we have in planning and promoting God's work, but let us never forget "God gives the increase." (1 Corinthians 3:6)

Again,
> The horse is made ready for the day of battle,
> but the victory belongs to the Lord.
> (Proverbs 21:31)

Perhaps our greatest need is to recognize the energy available to us and to use it in serving God. Or, perhaps we should say, let God energize us for his work.

Let us remember the power of Jesus is given us as we make disciples. As we are faithful in baptizing and teaching them we can expect the blessing of his presence with us.

George H. Davis

A part of our energy crisis is due to our own laziness. We have become a society of spectators. We like to watch somebody else do a good job or, criticize him if he doesn't.

This attitude has affected our churches. We attend services to watch performances by the music director, choir, and preacher. If they don't suit our fancy, we wonder what was wrong with <u>them</u>. It may not occur to <u>us</u> worship is an individual as well as a congregational affair.

May God grant you the joy of Christmas throughout the new year!

May you learn again to lean upon God for power for service as you did for power for salvation.

December 1973

Bible Study

My family joins me in thanking you for the generous Christmas gift. You were very thoughtful. Many of you also sent cards. Thank you. It has been a joy to share in your lives during this past year. I look forward to many more.

I persuaded my wife to let me use some of the money to buy a turntable for a stereo AM/FM radio we have. I had wanted one for some time but hadn't been willing to part with that much money. Now we are enjoying some great music with our meals.

The only problem is my kids prefer music with a pretty heavy beat and I like something quite a bit smoother. Maybe the answer is the set of headphones they have been wanting.

Bible study is at the heart of the work of the church. Perhaps nothing we do is more important than helping people understand and apply Bible truth to everyday life.

But, there are some dangers in Bible study. Sometimes we study only out of idle curiosity. We don't intend to apply God's truth to our life. We just want to win our argument.

I see a danger in making God's Word fit our pet ideas. We take a verse here and another there and prove we are right! We need to approach the Bible with an open heart and mind. We have to learn from God before we can teach others.

Another danger is to consider the Bible a closed book – to feel the average Christian cannot understand it. Some seem to feel that only a few "initiated" preachers really know what the Bible means. Hogwash!

I get upset when I hear people say they don't believe some part of the Bible was meant to be understood. Why do we have it? Was it just "an exercise in futility" when God gave it to us?

If only a few were meant to understand the Bible, we would still have to study it in the original languages. But the Bible was written in the language of the street. The pressure is still on to have the scriptures in language that can be understood. It is not enough the language be beautiful – it must also be so clear every man may understand

by George

Have you heard about the man who got rode out of town on a rail? Someone asked him how it felt. "If it hadn't been for the honor," he replied, "I'd just as soon have walked."

That's the way I felt when I was elected president of the Illinois missionaries last month. . I have a lot to learn about associational work. I hope something will rub off in my fellowship with other missionaries.

January 11, 1974

Do It My Way

Daylight time sure makes getting up dark. I'm not too crazy about getting up two hours before the sun does!

I guess I'm basically an A. M. person. I like to get up early and get going. One reason is I'm slow enough I've got to get a head start.

My wife happens to be a P. M. person. She can stay up all night if she can sleep late.

This sometimes creates problems. Especially when I stay up to watch a late show with her. I like to get to bed early. When I don't, it's even harder to get up in the dark.

Should we insist that everyone follow our life style?

Or, is there room for varying patterns among the disciples of Jesus?

The brothers, Andrew and Peter seem quite different. Andrew works quietly behind the scenes and brings people to Jesus.

Lovable, loud-mouthed Peter is always "rushing in where angels fear to tread." Maybe this is why it's so easy to identify with him.

Do you wear the same clothes every day? Most of us like the variety a change of color or style offers.

Shouldn't we also respect the Christian who happens to hate a different pattern of life? Even if he doesn't get up as early as we do?

January 25, 1974

Sharpen Your Axe

One of my favorite Bible teachers is Clyde Francisco, Professor of Old Testament at Southern Seminary in Louisville, Kentucky.

One of the stories he likes to tell is of Elisha building a larger dormitory for his seminary students. As you read 2 Kings 6:1-7, and let your imagination work, maybe you can see it.

Then Dr. Francisco tells the purpose of a seminary. "Our job is to sharpen your axe," he explains. "We cannot make preachers out of you; if you are preachers, maybe we can help you become better preachers."

I can hear him now with his special way of speaking. (How he overcame stuttering to become a powerful preacher is a story in itself.)

George H. Davis

I believe he's right. Our gifts and calling come from God. It's up to us to develop the abilities God gives us. Training and education can sharpen our skills and enable us to do a better job.

"You have a tough job cutting down a tree with a dull axe," Dr. Francisco says. "Education can help sharpen your axe."

The idea that education and the leadership of the Holy Spirit are enemies needs to be exposed for what it is – hogwash! I believe the Holy Spirit can lead me better when I have studied. It's hard for even Him to bring things to my mind I never knew.

Granted, I cannot rely <u>only</u> on what I know. My education and knowledge are limited. My opinions are fallible. But I must learn what men through the years have come to know about God and His ways. Isn't this part of what the Bible is – the record of men experiencing God's revelations?

I can understand the Bible better if I know something of the way people lived then. Knowing something about their marriage customs, the place of women, and religious ceremonies can make the Bible mean more to me.

Our congratulations to Roy Rogers upon completion of the Pastoral Training certificate with the Seminary Extension Department. He began in a class I taught. After that he finished by correspondence. There must be a message in that! Did I do such a poor job he said, "There is surely a better way." Or, did I do such a good job he said, "I think I can make it on my own now." I suspect the truth is somewhere between the two. He has received the benefit and that's what's important.

February 5, 1974

On Time

There's an old saying around Baptist churches: "Stay away from the door about 9:25 Sunday morning – you might get run over."

Many people have the habit of rushing in at the last minute. Some never quite make it on time.

Imagine my surprise recently when I arrived at a church about 9:25 and was the only one there!

I soon decided they didn't begin Sunday School until 10:00. About 9:35 people began coming. By 9:55 almost everyone was there. I don't remember anyone coming in late.

I was impressed that people got there early and had time to visit before Sunday School.

I'm attending a Leadership Growth Seminar for missionaries at East Bay Camp, Bloomington this week.

The focus is on understanding and developing one's leadership potential.

February 20, 1974

by George

Faithful Fellowship

"Let's all cooperate and support our Association by attending this meeting."

Have you heard or read words similar to this? How do they strike you? Frankly, this kind of appeal leaves me rather cold.

In the first place, I don't see the Association as something that has to be supported (propped up). I see the Association as churches in fellowship. This kind of fellowship is as voluntary as faith. It cannot be coerced or demanded.

Fellowship grows out of faith. Faith in Christ makes us brothers to other Christians. We do not choose our brothers. They are given us by our parents.

Fellowship is not an elective for Christians. This is true for the individual and for the congregation. We are in fellowship. Our concern is with the quality of that fellowship.

I am committed to deepening and strengthening our love for each other. It's hard to love people you don't know. (Sometimes, it's hard to love those you do know too!) One of my concerns is to help us get better acquainted.

Until I came to this position, I didn't know where half of our churches were located. I have found all the buildings now, but that doesn't mean I know where the churches are.

I want to know more about our churches and to help us know each other. One of the projects I have worked on is a map of our Association. I hope we can publish one in the near future.

Russell Bennett, of the Home Mission Board staff, suggested that associations might circulate associational letters to their churches. This would be a message to the churches about mutual concerns. It might contain a call to prayer for a special need. There might be warnings about dangers facing churches.

Mull this idea over in your mind and let me know what you think of it. Bennett's suggestion was that this letter be prepared and adopted at an annual meeting. It would go out as a message from the Association rather than from an individual.

High school JUNIORS and SENIORS, their leaders, and pastors are invited to meet with a representative of Hannibal-LaGrange College at 7:30 P.M. on March 18 at the First Baptist Church in Carmi.

CONGRATULATIONS to David and Carolyn Dean on the birth of their third son. Timothy William arrived on February 20. David is pastor of Fairfield's First Baptist Church and is moderator of our Association.

March 6, 1974

Sensitivity

Ben Connell of the Brotherhood Commission tells of a practice of Renaissance sculptors:

When the artist had finished cutting away the stone, he would polish the statue with pumice. To check the smoothness of the surface, he would tear a finger nail off into the quick and rub the tender area over the surface.

George H. Davis

In this way, he would be extra sensitive to any roughness. He would know if he needed to polish the statue more.

I wonder if we have the nerve to pray – Lord, cut me to the quick so I may be sensitive to the needs of others. It's not that I want to be a sucker for every "bleeding heart", Lord. But, I do want to help men over the roughness in their lives.

Next week (March 24-31) I will be in a World Missions Conference in the Kaskaskia Baptist Association. The following week I will be with the Temple Baptist Church in Centralia for a revival.

March 20, 1974

Highest Call

I'm convinced we've got some things turned around concerning God's call. We assume the highest call a person can receive is the call to foreign missions. The next best is to be a home missionary – especially if you work with Indians. The next choice is to be a pastor and the layman is on the bottom of the totem pole. "I'm only a layman" I've heard some say.

The highest call any person can receive is the call to be a Christian. This is a call to follow Jesus and to witness to his grace and forgiveness. Trueblood says the person who fails to witness is not in the company of Jesus no matter how kind and good he may be.

Our vocation is to make Christ known. Whatever job we have, we are to live out the Gospel. There is no more important calling in the world than to share our faith in Jesus.

There are special needs in church vocations today. Persons who are committed to Christ and prepared to serve through his church are in demand in many areas. Pastors and persons trained in music and education are needed both here and overseas.

The 1974 Life Commitment poster has this introduction:

"Youth and young adults are following God's leadership into church vocations. Some of these are still in high school, others are in college and many are adults already in the work world.

"Many of these church vocations volunteers are anxious to get on with their life. Therefore, they are bypassing education for involvement in ministry. But involvement and education should run concurrently. Involvement is limited without education.

"Theological education is a necessity for the minister who must speak to the spiritual needs of today's congregation with their varied backgrounds of education and experiences. The minister must be armed with the Word and know whereof he speaks."

April 11, 1974

by George

New Ideas

One of the things that bugs me is for someone to appeal to me to prove his way is "THE way Baptist churches" operate.

Baptists are a freedom-loving people. But, sometimes we try to persuade others our way is right by appealing to our tradition.

Someone has suggested "We can prove a lot of things by Pendleton's Church Manual we can't prove by the Bible."

I would like to be like the scribe Jesus described bringing "out of his treasure what is new and what is old." (Matt. 13:52)

I'd like for us to be able to hold on to the good of the past without being hidebound by tradition. At the same time, I'd like for us to be willing to try new ideas and approaches – to be willing to fail, if necessary.

The same Bible that likens God's children to sheep refers to diversities of gifts among believers. Each one is to use his peculiar gift for the good of the body.

The same truth applies to churches. Each one has peculiar characteristics and a particular ministry. We should not be slavish in our imitation of each other.

We can learn from each other, but we also need to dare to be what God wants us to be in our community.

I don't see the Association as making a mold to fit her churches into. I hope the Association can become an enabler for "churches in fellowship on mission in their setting."

April 23, 1974

A Good Idea

As you read this I will be at Ridgecrest for the National Convocation on the Association. This meeting is held every ten years. The last such meeting was held in 1963 in Gulfshore, Mississippi.

Associational leaders and denominational workers from across the country will be meeting in conferences and study groups to deal with various phases of our work.

I will be working in a study group on the role of the superintendent of missions. Gene Strahan of Champaign will be leading this group.

About 39 will be attending the Convocation from Illinois. I expect the total attendance will be in excess of 1,000 (and that's not speaking ministerially).

One of the features I'm intrigued with is the Associational Auction. This is a brainchild of Russell Bennett of the Home Mission Board, a pretty brainy guy.

The Associational Auction is a team game. Each team is to develop ideas it can sell to the other teams. They will write up an idea they think is useful but not widely known.

The idea is then sold to the highest bidder. The team with the most money at the close of the auction is the champion.

Had any good ideas lately?

George H. Davis

May 6, 1974

Our Loss, Heaven's Gain

It's still hard to believe they're gone!

It was a good day Monday at the Mid-Year meeting. We enjoyed the fellowship and the reports.

Mrs. Ivy spoke for Stewart Street. Mrs. Gill spoke again and was warm in her praise of her pastor. She good-humoredly warned pulpit committees to leave him alone.

Then we enjoyed warm fellowship around the supper table. God's Spirit gave unusual freedom as I preached that evening.

We went home tired but grateful for God's goodness. At midnight the telephone woke me from a sound sleep. My wife answered. Peggy Huff was calling to tell us three people had died and Dewitt Kelley was seriously hurt in a car wreck on their way home.

I called David Dean and we drove to Carmi. Soon after we arrived at the hospital, we learned Dewitt had died enroute to an Evansville hospital.

We visited with Brother Ivy briefly and with the Kelley's. Then we returned to Fairfield still stunned.

On the way home, David remarked about what a contribution to heaven that church had made in so short a time. And I thought, Mrs. Gill still has her beloved pastor ... in heaven.

We share our mutual woes,
Our mutual burdens bear;
And often for each other flows
The sympathizing tear.

May 21, 1974

To fail to plan is to plan to fail!

One of the great needs of associations and churches is the willingness to discover our needs and then plan to meet them. It is my intention to revive our Associational Council to look at where we are and where we're going.

Our first meeting will be next week with associational officers, program directors (SS, WMU, Bthd., Music, and TU), and committee chairmen invited. We will not attempt to conduct the business of the Board but we will attempt to determine some directions we should go.

Some of the questions we should try to answer are: What are the needs of our churches and communities? Which of these could we meet? Which needs are most urgent?

I hope we can begin to plan our work along these lines rather than just asking what the state or SBC calendar says we should be doing. We can continue to look to them for resources (programs and personnel) as we seek to meet felt needs. But, no one else knows what we need quite as well as we do.

by George

I have a new 18-minute, color film entitled "The Devil and the Baptist Association." It features Loyd Corder of the Home Mission Board and his friend, Joe the Baptist. Joe is the only genuine, <u>certified</u> wooden-headed Baptist preacher in the Convention,

I'll be showing the film at our quarterly Board meeting, July 15 at Elm River. After that, I'll be asking for an invitation to show it in your church.

Don't forget to mail three copies of your Vacation Bible School report to: (1) George Davis, PO Box 186, Fairfield, IL 62837, (2) John Perkins, PO Box 3486, Springfield, IL 62708, and (3) Baptist Sunday School Board., 127 Ninth Avenue, North, Nashville, TN 37234.

June 12, 1974

"Why do they want to change the name of the Association?"

I've heard this question asked a few times, so I'd like to tell you what I think about it.

I think we're seven years late in getting around to it. In 1967, the Wabash Valley Baptist Association dissolved and six churches became a part of the Mt. Erie Association. The six were Carmi, First; Grayville, First; Grayville, Northside; Burnt Prairie, Liberty; Crossville; and Mt. Vernon, Casey Avenue.

It seems to me <u>that</u> would have been the ideal time to change the name of the Association. But, since seven is a perfect number, maybe <u>this</u> is the ideal time!

I believe the proposed name, Greater Wabash, would identify our total area better. The churches formerly affiliated with the Wabash Valley Association could identify with it. The whole area is in the Wabash-Little Wabash River Valley.

As hallowed as "Mt. Erie" may be in our memory, it does not identify us. When the Association was organized, Mt. Erie was near the center of the churches. Now it's on the northern edge. We don't have a church there.

I'm for the change. It's not a "vote of confidence" for me. I'm not going to resign if it doesn't carry.

Messengers from your church will get a chance to vote on the change at our annual meeting, October 7-8 in Mt. Carmel.

June 25, 1974

"Don't get your wires crossed!"

I had put my Volkswagen back together and it wasn't running right. I tried everything I could think of and then called my friend and VW mechanic par excellence, Nile Deputy in Mt. Carmel. He took one look at it and asked, "Do you have your spark plug wires crossed?" Sure enough, it ran much better when he switched them!

George H. Davis

I told Nile I was hoping it was something simple, but not that simple. "Oh, I won't tell anybody – unless I see them," Nile promised. And sure enough, he was as good as his word. He charged me a cup of coffee for his work. At the coffee shop a fellow came in and sat down beside him. "What would you think of a preacher, who thinks he's a mechanic and gets his spark plug wires crossed and drives all the way to Mt. Carmel to get them uncrossed?" he asked his friend. He didn't tell anybody – until he saw them. As I drove away, Nile called out, "Don't get your wires crossed!"

Well, I guess we all get our wires crossed once in a while, but I sure foolt feelish!

I haven't gone to the wrong church to preach, yet. I did fail to show up one Sunday morning when a pastor was expecting me. I had failed to put it down in my "little black book."

I am more concerned about more serious consequences of getting our wires crossed, though. Like, thinking of the Association as an end in itself rather than an instrument through which the churches minister in their area.

It's also possible we get to thinking of the churches as ends in themselves. I'm convinced churches exist to serve people and not people to serve churches. Jesus said something about the Sabbath being made for man and not man for the Sabbath. We are slow to learn and apply this in our day. God loves people and uses churches to minister to them.

When we begin crying that people are not supporting our programs, maybe it's because our programs are not serving people. Maybe they're not big enough. Maybe we need to be sure our programs are tools and not goals. Our goal is to serve people. We <u>use</u> programs to do that.

By the way, I'm going to be on vacation July 16-23, if I don't get my wires crossed!

July 10, 1974

Youth Camp '74

Several weeks of planning and preparation are coming to fruition this week in our Associational Youth Camp. We are grateful to pastors and others who have helped promote Camp. We have one of the best staffs I have known about.

Several are working this year for the first time. We're grateful for their willingness to give a week of their summer.

There are a few people we're going to miss this year. Dewitt Kelley was Director for five years. We can't help missing him. Theron Arnold wasn't able to help this year because of his health. He has been a good counselor for several years. Mr. and Mrs. Earl Sanders didn't feel they should work this year. They have operated the concession stand for some time.

August 12, 1974

by George

"Thank You"

I want to share a letter with you from Anna Collins of Fairfield. She was the first one to register for Youth Camp. She was also our Children's Bible Drill winner from Mt. Erie Association.

304 W. Douglas
Fairfield, Ill.
August 19, 1974

Dear Bro. Davis,

I would like to thank you and the Mt. Erie Association for having Church Camp this year.

I attended camp last year, but I enjoyed the services better this year. I also think that Don Price did a very good job of preaching. I think the cooks did a very good job of cooking the food. I think the bonfire was very nice.

Dorm Prayer, Fun Time Show and Tell, and Recreation were all great. I would like to thank the ones for having this camp, and also the counselors. I also hope we can have camp next year too.

Thank you,
Anna Collins

I'd appreciate any other reactions, comments, or suggestions about Youth Camp. If you do not want your letter made public, please say so.

August 23, 1974

Read the Bible

Read the Bible Through in 1974-75 is one of the most worthwhile programs I have heard about in some time. It is a plan to read the entire Bible in one year beginning October 1. The outline for daily reading will appear in 23 periodicals including <u>Open Windows</u>, <u>Home Life</u>, and most teacher's and Adult member's periodicals.

I hope many of our churches will promote the use of this plan. I know North Side in Fairfield plans to devote some time each Wednesday night to the passages for that week. Even if your church does nothing to encourage it, you as an individual can use the plan to read your Bible through. You can follow the readings outlined in your Sunday School periodical or <u>Open Windows</u> or <u>Home Life</u>.

I believe some parts of the Bible are more important than others. But I also believe we should be acquainted with all of it. How long has it been since you read through the Bible? It's been a while for me and I'm looking forward to beginning October 1.

George H. Davis

Speaking of the Bible, I hope you're making plans to study Acts in January. Whether you use January 6-10 as Bible Study Week or work out some other plan, I hope you'll plan to involve your church in a serious study of this record of the apostolic church.

I plan to teach the Seminary Extension course on Acts beginning September 26. We will meet for nine weeks. We will meet either on Thursday nights or Saturday mornings, depending on the wishes of those enrolled. If you want to get a head start on studying Acts, I invite you to enroll in this course. It is open to youth, laymen, and preachers.

Speaking of the Bible again, I've still got a basketful of fragments left at Youth Camp. If you're missing a sheet or a swim suit or whatever, check with me.

September 9, 1974

Ugly Thoughts

About this time of the year I get to thinking ugly thoughts – like "Let's abolish the Associational Letter!"

So often the numbers mean so little and sometimes they are misleading. We seem to change our way of counting people every few years.

And then we get all upset because the numbers are down. Wouldn't it be simpler just to do away with the Letter! Maybe then we wouldn't get so upset!

How the calendar happens to fall can also affect our statistics. If the money doesn't come in until the next month or the next year, our precious figures are distorted.

Yes, I'm halfway serious. I'm not sure we should take our statistics so seriously. They are not always accurate reports of what we have done.

I know figures don't lie (though I've heard that liars figure). I also know that just as you can find a verse of scripture to prove about anything you want, you can also find figures to prove your point.

You may get the idea I don't trust statistics. But it's the guy using them I want to know about. What's he trying to prove?

Maybe we should come up with a better way of knowing when we're doing a good job. Maybe we should get our support from the assurance we are being faithful to our calling. Maybe along with our Letters we should rely on the witness of the Holy Spirit to know whether we are pleasing the Lord.

September 24, 1974

Annual Meeting '74

Extraordinary preaching, meaningful sharing experiences, and splendid hospitality were the features of this year's Annual Associational meeting.

The Mt. Carmel church did an outstanding job of entertaining us. The leaf name tags were a delightful thought. The decorations and the meals were superb.

by George

Members from at least 16 of our churches shared some highlight or concern of theirs. We shared in moments of prayer and praise. It was good to get to know each other's interests better. I believe we can pray more intelligently if we know the situation better.

The preaching this year was exceptional. Theron Arnold challenged us to be better preachers. Jack Pierce led us to look at the Biblical teaching on reconciliation.

James Davis reminded us he was honoring the one who had been asked to bring the Memorial sermon, Dewitt Kelley. If there were any doubts about Ken Carter's preaching ability, they were quickly dispelled Tuesday night.

I guess my only disappointment was that so little interest was shown in the name change proposal. I got the feeling most people didn't really care what the Association is called.

I guess I was reminded again changing the name won't work any magic. We still have quite a job to do in educating and challenging people concerning the nature and work of the Association. But, I feel we can do it, <u>with the Lord's help</u>!

October 21, 1974

Budget

Budgets are important pieces of paper. They are a plan for spending money. They show what a group thinks is important.

Listed below you will find an estimate of what the Association expects to receive next year. On the next page is listed the plan for spending this money.

I don't think of a budget as an inflexible document, but as a statement of intention. We plan to use our money in this way. This doesn't mean if we don't spend everything in a certain category this year, we can carry it over to next year. Nor does it mean we absolutely can't go over the amount allocated for a category. If the need arises, I believe we should be flexible enough to adjust to it. I would hope we could stay within the overall figures and certainly within our income.

Mind you, what I'm saying is strictly my own interpretation. This is not from the Lord – nor from the Board! If they want to set a different policy, they certainly may do so.

I'm certainly grateful for the support of the churches. We could have the Association without money, but it would be very difficult for me to work without pay. Your support is also necessary to carry on the various kinds of programs you see listed on the next page. If churches will give 4% of their undesignated income for associational work, we can do everything that needs to be done.

I'm also grateful for the Committee's proposal to provide for a part-time secretary next year. I believe this would be a real help in getting the office work done. It seems to me, you're paying me too much for me to be just a glorified secretary! I believe there are other things I need to be doing if I can be freed from the office some.

November 4, 1974

George H. Davis

Our Mission

Is it possible for a church to give too much to missions?

I doubt it. But I do think churches sometimes get their priorities out of kilter.

Consider a church that gives 5% to the Association, 5% to the Children's Home, and 5% through the Cooperative Program. I recognize that each church sets its own pattern of mission giving. But I doubt that church has responded adequately to needs outside its own area.

You would not expect me to advocate decreased giving to the Association or the Children's Home. What I am pleading for is increased support of state, home, and foreign missions through the Cooperative Program.

The needs of our state are staggering. I hope we can get better acquainted with them this year. 60% of our Cooperative Program dollars will be used in Illinois next year.

Foreign and home missions and our seminaries are supported with the other 40% we give. The needs of the world demand more than a token contribution.

Let's look again at how we give to missions. Just giving every cause the same amount isn't necessarily fair. The fields served through Cooperative Program monies are vastly wider than either the Association or the Children's Home.

I'm for the Association and the Children's Home, but I also know the world doesn't end here. Let's reorder our response on the basis of need.

November 25, 1974

What's the most important word in the Great Commission?

Most people would underline "Go ye therefore and make disciples of all nations: baptizing them in the name of the Father, and the Son, and the Holy Spirit, teaching them to observe everything I have commanded you."

However, Jesus used one imperative and three participles in the commission to his disciples. "Make disciples" is the imperative. "Going," "baptizing," and "teaching" are the participles. His emphasis was not on going but on discipling. The going was incidental, the discipling was imperative!

If Jesus had spoken our dialect, he might have said, "Bein' as how you're goin', make disciples..."

Jesus is not so concerned with feverish activity as with the quality of our life and witness. His command was not just to do witnessing but to be witnesses.

Granted that we never live an adequate witness. We must always acknowledge that our life is not an accurate reflection of Christ. We must always point beyond ourselves to the perfect Lamb of God. But there must also be some resemblance of the Lamb in our lives. Else our words of witness are wasted,

Granted too it is the Spirit of God who makes our witness fruitful. But we must be careful it is believable. If we talk about God's forgiveness and at the same time nurse a grudge, what are people going to believe?

by George

I believe our primary concern is to be letting Jesus live in and through us. Our attitudes and motives should reflect His. I believe this is more important than running around like a chicken with its head cut off "serving the Lord."

Baker James Cauthen of the Foreign Mission Board reminds us that sending a person overseas does not make them a missionary. Unless they are a missionary where they are, a geographical transplant does little but uproot a family and place it in a strange culture.

Christ's work is one – whether we call it foreign missions, or home missions, or state, associational, or local missions. Our task is one – to bear witness to God's love for us in our sinfulness. We are to use our unique gifts to glorify the God who saved us.

I think it's significant that Jesus told his disciples to begin in Jerusalem. I suppose they might have protested, "But, Lord, don't you realize that the same power structure that crucified you will make life miserable for us? And don't you remember the crowds you drew in Galilee? Why can't we go back home and get into this thing gradually?"

Jesus seems to be saying, "You begin wherever you find yourself — wherever your work or your family or your schooling takes you. You have one job — to be my witness!" Maybe it's this sense of vocation (calling) we need to recover.

December 9, 1974

I hope your holidays are holy days!

I hope amid the family gatherings, meals, presents, hunts, and football games you will recognize God as the giver of all good and perfect gifts.

I guess I enjoy the holidays as much as anyone. I look forward to seeing the larger family occasionally. I guess we're probably closer now than we have ever been. Maybe absence does make the heart grow fonder.

I look forward to seeing my brothers and sister and their families. Since we're scattered across Illinois, Missouri, Tennessee, and Alabama we don't get together too often.

But I thank God too for deep Christian friendships wherever He has led me to serve. I suppose pastors are more fortunate than others in finding close friends in several different places.

I get to meet some fine people from several churches and I thank God for these friendships.

Let's recognize our families and friends as gifts from God and vow to accept them gratefully. A book came out a few years ago entitled "You Can't Be Human Alone."

I believe it's also true "You Can't Be Christian Alone." Just as we need each other to be fully human, we need each other to be fully Christian. The day of the Lone Ranger Christian is over. As individuals and as churches we need each other.

Thanks be to God for giving Himself to us. And thanks to Him for giving us to each other!

December 24, 1974

George H. Davis

A New Name

I suppose it'll take some getting used to, but now we are officially the Greater Wabash Baptist Association. Some have jumped the gun and started using the new name before January, but it became official with the beginning of the new year – a new year, a new name!

I suppose there will be some slips of the tongue. On occasion we may refer to the Mt. Erie Baptist Association. I notice one of the radio announcers the other day hesitate as he read "Greater Wabash Baptist Association." I had to correct the first Baptist Hour schedule I typed because I had listed the sponsor of a program as the Mt. Erie Baptist Association.

My family joins in thanking you for your generous Christmas gift. Andy Moye brought me the weekly salary check and an extra check for $100. It didn't take long to spend it – we used it on a new electric range. So we're all getting good use of it. Thank you again. You are a most generous and thoughtful people to serve. We received many cards and enjoyed them all.

I don't think I've ever been happier or enjoyed my work more. I feel I'm doing what I ought to be doing — what God wants me to do. I know I'm not getting everything done I ought to do or want to do. But, I do have some sense of accomplishment in my work. You are a good people to work with and I appreciate you more than I can say.

I recognize we're just beginning to scratch the surface of what we ought to be doing as an Association. We are getting some direction though and I'm grateful for that. I believe it's important to have our concepts right as well as to be doing something. So I've given some attention to developing my own philosophy of associational work. I've shared some of these ideas with some of you. I'm going to be doing more of this. But then I hope we can put some of them into practice.

I'll be going to Indianapolis January 10 and 11 for a strategy meeting planning an outreach thrust in the North Central states in 1977 through 1990. Then on January 20 and 21 Larry Werries and I will be taking a faculty to the State Vacation Bible School Clinic in Springfield. We come back and plan and conduct our own Associational V. B. S. Clinic on April 1.

I'm enjoying teaching Acts this week at First Baptist Church in Fairfield. In two weeks, I'll be teaching at North Side here. If I can help you, please let me know. There's not much I enjoy more than trying to teach (unless it's trying to write).

Time spent in Bible study can be valuable if we can learn to apply the message to our situation. We need to ask first, "what does the Bible say?" Then we can ask "what did it mean when it was written?" Then we are ready to ask "what does it mean to us today?"

January 8, 1975

Sour Dough

When we lived in Grayville, my wife had a batch of sour dough. It was a kind of perpetual supply of home made yeast. She used it to make rolls and bread. Every so often she would add some flour and milk to the bowl so it would keep growing.

Once when we were going on vacation she asked Stacey Wilson to keep it while we were gone. She took it over to her house and finding no one home, she set it between the storm door and the inside door.

Bud Wilson got home before Stacey did that day. He noticed the Tupperware bowl. A note on the lid said, "I fed it this morning." Bud's curiosity about got the best of him. What could be in this small bowl that needed feeding? Was it safe to open it? Could it get away?

When his curiosity overcame his caution and he opened the bowl, he still didn't know what he had. It wasn't until Stacey came home that he understood what was going on.

I wonder if you've ever had that kind of situation on your hands? You weren't sure whether to simply pick it up or look for a ten foot pole!

I can sympathize with Bud because I sometimes feel that way about kids – my own and others. I'm not sure whether they've just been fed or whether they might bite!

I guess it's a sign of old age when you don't understand kids. It may also be a sign of poor memory – forgetting your own childhood!

January 20, 1975

The church is alive and well on the planet earth.

Despite her detractors and critics, the church is not taking the news of her impending death lying down. I believe it was Mark Twain who said, "The reports of my death are greatly exaggerated."

Some are beginning to realize the church is in the most important business there is: sharing the Good News. We're not so concerned about what the world is coming to as we are about who came into the world.

William Hendricks of Southwestern Seminary in Fort Worth, Texas has pointed out the Sermons in the early chapters of Acts can be summarized:
1. Jesus Christ came from God according to prophecy,
2. You killed him,
3. God raised him up,
4. He sends his Spirit to bear witness, and
5. He who began it all is going to wrap it up.

It may still be more relevant to preach this message than it is to preach on the latest ecological or social concern. Man's basic need is for forgiveness and the restoration of right relationships. He needs to be set right with his fellow man and with God.

I'm convinced the average person does not know God loves him and he is accountable for his response to God's love. We have beat around the bush with people so long. We've invited them to our services. We've condemned their habits that are different from ours. (What you do and I don't do is sin.)

Churches are beginning to realize people are more important than budgets or buildings. We're seeing personal relationships are more basic than organization. The only reason the church needs money or buildings or organizations is to share Jesus' love with people. I believe God is reviving his church.

February 3, 1975

Growing a Loving Church

I spent three days last week at a Personal and Professional Growth Conference for associational directors. It was a very helpful meeting emphasizing pastoral care.

I like the retreat facilities at DuBois (about nine miles south of Ashley). They are owned by the United Church of Christ.

But the people involved were more important than the setting. Don Dillow had enlisted Bob Dale, a pastoral ministries consultant with the Church Administration department of the Baptist Sunday School Board. Bob is author of a new book on pastoral care "Growing a Loving Church."

The thing I'm excited about is that Bob will be back to lead two Pastor's Personal Growth Conferences in our area:

May 26-29 in Carbondale, and

September 15-18 at DuBois.

The cost will be $30 to $45. I hope you will make it possible for your pastor to go and encourage him to get to one of these. Tell him the deacon's will take care of prayer meeting.

Get him registered and send him off and he'll be a better person and a better pastor when he gets back.

Bob says, "You can learn a lot in the school of hard knocks, if you don't mind the school colors – black and blue!"

February 19, 1975

Here we go again!

We're back on daylight savings time.

We're supposed to stay on it until the last Sunday in October.

After that we'll go back to the six month cycle (six months of standard time and six months of daylight time). That is, we will unless Congress changes its mind again.

Congress put us on year-round daylight time for a 22-month trial period. Public pressure torpedoed that and they put us back on standard time for four months. Now we have eight months of daylight time. I remember a neighbor of ours at home who used to talk about "God's time" and "Democrat time." At least you didn't have to guess where his loyalties were.

Congress has also taken to juggling the calendar. When I was in school, I learned Washington's Birthday was February 22; Decoration Day was May 30; Columbus

Day was October 12; and Armistice Day was November 11. Now we've got to have Monday holidays:

February 17 – Washington's birthday,
May 27 – Memorial Day,
October 13 – Columbus Day, and
October 27 – Veteran's Day.

Of course, these dates are good only for 1975. Next year you'll have to look them up again.

One other exception – our Illinois legislature got sentimental and changed our Memorial Day back to May 30. But now they're getting public pressure and a number of bills have been introduced to put us back in with the rest of the country.

But it seems to me with all our twisting of the clock and juggling of the calendar, we still have not learned to manage our time. It's not that we don't have enough time – we've got as much as anybody else. It's just that we don't use it well.

We tend to fritter away time on worthless things and then scramble nervously through a hectic schedule. We need to decide what's important and devote our best time to that. So often we give our leftovers to some of our most important tasks.

But what I really want to know is – what time is it?

March 3, 1975

Outreach

At our evangelism conference Ken Carter suggested a church put emphasis on outreach – this will demand training.

I expect he's right! Too long we've told people they ought to come to Training Union – we haven't told them why.

I'm afraid much of our training is going the way of Humpty Dumpty – all the king's horses and all the king's men can't put it back together again.

Some one said, "You can lead a horse to water but you can't make him drink." But an old-timer added, "You can salt him!"

We need to challenge people with tasks that demands training – then offer it.

March 19, 1975

Who's your Pastor's Pastor?

Who shares his discouragement? Who rejoices with him over his accomplishments? Who ministers to his family in sickness or death?

Of course, God ministers to him. But, how does God minister? Just like He ministers to you — through someone else!

We do not honor our pastors when we place them in a category separate from the common problems of life. They share our humanity. One writer refers to a pastor as a "wounded healer."

George H. Davis

Recently a passage in Acts grabbed me. Paul and Barnabas had preached in Lystra. The Jews were jealous of their popularity and stirred up the people to stone Paul. They dragged him out of the city and left him for dead. But Luke tells us "when the disciples gathered about him, he rose up and entered the city…" (14:20)

It seems significant to me that Paul revived <u>when the believers gathered around him</u>. He might have died if they had not cared enough to risk their lives to minister to him.

Your pastor sometimes needs someone to share his joy or his grief. Sometimes he simply needs someone to stand beside him. Sometimes he needs encouragement. <u>You can help</u> him.

When I came to this work, I was asked to be a pastor to pastors. I continue to have a real interest in this area of my ministry. I want to stay close enough to be a pastor. I want to help equip the man of God.

But you can <u>share</u> in this ministry. You need to be aware of your pastor's needs and desires. You can't give him everything he desires, but you can meet his basic needs. His ministry will be crippled if he is constantly worried about making ends meet! You can't pay him what he's worth, but you can <u>support</u> him as he serves.

You can also recognize he is a growing person with the same kinds of needs you have – emotional, social, spiritual, and physical. You can be his friend.

April 7, 1975

"For the Shortest Preacher Who's Been Here the Longest"

That was the inscription on the loving cup the First Baptist Church in Carmi presented her pastor recently.

L. M. Huff, Jr. has been their pastor seven years and that's longer than anyone else has stayed. Those of us who know L. M. know he's short in stature but not in ability or enthusiasm.

I think it's great for a church to recognize her pastor's anniversaries and other special days. In fact, I think it's so important, I'm promoting a Pastor Appreciation Day in June.

I think you ought to appreciate your pastor every day but I'm suggesting one day be set aside for church-wide observance and celebration. Though June 1 is the suggested date, your church may want to choose another date – your pastor's anniversary with your church, his birthday, his wedding anniversary, etc.

I'm glad First Baptist in Carmi "jumped the gun" and got things rolling. I hope you'll follow their lead.

I think it's great, too, that L. M. has stayed seven years. I'm convinced good work is done in longer pastorates. If you can stay through the difficulties and discouragement, you can get things done.

April 25, 1975

by George

Baptist Children's Home

The work of the Baptist Children's Home is changing.

It's changing because children (and youth) are changing and because our society is changing.

We used to talk about the Carmi Orphanage. It's been a long time since we were caring for orphans. We moved into caring for dependent, neglected children. Now we're caring for more and more older children and youth. Many are in our care for only a short time.

Some of the children and youth we minister to now have a history of being rejected and unwanted. They bring a special set of needs and problems.

It is more difficult and more expensive to care for these young people. It is also more expensive to keep a person in prison than it is to keep him outside.

I hope as you make your Mother's Day offering for the Baptist Children's Home you will also pause to pray for staff and houseparents who have a difficult task.

I remember a Bible School worker taking an especially troublesome girl home and apologizing to her grandmother, "I'm sorry, but we can't do anything with her. I had to bring her home." "You can't do anything with her. What do you think about me? I've got her all day," the grandmother responded.

If you think you've got your hands full with your kids, remember the workers at the Children's Home. I salute them and their devotion to child care.

May 7, 1975

How Can We Help?

I was impressed with the needs of northwestern Illinois as Jack Fritts spoke to us last week. He told of 30 towns and cities with a population of 1,000 or more with no Southern Baptist churches. The largest of these is Rock Island with 50,200 people.

He suggested we could help as churches or as an association by sending people to help:
1. begin new work
2. strengthen a mission in Freeport
3. complete community profiles on towns
4. make telephone surveys of towns to determine specific needs and possibilities.

I know our missions director and council will have some recommendation for us. I hope we can get better acquainted with our brothers in northwestern Illinois.

Many of us already know Lowell Regains and Sam Harris who used to pastor at Albion and Grayville First. They are both serving in Rock Falls now.

May 20, 1975

George H. Davis

SBC '75

The annual meeting of the Southern Baptist Convention has all the excitement of a county fair — people milling around, sideshow attractions, spotlight seekers, etc.

I wonder if we really do anything so significant it couldn't be done once every three or four years. The resolutions seem to repeat themselves at least that often. As for the pageantry and celebration, I soon get enough of that.

Whenever I start criticizing what someone else is doing, I remind myself to look at what I'm responsible for. Some of us were talking recently about our annual associational meeting.

Should we eliminate the day session and have two night sessions in two different churches? Would this involve more people from more churches in our fellowship?

I'm not advocating a change this year, but let's think about the future. We're planning for 1976 and beyond now. Perhaps our Mid-Year meeting should be limited to a night session.

I'd appreciate your reactions to those ideas.

June 27, 1975

A Matchmaker

In one of my favorite movies, "Fiddler on the Roof" the matchmaker arranges marriages. This doesn't mean the men and girls can't court without her, but if they're having trouble finding someone she will help.

Is the missionary a matchmaker?

Is it his job to help churches get pastors and preachers get churches? I guess I would have to answer with a qualified "yes."

Calling a pastor is one of the most important decisions a church makes. This is the one time in the life of a church when they do not have the leadership of a pastor. Some churches have adequate lay leadership. Others simply do not know how to go about seeking a pastor.

Perhaps the greatest help a missionary can be is in helping a church or committee know how to go about looking for a pastor. Most people have very little experience serving on a pulpit committee.

I prefer to make suggestions about how the committee works rather than to suggest who they consider. If they ask me about preachers available, I will tell them.

One thing I don't want to do is to recommend only one man to a church. I don't know any church well enough to know what kind of pastor they need. And I probably don't know any man well enough to give him a blank endorsement.

I prefer to give a church several names for them to check out themselves. I recognize the fact that I give them the names implies some kind of endorsement. I can live with that. I just don't want to get in to the business of playing "one on one."

I want to maintain a healthy respect for a church's autonomy and her ability to know and follow God's leadership.

I have lots of preacher friends. But I recognize some times the most "available" preachers may not be the most desirable.

There are about four times as many preachers wanting to move as there are churches looking for pastors. Something is wrong with this situation.

July 11, 1975

Speak Your Mind

A deacon told me, "Bro. George, we've never had a unanimous vote on anything."

I'm not sure that's bad.

I don't mean people should be cantankerous and against everything. You've probably heard about the church who was discussing buying a new chandelier.

One member arose to express his opposition, "I'm against it for three reasons: (1) we haven't got anybody to play it; (2) nobody knows how to spell it, to order it; and (3) what we really need around here is more light."

As individuals we are different and have different viewpoints. Becoming Christians didn't change that. I believe we should be free to express our opinion in a business meeting.

I would rather members speak up and argue their case there than go away unhappy without saying anything.

I believe we all ought to seek God's leadership but that's no guarantee we'll all agree about it. Until we're infallible, we cannot be absolutely sure of God's will. We can only know what we believe to be His will.

Once a decision is made we should be ready to support it. I know the majority isn't always right. But, neither are we!

July 22, 1975

Planning for Youth Camp

I'm grateful to our Youth Camp committee for all their work. They have met and dreamed and planned. They have drunk coffee and chased rabbits.

Norris Price, J. Ron McGee and Jack Pierce have been faithful to their job. We have been working since early this year to get ready for Camp. We've had several new situations to deal with.

We're going to a new place and we're going to try some new ideas at Camp this year. I'm sure we'll learn some new things, too!

We're not trying to get every camper to make a decision this week. We are interested in helping them grow. Some will become disciples. Others will renew their commitments to God. Hopefully, all will grow in their understanding of and love for God and His people.

George H. Davis

One of our concerns is to help families. We've scheduled classes in family enrichment. We're hoping to help campers in their families. From what we've seen in the last two years, there's a real need.

It's our hope Youth Camp can be a growth experience as well as a good time for everybody involved. Please remember us in prayer during the week.

August 5, 1975

"I'm 49 and this is my first youth camp!"

Charles Collins of Fairfield was speaking at the campfire service the last night of camp. He had taken his vacation so he and his wife could help at camp. He went on to say with much emotion, "It's been worth it all because my boy was saved tonight."

I believe our staff made this year's camp. Ron Brand, also of Fairfield, also took his vacation to work in camp. School teachers Gail Addison, Lyndall Rickard and Jerry Hefley spent part of their summer at camp.

Housewives Betty Qualls, Bessie Burkett, Linda Jones, Yvonne Lathrop and Cindy Withrow gave of their time when they had plenty to do.

Young people Cindy Alcorn, Curt Wood, Judy Ellis, Evelyn Fenton, Jane Johnson, Laura Kincart, Judy Wohler, Mark Davis and Rick Lathrop helped relate to youth.

Pastors Charles Boling, David Dean, Larry Gwaltney, Jim Crask and Norris Price helped guide us. Donna Price accompanied Norris to cook and to spend their wedding anniversary at camp. Wilma Crask, Lucille Cunningham and my wife also cooked.

Staff members J. Ron McGee and Dale Sloan contributed much to us. Former pastor Tom Cummings also helped.

I don't know where you'd find a better staff anywhere. Let's hear it for the staff!!!

August 20, 1975

You Are a Missionary

Missions, like charity, begin at home. Of course it doesn't end there. But, we got romantically excited about missions overseas. For some reason, this excitement doesn't always carry over to missions at home.

What's the difference? I'm not sure there is any basic difference. I believe missions is pretty much the same wherever it's done. Designations such as associational, state, home and foreign are more geographical than anything. They tend to be artificial. The work is very similar. There is some justification for calling an associational worker a "missionary."

Maybe the reason we get more excited about missions as they become more remote is there is less chance of our getting personally involved. We can give our money but can't see what else we can do.

We tend to want to hire someone to do our missions for us. We seldom even get deeply involved in prayer for missions or missionaries. One of the threats of missions nearer home is the call for participation.

September 10, 1975

Needed: Space

When the idea of securing an associational office building was discussed several years ago, I was opposed to it. Strangely enough, now I'm in favor of it!

What made me change my mind? I guess two things: (1) I'm more personally involved now. I see the need because I'm trying to do the work. (2) I believe the work has changed some. Our emphasis is on communication and fellowship. Promotion is secondary.

If we're going the right direction in the Association, I believe we need adequate space to work in.

And, by George, that's all the space I've got to write in here!

September 23, 1975

Education Doesn't Make A Preacher

Gerald Wright said, "I've been going to school every since I entered the ministry. I took two courses in grammar in college and one in seminary. But, I ain't sure I've got this grammar yet." Then he preached on the grammar of salvation at our annual meeting.

I've thought a little about the difference education makes in preachers.

It seems to me education gives a person the tools to work with. I recognize not all education is gotten in the classroom. Two persons can read a book and what they learn can be quite different.

Some preachers are dependent on books of sermons and sermon outlines all their lives. Their illustrations come from books rather than from life. Most preachers begin heavily dependent on the work of others. A few never graduate to faith in what God can do through them.

Now, I'm not against books. I am concerned about over dependence on them. A preacher needs to know how to use the basic tools of Bible study and ministry.

I'm grateful for all the help others have given me. But, the greatest help I've had is in getting to know myself. Some have helped me find out what my gifts are and how to develop them.

I heard in school, and I'm more and more convinced it's true, education can't make a preacher out of you. If you are a preacher, education can make you a better one.

October 16, 1975

George H. Davis

When are we going to move into the new office building?

I've answered that question several times lately.

We're waiting for the abstract to be brought up to date. After that, an attorney will give a legal opinion as to whether it's a good one. After that we'll be ready to borrow the money necessary and close the deal.

Some money has already come in from the churches. Others received an offering November 2 and will send it along soon. A complete report on church gifts will be made later. The goal for this offering is $2500. This amounts to a little over $50 for each resident member. This offering will be used as a down payment on the building.

By November 15 the trustees will have completed the purchase of the former Career Development building on Route 45 south of Fairfield.

Shortly after that we will begin mowing and cleaning. We'll move in as soon after that as possible. Some office furniture has been ordered. More will be ordered. I'm excited about the possibilities the larger quarters will offer us.

It will be good to get the mimeographing and addressing operations in a separate room – away from phones and traffic. It'll also be great to have room to store supplies all in one place. Separate offices and a reception area will also be a boon to those coming to talk.

I'm excited about the possibilities of the two large open rooms. I believe we can develop these in many ways. They will make ideal rooms for conferences or classes. They can be used as work rooms for many projects. They might be developed as a learning resource center for all the churches.

I don't believe anyone is more anxious to get moved than I am. I want us to plan to have an open house when we get in and settled. I want you to come and see our new associational office building.

But, I think we'd all be negligent if we failed to say a big "THANKS" to First Baptist Church in Fairfield. For the past 2½ years they have provided space, utilities, janitor service and fellowship. I'll miss this!

November 4, 1975

Moving?

By the time you read this, we may be moving into our new associational offices. Then again…

Right now we're waiting the processing of our application for title insurance. As soon as everything is in order, we'll complete the purchase and get possession of the former Career Development building at the south edge of Fairfield.

The First Baptist Church in Fairfield has provided office space for the Association for the past 32 months.

Money continues to come in from the churches for our down payment. So far we have received over $1300 with a few churches still to send their offering. We'll list the gifts by churches when all are in.

by George

I'm not sure how much I'm looking forward to moving. I'd like to wake up one morning and be there. But I'd like to be able to find things when I get there, so I guess I'll go through the process.

One of my bywords is, "Moving is for the birds." They have so little packing and unpacking to do. But then one can hardly be a preacher and be unwilling to move.

If you're wondering how much there can be to move in an office, I'd be willing to show you.

November 19, 1975

Still Moving

Well, it looks like we're finally about ready to complete the purchase of the office building!

I had begun to feel a little like an expectant mother. Every few days someone would ask, "When are you going to move?" It was a little like asking a mother-to-be, "When are you going to have that baby?"

It's not that I mind people asking. It's just that I couldn't give them a date! I know I'm not carrying the burden of a prospective mother, but I'll certainly be relieved to get moved.

We had been waiting on title insurance. Now we are ready to sign papers Saturday morning, December 6. We'll plan to move sometime the following week the Lord willing!

As soon as we can get heat and water turned on, we'll begin cleaning. We don't plan to do any extensive remodeling now. We'll use the space pretty much as is for the present. We already have four tables and twenty-four chairs to use for classes or conferences. Another desk and chair will be delivered whenever we ask for them. So we're raring to go!

I've been thinking recently about the possibility of developing a training center for the churches at the new building. Audio and video cassettes as well as films and filmstrips are becoming available on a wide variety of subjects. I believe there are some real possibilities for training church leaders.

I'm delighted with the response from the churches to our request for extra money for a down payment on the building. We've already received almost $2000. 21 of our 30 active churches have given. Others may be on the way. We'll still take it. Gifts should be sent to Andy Moye, Route 3, Fairfield. Please mark them for the building. In the next issue of The Tie we'll list the gifts by churches.

I hope you'll be patient with us while we're moving. We want to be able to serve you better from our new facilities. Our whole purpose is to serve the churches. If you can't reach me at the office, call me at home. If I'm not there leave a message. My kids are usually pretty good about giving them to me - within a day or two!

And come and see us – with your broom and mop!

December 5, 1975

George H. Davis

We're In

An announcement: We've moved into the new associational building. We're located on the west side of Route 45 at the south edge of Fairfield. There's a red barn in our front yard (temporarily).

An invitation: Come and see us. We'll be happy to show you around. We're delighted with the space. Although we're still straightening up, we're presentable.

A request: Please keep our drive open. There is a drive between us and the trailer to the south. It must be kept open for the people behind us. Please park parallel beside the building, or behind the building.

We're here to stay! It's not just that I don't want to move again soon. I believe this move says to the community and to the churches, we're here to stay. The Association is not a fly-by-night operation that can be ignored or forgotten.

We've committed ourselves to Jesus Christ <u>and</u> to each other. We <u>are</u> in fellowship. Our building and our association must build that fellowship.

THE ASSOCIATION IS FREE CHURCHES IN FELLOWSHIP ON MISSION IN THEIR SETTING.

By the way, I've got a new filmstrip on "The Baptist Association" I'd be glad to show in your church. I also still have the "Joe, the Baptist" film on associational work.

December 19, 1975

Logos

I seldom watch television news. I'm not bragging – just stating a fact. It's partly habit and partly being fed-up with "investigative reporting."

Trial by television is a radical departure from our American heritage. I've come to distrust the media. Pardon me if my politics is showing.

But that's not what I want to talk about. I did watch Harry Reasnor last night and particularly enjoyed his last story.

It seems NBC was looking for a new logo (an emblem). According to the story they paid something less than a million dollars to an agency for their new stylized N.

It turns out Nebraska Educational Television was looking for a logo. They paid something less than a hundred dollars for a stylized N that looks almost identical to NBC's. The main difference seems to be in the color.

Since Nebraska Educational Television began using their logo several months ago, they are objecting to NBC's use. Their attorneys are meeting on the matter.

All this made me more grateful to the art department of the Home Mission Board. They designed the logo we have been using for the past several months.

We are using the stylized GW as our emblem. It appears on almost everything we send out. We hope it will identify us as GREATER WABASH Baptist Association.

January 8, 1976

by George

"Warsh Day"

I enjoy driving through the country on a winter night. The leaves have fallen and you can see forever on a clear night. Mercury vapor lamps dot the countryside.

It reminds me of when I was growing up. You could look across the pastures and fields and see if your neighbor was home. His pole light or his house lights gave a warm reassurance.

Oh, I got my lessons by an Aladdin lamp. But as a youth I helped wire our house. I remember converting our Maytag from a gasoline engine to an electric motor. I also remember an old hand-operated washer. It's not that I'm old – I just have a good memory.

Remember "wash day?" We called it "warsh day." It took all day to heat water, wash the clothes, and hang them out to dry. My job was to start the engine on the washer and then clean the clotheslines. A small rag with a little kerosene worked wonders on the lines.

Now we wash every day. But, we can do everything else while we're washing. Automation has made "wash day" obsolete.

Another thing I haven't done for a while is harness a horse. I used to struggle to get the collar over his head and then to sling the harness on his back.

I wonder if we're still operating on obsolete skills in our churches. Or, have we learned to communicate the changeless gospel to our changing society.

January 21, 1976

Five Fabulous Sundays!

February is a rare month this year. It has five Sundays. That happens only once every other blue moon!

Many churches are encouraging members to be present all five Sundays. They are recognizing those who come. (Someone reminded me recently: we used to have half-time preaching – now we have full-time preaching and half-time members.)

The preacher to the Hebrew Christians reminds them of their responsibility to encourage each other. One of the ways they can do this is by continuing their habit of meeting together.

I don't think it's any accident he goes on to warn: "For there is no longer any sacrifice that will take away sins if we purposely go on sinning after the truth has been made known to us. Instead, all that is left is to be afraid of what will happen... It is a terrible thing to fall into the hands of the living God!" (Hebrews 10: 26-27, 31 TEV)

If this is true, church attendance must be more important than we have made it, Charles Trentham writes, "The person who takes his loyalty to Christ lightly is such an easygoing relaxed person that he imagines God also to be easygoing. Because he has never taken his promises to God seriously he thinks God does not take them seriously," (Broadman Bible Commentary, XII, p.76)

February 6, 1976

George H. Davis

Reality

There seems to be an epidemic of catastrophe movies around: The Poseidon Adventure, Towering Inferno, Jaws, The Hindenburg, Earthquake plus a host of science-fiction tales.

I'm not much of a movie fan, but I do have an idea why we're so addicted to disaster.

Could it be that reality is harder to face than tragedy? It's easier for us to escape from the sometimes boring, monotonous routine to the thrill of tragedy. There's a perverted kind of excitement about calamity.

You may protest and say life is filled with tragedy. I don't believe it. Tragedy is the exception – not the rule. I know we all have tragedy, but our lives are not filled with it.

It's true, the news media emphasize tragedy. It's what we want to hear. That only proves my point. News is not what's happening – it's what will sell. News has become a commodity.

Our tastes have turned to the bizarre. The weirder a story is, the better copy it is. I believe we've become a society of escapists.

A concern of mine nearer home is that this same spirit has invaded our theology. We have become escapist here too.

There is a popular religion that emphasizes escape from trouble. "All of us good guys are going to be rescued while the rest of you bad guys have to suffer." We even have a number of gospel films portraying this.

I don't believe this is biblical. Jesus' prayer for his disciples was not that they would be taken out of the world but that they would be victorious over evil. He was speaking to his disciples when he said, "In the world you have tribulation; but be of good cheer, I have overcome the world."

I know the discipline required for Christian discipleship is demanding. But let's not try to escape by inventing a theology to fit our violence-oriented society.

I believe living the Christian life demands our facing the realities of each day. Some are good and some seem full of sameness and routine. I believe Jesus can help make each day significant.

The promise of "pie in the sky by and by when you die" is not the whole gospel. Jesus also gives strength for daily discipleship. I don't read where he asked, "Who wants to go to heaven?" I do hear him calling, "Follow me."

February 24, 1976

Sunday School Enrollment

I listened to Andy Anderson with some skepticism. But before the three hours were up, I was a convert.

Andy Anderson is the father of the ACTION plan for enrolling people in Bible study. He was in Mt. Vernon February 28 to explain the plan.

by George

He begins with the knowledge that Sunday school attendance averages 40-50% of the enrollment. The way to increase attendance he says is not to take people who aren't coming off the roll. The way to increase attendance is to increase enrollment.

Churches in the program are increasing their enrollment by 19% and their attendance by 10%. A task force is enlisted to visit every home in a community to enroll people in Bible Study. The "Open philosophy of Enrollment" includes enrolling:
- Anyone (even those who have not been to church)
- Anywhere (even away from the church building)
- Anytime (even other than Sunday school time.)

who agrees to be enrolled.

I'm convinced that a church who follows through on this program, will grow. It's just good, basic Sunday school work. And that's the way churches grow.

March 9, 1976

Communication

One of my jobs is to be a communicator. It's hard to build fellowship between churches if they don't know each other. As I share information and ideas, we become better acquainted.

I enjoy telling good news. I like to share the good things churches are doing. Most good church programs do not come out of Springfield or Nashville but out of churches. Springfield or Nashville hears about them and begins promoting them. That's the way it should be!

One of my goals is to keep up with what's going on in our churches. I need your help. If you're doing something, let me know. I won't always put it in The Tie, but I want to know.

Through The Tie and through personal contact, I want to help us know and care about each other. I believe this is one key to effective intercessory prayer.

I heard Bob Hastings say, "To pray for all the lost people in the world is spreading it kind of thin. We need to pray for individuals by name." I believe we need to pray intelligently for each other.

April 7, 1976

Do You Drive an Auto or a Car?

What's the difference? About forty years! Do you still call your refrigerator an ice box?

Do you teach Primaries or Children?

What's the difference? About ten years. About ten years ago the Baptist Sunday School Board adopted a simplified grouping-grading plan. Many people and churches have not yet caught on.

Let's compare the groupings used since 1967 to old ones:

Old	New
Nursery (birth-3 yrs.)	Preschool (birth-5 yrs.)
Beginner (4 & 5 yrs.)	
Primary (6-8 yrs.)	Children (6-11 yrs. or grades 1-6)
Junior (9-12 yrs.)	
Intermediate (13-16 yrs.)	Youth (12-17 yrs. or grades 7-12)
Young People (17-24 yrs.)	
Adults (25 yrs. up)	Adults (18 yrs. up)

The new plan is obviously much simpler. It offers many advantages to the smaller church. The broader groupings mean a church can have as many or as few classes as it needs. Instead of seven basic groups there are four. The smallest churches may not need seven classes. The larger churches can still provide as many classes as they need. They can have multiple departments in each age group.

Another advantage of the new plan is the possible use of school grades. Preschoolers are just that. Children are in elementary grades. Youth are junior high and high school students. Adults are above high school age.

All the literature and teaching materials are being prepared for the new groupings. If you're still teaching Primaries, you have to figure out what literature to get. You have to try to adapt teaching suggestions for Children to Primaries. Why not get out of that auto and step up to a car?

I believe there's one more step the Board needs to take. They need to carry the school alignment to its logical conclusion. Literature should be published by quarters beginning in September. (Sept., Oct., Nov.; Dec., Jan., Feb.; Mar., Apr., May; and June, July, Aug.) Promotion Day should be moved to the end of the school year. This makes more sense than waiting until the end of September – a month after the new school year has started.

April 20, 1976

Pastor Appreciation Day

Mother's Day is traditionally time of remembrance and appreciation. I think it's great!

I want to see it extended to another group – pastors and church staff. I know we are grateful for them. But, like mother, we often fail to tell them.

Pastors are human. They hear a lot of gripes and criticism. I believe they should also hear praise. I'm not too worried about them getting the big-head. We're pretty good about keeping them humble.

We need to learn to remember birthdays, wedding anniversaries and anniversaries with the church. Why not begin making plans for a Pastor Appreciation Day – June 6 or another convenient time. Really let your pastor know you love him.

About 90 persons attended the open house at the associational office Sunday afternoon, May 2nd. Most were from the Fairfield area.

by George

Special thanks go to ladies from eight churches who furnished homemade cookies: Barnhill; Elm River; Fairfield, First; Fairfield, North Side; Mill Shoals; Mt. Zion; Pleasant Grove and Sims.

Mrs. Jerry Dickey, Mrs. George Davis and Angie Dickey served refreshments. L. M. Huff and J. Ron McGee helped paint on Friday.

Those who missed the open house may stop by anytime to see the office. The office is open every morning – Tuesday through Friday from 8 o'clock to noon. It is also open many afternoons and Saturdays.

May 11, 1976

What's it feel like to be a pastor?

Good… Bad… Sad… Glad… Mad… Happy… Great… Terrible….

A pastor feels about everything you do. He has the same joys and sorrows and concerns. He is frightenly human – and vulnerable.

There are many joys in being a pastor. It's a joy to watch people grow and develop. It's a joy to work with good people. It's a joy to let God work through you.

There are also a fair share of sorrows and disappointments. There's the sorrow of people who shut God out of their life. There's the disappointment in yourself – you don't do all you should.

Pastors wrestle with discouragement and loneliness. Faith in an unchanging God, an understanding wife and a loving congregation help you to be faithful to your call.

I used to think I'd rather work anywhere than on an assembly line. Then I began to realize being a pastor was a lot like working on an assembly line. You never get to see a job completed. You work along the line and see some progress but don't see the job finished. Paul said, "I planted, Apollos watered, but God gave the increase."

There's always a job somewhere else on the line. There's more work than you can do. Then there's the temptation to try to do everything. There are things somebody needs to do and nobody's doing them. I guess it's the temptation to play God.

Slowly the pastor learns to try to give himself to what God called him to. He seeks to call the people of God to do the work of God. He tries to prepare them for this work.

How does it feel to be a pastor? It feels like the greatest privilege in the world. And even when it doesn't seem like a privilege, God reminds you of your frailty, too.

How do I know how it feels to be a pastor? I've spent a third of my life as a pastor. I still feel like a pastor… to pastors.

May 25, 1976

Sticking My Neck Out

I've heard a turtle never gets anywhere unless he sticks his neck out. I'm not a turtle but here goes!

George H. Davis

I believe churches should voluntarily pay taxes on their parsonages. Not on their buildings used for worship and education – but on homes for their pastor or staff members.

If I interpret Jesus' teaching right – He said if we are going to use Caesar's coins to trade with, we should be willing to pay the tariff. I would imply that principle to mean we should be willing to pay for police and fire protection and other civic improvements.

But, why pay taxes on the church-owned homes only – why not on the places of worship too? I believe there's an important principle involved here, too. Churches should not have to pay taxes on their essential functions. I believe auxiliary businesses may be taxed – buildings rented to commercial firms or a business operated for a profit. A business owned by churches and operated solely as a service to the churches should not be taxed.

Church buildings seem to he an integral part of the work of the churches now. I know a church can function without a building, but to reach and minister to many people, buildings seem to be necessary.

I'm not at all sure parsonages are essential. In some cases a housing allowances can be provided and the pastor or staff member buy or lease his own home or apartment. Many part-time pastors will live in their own homes. I believe as a matter of equality, all homes should be taxed.

The time may come when churches will be asked to pay taxes on all their property. I believe we should volunteer to pay on church-owned homes. You may quote the proverb about the camel getting his nose in the tent. But I'm not sure we have to let him camp with us. It may be that voluntarily paying would show our civil leaders we do want to be an asset not a liability.

I'm neither an attorney nor the son of an attorney. I do claim to be a prophet and a church man though. I'm not a predictor of the future but a speaker for God. And I am committed to the church. I believe it is in our best interest to take the steps I've suggested.

But I'm willing to listen to your opinion. As Paul said, I have no word from the Lord on this; I'm giving my opinion.

July 23, 1976

Youth Camp '76

The weather was delightful; the food was delicious; the counselors were dedicated; the campers were something else!

Our youth camp this year was the best in my experience. We had 13 saved and 12 rededications. We had very few problems, very little sickness and only minor injuries.

I'm deeply grateful for the fine workers we had. It's so much easier to have a good camp when you have enough help.

David Claybrook did a tremendous job speaking to us. Leona Davis and the cooks kept us well fed. Charlene Knight kept us feeling well and Jerry Hefley kept us busy playing.

We worked our counselors harder than ever before. Almost all of them lead either a Bible study or small-group session. Many were involved in the recreation program. But I didn't hear any grumbling or complaining. Some of them took a little longer getting over the hills Friday morning – but no complaining.

The campers were the best behaved group I've worked with. They were serious-minded. I appreciate the homes and churches they came from.

This was one time I believe everybody came away from camp looking forward to next year. We're beginning our evaluation and planning next week. I hope you'll be at our Camp Reunion at Pleasant Grove on September 18 whether you were at camp or not. Maybe some of the enthusiasm will rub off.

August 26, 1976

Youth Camp Letters

I enjoy receiving letters. I'm not the best at writing, but I enjoy getting them.

I got several letters and notes from counselors about camp. And I appreciated them. But, I'd like to share a couple letters I got from campers. Charles Collins II wrote:

> Dear Mr. Davis,
> Thank you for having camp this year.
> I enjoyed the games, the funny stories the preacher told, the food. I liked finding out who would be called to eat first.

Then his older sister, Anna, expressed her appreciation:

> Dear Mr. Davis,
> I really enjoyed camp a lot, it gets better every year.
> I'm glad you were the camp director. I think the games were great, especially softball & ping-pong. The church services were the best of all though. The speaker was really a great guy. I enjoyed his little stories he told at the church services to express or point out a learning to us. My counselor was really a nice person. Devotion was a special time for me because I got closer to God and the other kids in our cabin. I hope I can go next year.

I'll have to confess – before Camp I was beginning to wonder if we really should put all this time and energy into this one week. It's probably the biggest single project we undertake each year.

September 9, 1976

George H. Davis

A Great Association

In accepting a TV Emmy award, Peter Falk said, "Hundreds of people are involved in a TV show – writers, producers, cameramen, sound men and crew – but when a show is a hit, the spotlight narrows down to one person, the star. This is a very sensible system, and I don't want anybody to change it."

It takes more than one man to make a great association. Many people contributed to our annual meeting. It was good to have Rod Latta, our state music director, with us for the entire meeting. He led our closing service Tuesday night. He made singing fun. He taught us some things about using music in worship.

He suggested we may need to have congregational rehearsals as well as choir rehearsals. "Baptists may be ritualistic," he observed. "In one church, no matter what I did, the ushers came forward after the third song."

It was good to see Billy Allen, if only for a minute! He's our state Sunday school director. He came by to leave a videotape and a videotape player. Rod convinced him to share what ACTION is doing across our state. He'll be back this weekend and next week to direct ACTION at First Baptist Church in Fairfield. He's been a busy man trying to keep up with ACTION.

I was glad to see Edgar Schulz and the Northside Baptist Church of Grayville recognized as the rural church of the year. This is not the first time for Ed. He led the church in what he knew would help them. And it did! Their mission giving increased by 71% last year. I hope other churches will talk to Ed about the Rural Church Achievement Ministry. Or, call Walter Mihlfeld in Carbondale. He's our Rural/Urban missionary. He says that means "country preacher."

It was good to see so many churches represented at the annual meeting. Many shared what God is doing in their congregations. I am more convinced than ever that an association is "free churches in fellowship on mission in their setting."

God has given us to each other. Our churches are different as we are different. But God has made us brothers and sisters. Our fellowship is in Him. Our mission is His. We are not just "our kind of people" doing our own thing. God has given us to our communities. We are to make Jesus Christ known. If there is to be a "star" let it be Him.

October 6, 1976

How do you spell ACTION?

I spell it W-O-R-K.

ACTION is a reach out enrollment plan for Sunday school. The heart of the plan is to enroll people where they are. Then the Sunday school workers encourage them to attend.

It's not magic! It's not easy! It's not all that new! It is good, basic Sunday school work.

by George

It takes detailed preparation to make the campaign work. Many people must be involved to visit every home in a community. Sunday school teachers and officers must be committed to welcoming new people.

None of this is easy. But then, reaching people has never been easy. But, it is worthwhile. We don't reach everyone we enroll. But, if we reach 40% it's worthwhile.

It's a way to get out of our shell and reach out to people where they are. And that's work for most of us. But, I believe it's God's work.

October 20, 1976

Fringe Benefits

There's been a lot of talk lately about fringe benefits. I'd like to talk a little about fringe benefits of the ACTION campaign.

Last month four of our churches participated in a Sunday School ACTION Enlargement Campaign. They attempted to contact every family in their communities to enroll unenlisted families in Bible study.

One of the things that happened was the building of good will in the communities. People were glad to see church members out working. I ran into several people who said they went to North Side when they went. I encouraged them to go. The next Sunday they had 123 present. That was 20 above their average. 60 people visiting in the community helped all the churches.

In Barnhill, Bill Camp and his people visited every home meeting people and inviting them to church. They have begun a Bible study group on Wednesday afternoons. They have also started ringing the church bell at 9 and 9:30 Sunday mornings.

I believe whatever we can do to get our churches before the people of the community in a favorable light will help. They like to see God's people doing something. This may help much more than passing resolutions condemning what is going on in the community.

November 5, 1976

What is an Association of Baptist Churches?

What is our work? How can we know when we're doing a good job? Are there things we should be doing?

An association exists not only to help the churches do their work but also to do things the churches cannot do individually. The association conducts meetings to help train and inspire church leaders. It plans and coordinates cooperative work – like an associational ACTION campaign, or simultaneous revivals or a world missions conference. It provides services to the churches.

George H. Davis

It is not the association's job to keep everybody busy. Perhaps the best barometer of the effectiveness of the association is the temperature of the churches. If an association is helping churches do the work God wants them to do, it may not be noticed. It may not be in the spotlight. The focus may be on what's going on in the churches. Perhaps that's as it should be.

I don't see the association as primarily a promoter of programs. I believe in and support many programs. But, I doubt that's the most important thing I do. I hope my basic thrust will be to grow and develop people – particularly pastors and church leaders, I realize this includes the development of skills and that programs can contribute to this. But personal relationships are basic to all our work.

The associations came into being to foster fellowship and maintain doctrinal purity among the churches. They also existed for cooperative mission work. For many years "missionaries" in our area were expected to preach the gospel in "destitute places" and in struggling churches. They also served as associational evangelists. Some of these needs are not so great now in our area.

Our need for fellowship and for doctrinal purity may be greater than ever. I believe it's still important for the association to provide a forum for fellowship and the discussion of doctrine. If we don't know and trust each other we're surely going to be afraid to talk about our differences. We won't risk disapproval.

It's not that we all need to look just alike. Or, that someone needs to straighten us out so we all think alike. But, our opportunities and problems are similar. Perhaps God can use us to help each other find ways of dealing with them. Perhaps it's significant that almost half of Paul's church letters were sent to groups of churches.

November 23, 1976

Does Missions Like Charity Begin at Home?

I suppose it does. Perhaps it really begins in the heart. If a man is inwardly selfish, he'll only give grudgingly. He'll want his church to reflect his spirit, too. He'll be more interested in the things that benefit him than in those directed toward others.

In most churches it's a constant fight to keep mission giving at a healthy level. Our selfish nature is always asking, "What do we *get* out of that?" The assumption that we should give only to those things we benefit from is foreign to the spirit of Christ.

Missions is the work of the church beyond its field. It's reaching out to touch others. The benefit we get is in knowing we are doing the work of Christ.

Many things are called missions. I suppose a church can call anything missions it wishes. But, I wonder if we're not just trying to salve our conscience by making it look like we're giving more to missions.

I believe the Cooperative Program is worthy of our support. It is Southern Baptists' means of supporting 2700 missionaries in 82 countries around the world. Through it we also support over 2100 home missionaries. We also help train pastors and other Christian workers in our six seminaries.

by George

I'm glad our state has increased the percentage we will share with Southern Baptist causes next year. 41% of all Cooperative Program money received will go for work outside our state. *But* Illinois is a mission field, too. 59% of our mission money will be used to reach the millions of lost people here at home.

The Baptist Children's Home also deserves our support. It does not receive Cooperative Program money. It depends on the churches for its support. Inflation has been especially hard on child care ministry. Many churches need to increase the percentage they give to this work. Others need to begin giving on a regular basis.

I'm amazed at the number of people who tell me they've never been to the campus in Carmi. This is not the only place our child care ministries are going on, but it *is* in our area. We need to be familiar with the work and needs. Maybe we can give *more than money*!

December 8, 1976

Here's Looking at You!

I seldom see some of you so I wanted to look at you this time.

Let me tell you a little about God's goodness to our family this year. My wife, Leona, has begun teaching consumer education at Fairfield high school. She teaches two hours a day. She continues to serve as a dietetic consultant to the Rest Haven Nursing Home in Albion. She has taught a course in food service sanitation for school cooks this fall. As many of you can verify, she also was chief cook at our associational youth camp at Lake Sallateeska again this summer.

Our oldest son, Mark, began his sophomore year at Eastern Illinois University in Charleston. He's enjoying pre-med studies and Campus Crusade activities (and the company of a girl from Peoria). He has begun part-time work at the hospital in Charleston.

Our only daughter, Jane, graduated from high school last spring. She finished in three years. I m not sure she's that smart – I think she just enjoys being busy! She is attending Wabash Valley College in Mt. Carmel. She's studying child care (and other things).

Jim is a sophomore in high school. He keeps us busy chauffeuring him to jazz band, science club, basketball games, etc. He's anxious for next fall and his driver's license. We have mixed emotions about that.

Mike is an eighth-grader. He enjoys independent studies, band and caring for his gerbils. He and Jim occasionally disagree about football teams (and other things).

We're looking forward to our family being together over the holidays. We'll enjoy the Davis clan Christmas in Patoka with my brothers and sisters. We'll also share Christmas with Leona's father in West Frankfort.

I suppose, outside of my Lord, my family is God's greatest gift to me. And our Lord makes them even greater.

May you and your family enjoy God's blessings, too.

December 20, 1976

George H. Davis

Brothers are Supposed to Fight - - - Aren't They?

My brothers and I used to have an occasional misunderstanding. Our kids don't always see eye-to-eye. When they do, they're usually standing toe-to-toe ready to slug it out!

But brothers can learn to love. One of the best things about Christmas is visiting with my four brothers and one sister. We're much closer now than when we were growing up. Our love has grown through the years. I wouldn't trade with anyone *now* – but I remember when I would have traded – *(with anyone)*!

Baptists are supposed to fight - - - aren't they?

We seem to have earned a reputation for fighting – and we've done our share. I guess any group that stresses personal freedom above doctrinal conformity is going to have differences.

Our tastes in music vary widely. Some don't even like to sing! Well-planned worship services leave some cold. Spontaneous services bewilder others. Churches don't come out of the same mold. Even Baptist churches! We are different. I doubt we should try to be alike. But I have no doubt about our obligation to love and trust each other.

Churches are supposed to fight - - - aren't they?

Baptists have sometimes refused to admit others are real churches. So it's a victory when we begin to see each other as competitors – at least we're in the same business. How long 'til we look on each other as sister churches?

Surely we don't have to agree on every jot and tittle for us to have fellowship. As Baptists we are committed to a common Lord. We share an allegiance to the Bible. We believe in a spiritual rebirth. Our churches are made up of those who have decided to follow Jesus.

A few would make certain evidences of the Spirit or a particular brand of millennialism tests of fellowship. But Baptists have repeatedly refused to set up a creed – either for belief or behavior. Our fellowship is in Christ – not in the way we serve Him.

Remember, it's hard to hug if you're wearing a strait jacket!

January 6, 1977

Think It'll Snow?

Aren't we having some winter! This has been a good time for "I remember when" stories. But I don't remember it ever being colder than this. I remember it getting down to -13 degrees when I was is college. But last week it got down to -18 and this week to -23 in Fairfield. Last Sunday the low was -8 and the high -4. That's a mean temperature of -6. And that's <u>mean</u>!

The local Dairy Queen had a sign I liked. "COME ON SPRING" it cheered. The morning it was 23 below someone saw a beagle out west of town with jumper cables trying to get a rabbit running!

by George

I remember hearing Jimmy Baldwin preach on "Hast thou entered into the treasures of the snow?" It was up in Effingham – I believe at a Louisville associational M night. He reminded us how beneficial the snow was. As I remember, we had had a snow storm that day!

I guess I need to hear that sermon again! I'm getting tired of it! By the way, that text is found in Job 38:22. The newer translations talk about the "storehouses of the snow." You may feel like you've been in the middle of the storehouse – especially if you've been stuck!

But, there's still enough farmer left in me to appreciate the snow cover on the wheat when it gets this cold. It acts as insulation to keep it from freezing. Strange, but true! Jimmy told us a lot of other benefits – such as the minerals the snow brings. But, I've forgotten most of them. Like I said, I need to hear that sermon again.

I've made it pretty good, though. Haven't got stuck - - yet! I'm grateful to the state police for keeping us informed about road conditions. And the state highway department has done a tremendous job on the highways. I guess I'm as quick as anybody to gripe. Let's remember to say "Thank you."

I hope in the midst of frozen water pipes and heating problems and cars that won't start you've found added warmth in your family. Our TV has been on the fritz so we've been forced to find some things to do together. And it's been good! Maybe you've had enough "togetherness" with school being out so much. But, I hope you've gotten reacquainted, too. It's so easy to live under the same roof and come and go without really noticing each other. Television is a poor substitute for a fireplace for family warmth.

January 21, 1977

Anyone for Barbecued Ground Hog?

The weather continues to penetrate our thoughts and plans. Some have tried ignoring the cold, hoping it'll go away. But six weeks of snow and biting cold is hard to ignore. And we're just now in the middle of winter! I think I'd have joined a party to blindfold that groundhog if it would have done any good.

If we could only save some of this for August. I'm sure by then this will be only a dim memory. We'll be wishing for some relief – from the heat. Remember the boy who said, "Every winter the distance my dad walked to school gets longer and the snow he walked through gets deeper." If we follow that principle, this will be some winter 20 years from now.

I guess I'll never forget what Cecil Fuson said one August afternoon at an annual meeting. We were at the First Baptist Church in Altamont. Air conditioning was unthought of. The discussion had been heated. Cecil got up in typical, diplomatic Fuson style. "I don't know about anybody else, but I'm about to come unsoldered," he reported as he removed his coat and loosened his tie. Well, some of that warmth would certainly be welcome now. I haven't seen anybody getting overheated lately. (Now don't tell me about your radiator freezing up and then boiling over.)

George H. Davis

But I'm learning some things. I've come to a new respect (awe) for the weather. I've found I can be quite helpless in the face of the elements. There are times when cars need a push – and so do I! We've all been reminded a person can freeze if he's not careful.

Some have been learning about "house churches." The First Baptist Church in Carmi encouraged their people to meet for neighborhood services one Sunday night. Our pastor asked us to worship as families. Some have had to dismiss Wednesday night prayer meetings.

Do you remember reading about "the church that meets in their house"? This was before churches had buildings. If fuel shortages continue we may have to revive that practice. I've had some of my most enjoyable experiences in home Bible fellowships. The informal atmosphere helps break the ice.

Oh, we'll always need a time for all of us to get together. There's encouragement in praising God in a congregation. But we may also need the small group time – even in warm weather. It may take us a while to thaw out – inside.

February 8, 1977

I Thought He was Kidding!

"I'm glad I'm raising my family in Chicago," he told me. I was visiting the Northwest Baptist Church it Chicago. It ministers to several cultures and economic levels.

As I listened, I realized he was serious. "I'm glad I'm raising my kids where there is more than one kind of people. I believe they're richer for it." He had moved to Chicago from southern Illinois and was happy. I had just spent four days with a black pastor and his family. I began to understand what he meant. I felt richer for my experience, too. I don't think I grew up prejudiced – perhaps a little provincial, but not prejudiced.

As I joined millions of Americans watching "Roots" I reflected on my own limited experiences with black people. I remembered my boss on a student janitor crew at Old Main on the campus of Southern Illinois University in Carbondale. He showed us how to do our job and expected us to do it. We respected him. (You had to respect a man who'd made 25 jumps over Italy during World War II.) He happened to be black.

I remembered my neighbor in seminary— Theophilus A. Adejunmobi. We called him T.A. He and his wife left five children in Nigeria to train here. I remember asking him how he happened to speak so good English. He told me he'd taught English in Nigeria. I felt foolish. I had assumed because he was from Africa he was ignorant! He told me his grandfather was a Baptist preacher!

I remembered umpiring a Little League baseball game with "Junior" Hatchett. He owned the notorious "Glass Bar" in Colp. He was under indictment on a drug charge. His "Ma" also had a thriving business. They happened to be black. We had little in common except that we each had a son playing ball. And parents were fair game to be drafted as umpires. We got along fine on the ball diamond.

by George

Then I remembered the Coleman's and a few other families in Markham and south Chicago. They'd opened their homes and hearts to me. They happened to be black. But they enriched my life. I felt I was a better person for sharing in their lives.

I couldn't help but wonder if they were watching "Roots" too. And I wondered how they felt. I felt ashamed and angry and hurt. As I reflected on my feelings, I realized Alex Haley knew infinitely more about his "roots" than I did about mine.

February 24, 1977

"Is this Kosher Ham?"

We were enjoying a fellowship meal during simultaneous revivals in Louisville Association. Carvin Bryant was clowning about the ham.

I like simultaneous revivals. They can make an impact on an area. The idea of several Baptist churches doing something together is heartening.

I enjoy the fellowship the pastors and evangelists have. I regret not all the members get to share this. But, maybe the preachers need it worse!

I especially regret more people will not get to hear Dr. Smith, our executive secretary. He'll be preaching at First Baptist in Fairfield. I wish more of our people could meet and hear him.

I hope we'll be remembering each other in prayer during these days of revival. We need it, especially as we try to break out of our neat, little shells.

It's so easy for us to get satisfied with what we're doing. Or, discouraged when nothing's happening. It takes the breath of God to breathe life and hope into us.

March 9, 1977

Spring Flowers

Are the flowers prettier than ever this spring, or does it just seem like it?

I hope the winter of '76-'77 is over. And I'm enjoying the daffodils more than ever. We've got more this spring than we've had since we moved to Fairfield. They were there all along. But this year they've decided to bloom!

I'm not much of a gardener so I don't know why they're blooming now. I wonder if the hard winter made them decide to shape up. My wife says it's because she wouldn't let us mow the tops before they died down last summer.

Whatever the reason, I'm enjoying them. I was ready for the flowers. And I guess that means I'll have to be cranking up my lawn mower. But I prefer that to shoveling snow. It's not that I hate winter. I just think I could enjoy it more in smaller doses.

I think of myself as a late bloomer. We seem to expect people to be "on the way up" when they're 25-35. I'm not sure about my climbing ambitions – but I think at 45 I'm realizing what God wants of me.

It's not that I'm satisfied. I'm just at peace. Maybe I'm just slow. It's taken me a while to get here. But I'm enjoying my work. I have a sense of mission about it.

George H. Davis

Oh, there's frustration and tension. But there's also joy and fulfillment. You've been kind and generous in allowing me to learn. I've made mistakes and failed. I think I've grown. I hope I've helped you grow.

April 6, 1977

The Annual Call

I'm sure there must have been some advantages to the "annual call." Many churches used to call a preacher in their annual business meeting – July or August.

When most of the preachers were bi-vocational (a term that's becoming popular) they weren't so upset by being voted on every year. If they didn't get called back they could continue farming or mining or carpentering. Then there were always other churches who'd decided not to call their preacher back. He might get called to one of these.

Failure to get called back to a church was not quite like getting fired. It was usually an acceptable way of saying the church and preacher weren't compatible. Russell Bennett says, "Most pastors leave because they do not fit the church culturally. If they are tough enough to stay three and a half years, the church tends to become like them."

Whatever the advantages were, I think the "annual call" has outlived its usefulness. To continue just because "we've always done it that way" is not justifiable.

If a pastor is doing a good job he should be encouraged and supported. If he's not, the church should pray that he will – either here or somewhere else. A call without time limits is not an invitation to laziness. It is an acknowledgment of trust.

A pastor can hardly get to know the people in one year. He's just getting his feet on the ground (and learning to avoid the mudholes). I'm told the average pastor stays 18 months. That's a scandal to the jaybirds! (That's one of my grandfather's sayings. I guess he thought blue jays had few scruples. They were notorious for stealing and creating a commotion. You didn't expect much good from them. When it got bad enough to have a scandal on the jaybirds, it was bad!)

Some churches don't practice an annual call but still expect the preacher to move every three or four years. Some of my best work has been done when I've stayed and worked through discouragement and problems. If the preacher leaves every time he feels like it, the church will elect a pulpit committee every few months. If he leaves every time someone in the church wants him to, the church will elect a pulpit committee every few months.

If a preacher's growing he can get some new sermons and learn new ways of dealing with people. If he's not, he's dead whether he stays or leaves and repeats his mistakes somewhere else.

We expect more of preachers and churches than sheep-stealing and causing a fuss. But sometimes we get scandal because we're not willing to treat each other as we want to he treated.

April 20, 1977

by George

I'm prejudiced

I'm prejudiced in favor of public education. It's not that I'm against private schools. I'm just in favor of public schools.

I keep hearing about the benefits of "Christian" education and a "Christian" environment. I even heard about a "Christian" college that advertised it was "40 miles from the nearest source of sin." Well, most of us can't get that far away from ourselves!

I also hear about atheistic professors. But, I've yet to meet one. That's right! I don't remember a single professor trying to push atheism down my throat or trying to destroy my faith. Some challenged my thinking, but that's their job.

As Christians, we're to create our own environment. We're not to try to protect our light but to let it shine. The Lord will keep it burning. I'm not convinced colleges should be a refuge from the world.

I'm not sure we as Baptists can afford our own colleges. I'm pretty sure I can't afford to send my kids to them.

But then, I'm prejudiced. I'm a graduate of a state university. And I'm proud of it.

June 9, 1977

Don't get too close!

Don't get too close!

I may be quarantined!

I could hardly wait to tell David Dickey about my Democrat vacation. For those who don't know David, he's a former Wayne County treasurer. He's still somewhat interested in politics. You need to understand he spells politics R-E-P-U-B-L-I-C-A-N.

He may quarantine me when I tell him we camped in Franklin D. Roosevelt State Park near Pine Mountain, Georgia. We also visited the Little White House at Warm Springs. Those of World War II vintage will recognize this as FDR's retreat.

My brother and I wanted to visit Koinonia Farm near Americus, Georgia. We learned we had to go through Plains to get there. Maybe you can understand now why I wanted to kid David about our trip.

My grandpa Davis was a staunch Republican. He said he wouldn't mind voting for a Democrat if he could find a good one. My brother and I fully expected to see the grass on his grave disturbed from his turning over.

We enjoyed visiting Koinonia. This experiment in Christian community was begun by Clarence Jordan in 1942. He sought a place where he could live out what he believed Christ taught. He tried to practice racial equality and non-violence. Of course he was misunderstood and maligned. He was accused of being a communist. He was churched and boycotted. He was threatened and bombed. But his ideals live on.

George H. Davis

I've been reading <u>The Cotton Patch Evidence, The Story of Clarence Jordan and the Koinonia Farm Experiment</u> by Dallas Lee. It's an exciting story. I'm not sure I'd always agree with Jordan but I am challenged by his commitment. He tried to live the gospel and not just preach it. I'm not sure many of us have the kind of courage (faith) that takes.

I doubt we should all join Koinonia. But I am convinced we should seek to experience it. Koinonia (pronounced coy-no-NEE-ah) is the Greek word for fellowship.

Jordan said, "Never did Paul or Peter or Stephen point to an empty tomb as evidence of the resurrection. The evidence was the spirit-filled fellowship."

June 24, 1977

I'm going to miss David

David Dean became pastor of the First Baptist Church in Fairfield just a few months after I moved to Grayville. He's been a good friend and a respected counselor.

He was chairman of the committee that recommended me for this job. The first two and one-half years I was here, my office was just across the hall from his. We talked almost daily. That's one of the things I've missed since moving into our own building.

I remember the night we drove to Carmi after a Mid-Year meeting at Pleasant Grove. We learned that pastor Dewitt Kelley and three members of the Stewart Street Baptist Church had been killed in a wreck on their way home. We visited briefly with the families. On the way home, David remarked about the contribution to heaven that church had made in so short a time.

I'll miss David's family too. Quiet, talented, and busy -- that's Carolyn. And Michael, Steven, and Timothy – they're fine boys.

I'll long remember Steven coming into my office to play with my toys. I nicknamed Timothy "Timothy Titus Ebenezer."

They'll be hard to forget. But then, maybe I won't try. Maybe I'll remember – and pray for them. After July 24 their address will be: 6 Upton Road, Framingham, MA 01701.

July 8, 1977

Power Outage

"If I ever make it through this winter, I'll never complain about the heat again."

Is that how the line goes? It seems like I heard it a few times about six months ago. But tunes change.

"If I ever make it through this summer, I'll never complain about the cold again" is the latest tune.

by George

Last January one of our gas department employees was telling about seeing a beagle with jumper cables trying to get a rabbit running. Recently I heard Frank Potts of Carmi match that. He told about an oil field worker throwing a chain off a truck the other day. The chain crawled over to the shade!

The power outage in New York City has reminded us again how dependent we are on electricity. Not only was the city dark. Elevators wouldn't run – and stairways were dark. Air conditioning wouldn't run – and windows wouldn't open.

I remember being near Leitchfield, Kentucky for a revival several years ago. (It was a two-week revival. Does that give you an idea how long ago it was?) My wife and I were staying with a family in the country. When we got up one morning, the power was off. Realizing she couldn't bake biscuits in her electric range, the wife said, "Well, we'll just have to have toast." It took her a minute to realize that the same power toasted her bread that baked her biscuits.

I wonder. If the power went off in our churches, how long would it take us to notice it? Oh, I don't mean the lights – electricity. I mean the power – Holy Spirit.

How much of what we plan and do could go on without the presence of the Holy Spirit to empower us? Could we simply go on with business as usual?

Maybe as we think about the year ahead, we should ask God to lead us into some impossible tasks. Maybe we need some jobs that can't be accomplished without him.

"Some trust in their war chariots and others in their horses,
but we trust in the power of the Lord our God." (Psa. 20:7)

July 21, 1977

Want to Know How to Cut Your Pastor's Salary?

Don't give him a raise. That will effectively cut his salary. The price of gasoline and a number of other items has doubled in the last few years. Who would have thought of paying $5 to $10 for a paperback book?

If you haven't raised your pastor's salary rather substantially, you've cut his buying power. Is that what you want to do? A church that fails to pay its pastor a living wage is short-changing itself. The energy he uses juggling his finances is lost to the church.

The Bible is abundantly clear about the need for full support. Paul argues:

Don't I have the right to be given food and drink for my work? Don't I have the right to follow the example of the other apostles and the Lord's brothers and Peter, by taking a Christian wife with me on my trips? Or are Barnabas and I the only ones who have to work for our living? What soldier ever has to pay his own expenses in the army? What farmer does not eat the grapes from his own vineyard? What shepherd does not use the milk from his own sheep? I don't have to limit myself to these everyday examples, because the Law says the same thing. We read in the Law of Moses, "Do not muzzle an ox when you are using it to thresh grain." Now, is God concerned about oxen? Didn't he really mean us when he said that? Of course it was written for us. The man who plows and the man who reaps should do their work in the hope of getting a share of the crop. We have sown spiritual seed among you. Is it too much if we reap material benefits from you? If others have the right to expect this from you, don't we have an even greater right?

But we haven't made use of this right. Instead, we have endured everything in order not to put any obstacle in the way of the Good News about Christ. Surely you know that the men who work in the Temple get their food from the Temple and that those who offer sacrifices on the altar get a share of the sacrifices. In the same way, *the Lord has ordered that those who preach the gospel should get their living from it.* (1 Corinthians 9:4-14 Today's English Version © American Bible Society. Italics mine.)

Paul later wrote, "The elders who do a good work as leaders should be considered worthy of receiving double pay, especially those who work at preaching and teaching." (1 Timothy 5:17 TEV) Jesus told his disciples "a worker should be given what he needs." (Matthew 10:10 TEV; see Luke 10:7b)

August 9, 1977

Camp: Worth the Effort

Every year before Camp I get to wondering if it's worth all the time and energy we put into getting ready.

Then Camp comes – and it's better than I imagined it could be. This year was no exception. It was our biggest camp. We had 137 campers and 48 counselors – a total of 185.

We had a great group of counselors and the best campers ever. 11 were saved during the week and 8 recommitted their lives to Christ.

The weather was unusually good. All the activities went well. Ask the campers who won the camper counselor softball game. I heard two scores: 14 to 2 and 11 to 2. (That adds up to 25 to 4.) Anyway, the counselors got to eat first that night.

We've come to look forward to hearing Rannetta Mullinax sing "Through It All" each year. It's a powerful testimony. Don Price summed it up when he said, "God has planned that those who give, receive." Those who give the most, receive the most.

I guess my greatest disappointment was those who felt no need of opening their lives to God. It's heartbreaking to see young people indifferent to God's call. Some life-changing decisions were made. But, I wish there would have been more.

By the way, I have a pretty nice assortment of towels and clothing left at camp. If you're missing some, give me a call.

August 26, 1977

Who Runs the Show?

I've noticed that the biggest problem churches seem to have is 'who's going to run the show?"

by George

Sometimes when a new pastor comes he thinks the church has called him to be their leader. He may lead out in several new programs and activities. Then he discovers there's a power structure who's always called the shots. Things aren't done without their approval

The pastor can buck them – and face dismissal. He can knuckle under and lose his self-respect. Or, he can find out early who the decision-makers are and try to work with them.

Not every church expects her pastor to be the leader. Some just want him to "stick to Preaching" and let them run the church.

What did the church elect the deacons to do? They probably don't know. Pendleton's <u>Church Manual</u> says Baptist churches are supposed to have deacons and they're supposed to serve tables. So, we elect deacons. But, nobody bothers to tell them what the church expects them to do. We don't translate the language of the New Testament into something we can understand today.

Church members sometimes have unrealistic expectations of deacons. If the church isn't doing well, it's the deacons' job to get it going. If they're mad at the pastor, they think the deacons should straighten him out – or, get rid of him.

I believe churches need to talk about who runs the show.

September 9, 1977

Kenneth G. Hall

I've known Kenneth G. Hall almost half my life. We met when I became pastor at the Second Little Prairie Baptist Church, north of Louisville, Illinois. He was missionary in the Louisville Baptist Association. My wife and I spent the week in seminary in Louisville, Kentucky and weekends on the church field.

Soon after I finished my seminary work, Brother Hall recommended me to the First Baptist Church in Altamont. It was in the same association and my appreciation for him continued to grow. But he moved to Fairfield about that time and I wasn't in close touch with him. I saw him regularly at meetings – particularly at Southeastern Illinois Pastors' Fellowship meetings. He had become missionary in the Mt. Erie Baptist Association (now Greater Wabash). He was the first to serve here on an indefinite call – as opposed to an annual call.

I continue to find tracks he left here. He changed the character of the association and everyone he touched. He gave stability to the work. A home was built while he was here. He left lasting impressions through his work with the Baptist Hour, associational youth camps and Seminary Extension classes. I owe him a great deal. I suppose more than any other person, he's given me an appreciation for the Association.

Brother Hall has had two loves – Southern Baptist Theological Seminary and the Southeastern Illinois Pastors' Fellowship. Some of us have accused him of knowing more about what's going on at Southern Seminary than President Duke McCall does. Their Alumni Association honored him in 1974 as Alumnus of the Year.

George H. Davis

He was one of the founders of the SE Illinois Pastors' Fellowship. It has remained a fellowship in the best sense of the word – a group of preachers caring about each other. I'll never forget some difficult times in my own life when that group gathered to lift me up in prayer.

Brother Hall left Fairfield in 1965 to become missionary in the Salem South Baptist Association in Mt. Vernon. After serving about seven years there, he officially retired. In his "retirement" he served the Fairfield Baptist Association in McLeansboro. I couldn't see any difference in his pace or his work load. In fact, it doesn't seem like Brother Hall has changed in the twenty-odd years I've known him.

Mrs. Hall has been at his side. She's taught study courses, worked in Woman's Missionary Union and youth camps. She's never been "too good" to tackle the hardest jobs. She's one of the finest ladies I've ever known. Now, after five years of "retirement", they've retired again. They've moved to Harrisburg – 1212 South Webster. But I doubt they've quit!

September 23, 1977

Deacons

Should deacon rotation be continued? Each church will have to make its own decision. But, I have some thoughts.

Deacon rotation plans boomed in the 1950's. Deacons had become managers in many churches. Their work was to make growing churches operate efficiently. Some times the pastor was responsible to them.

I've seen church constitutions which read, "No important business shall come before the church without having been presented to the deacons first." I'm not sure how this developed. I don't know whether the deacons or the congregation suggested this. I suspect they both agreed to it. Churches probably wanted to avoid embarrassing disagreements in their business meetings. They felt this would keep the peace. I doubt it ever worked.

Sometimes deacons were a self-perpetuating body. Others were elected only with their approval. In an attempt to break up this power structure, deacon rotation plans blossomed. Usually deacons were elected for three year terms under these plans. After two terms, deacons were eligible for reelection only after a year on inactive status.

These plans usually met heated opposition. Deacons felt they were ordained for life – or, good behavior. They resented being put on the shelf. A few were glad for the opportunity to bow out gracefully. They had dropped out and now could be dropped as a deacon without being disgraced. Sometimes churches were glad for the chance to get rid of deacons who didn't "deac."

In the last 10 to 15 years the trend has been to emphasize the ministry role of deacons. Pastors and churches will probably continue to look to deacons for leadership in some areas. But, we have committees to look after most business matters – finances, property, planning etc. Deacons are freer to minister to neglected persons and groups. This need apparently called the Seven into being in Acts 6.

by George

The Deacon Family Ministry Plan attempts to assign each church family to a deacon. He is responsible to visit and minister to them. He's there in crises times – both joyous and sorrowful. He makes the pastor aware of special needs beyond his own ability to meet. If a deacon takes his responsibility seriously, I doubt he should have over 15 families. Most churches don't have enough deacons to make this plan work. Why not forget about deacon rotation? Make all the deacons who are willing to serve active.

Admittedly, churches need to be careful who they ordain. Not every successful business man in our churches will make a good deacon. And, there may be more important questions than, "Has he ever been divorced?"

Most pastors wouldn't like an annual call. Why should the deacons be subject to a triennial call?

October 6, 1977

It Must be a Terrible Burden to be Infallible!

I'm glad I can work in an atmosphere where I can be wrong and still be right. I don't feel I have to know everything about anything. I'm glad I can express an opinion without everyone taking me dead serious. It would be dreadful if you felt compelled to confront me every time we didn't agree. And I wouldn't feel much more comfortable if you rushed to defend every word I spoke.

Now, I'm not suggesting a goof-off attitude. I'm willing to be responsible if you won't force me to be infallible. Recognize that I'm human – limited in my experience and understanding. Recognize that neither of us may know all the truth. We may both be wrong.

Sometimes we force preachers into a "sacred desk" syndrome – every word they speak must come directly from God. Now, I believe we *are* spokesmen for God. But, even Paul recognized "we have this treasure in earthen vessels, that the excellency of the power may be of God, and not of us." (2 Corinthians 4:7)

Can you allow your preacher to be wrong? I don't think it's a luxury. It's a necessity. He's going to be wrong. So are you. The question is, can you accept him even when he is wrong? Or, must he be cast out? Is every opinion suspect because he's wrong on one?

Some people seem to subscribe to the domino theory – if he fails in one area, he's a failure. I can't buy that. All of us fail sometimes. God is in the redeeming business. And we jolly well better be too.

Let's accept each other – warts and all. Let's help each other become all God wants us to be. We can't do that without love and forgiveness.

October 19, 1977

Halloween's Over. Take Off Your Mask!

Have you noticed that people, dressed up for Halloween, behave in ways they'd be ashamed to without a mask?

George H. Davis

We use masks in different ways. They make us look scary, or handsome. They hide our ugliness. I guess we all have things we'd like to hide.

One of the ugliest words I know is "hypocrite." It refers to an actor who wears a mask in a play. He may have several masks to play different characters.

The charge leveled against the church most often and most damagingly is hypocrisy. We've thought up all kinds of cute answers, but we haven't faced up to the charge.

Nobody wants to be known as a hypocrite. Yet there's some pretense about all of us. We'd like to look better than we really are. We're afraid if we let others see us as we really are, they'll laugh at us. The *good news* is, God loves us – warts and all.

Confession is recognizing that God sees through our pretense and knows us. The Bible also says, "Confess your faults to one another, and pray for one another, that you may be healed."

I'm not suggesting we undress publicly. But, we do need a few people we can level with. People who know us and love us anyway. If there's anywhere we should begin to lift our masks, it's in a company of forgiven people.

Are you willing to risk a peek?

November 3, 1977

I'll be home for Christmas!

One of the things I look forward to is getting together with my brothers and sister at Christmas. We enjoy catching up on what's going on in each other's family. We share happenings and plans. We also swap a few new stories and reminisce about the old ones. I've got a couple of second-hand deer hunting stories this year.

Though miles and months separate us now, I guess we're closer than ever. We've been brought together by sorrow and difficulty. We've known many good times. But, I suspect it's the tough times that have made us a family.

I guess Christmas and family are almost synonymous to me. I know family doesn't mean just relation. Sometimes we feel closer to friends than we do to family. They say, "Blood is thicker than water." But, the blood of Christ can make friends that stick closer than brothers. I know I'm fortunate to have a family that feels close. I'm also fortunate to have some close friends – people I've learned to love and trust.

In a book entitled <u>I Ain't Well, But I Sure Am Better</u>, Jess Lair says you need: (1) a spouse who loves you, (2) a job you love, and (3) five people whose faces light up when you enter the room. I hope you've got all three.

I'm thankful for my wife, my work, and wonderful friends. They help me become what God wants me to be. I believe they're God-given.

December 20, 1977

by George

Do Churches Need Pastoral Relations Committees?

I know we've got committees coming out of our ears now. And some of them aren't committing. But we have work that's not being done and we really haven't asked anyone to do it!

Pulpit committees go to great lengths to find out where a prospective pastor stands. They try to let him know what church policy is. They explore the proposed relationships. Sometimes vague promises are made. But once the man accepts the church, the pulpit committee fades into the woodwork. The pastor has no one to relate to.

I know he gets his orders from God and doesn't need anyone to tell him what to do. But occasionally there's a difference of opinion in interpreting God's orders. Pastors and churches need a way of settling differences. Even when there are no major differences, there needs to be a way to check signals. Preachers need a sounding board for their ideas. Church members need a way to question without attacking. Minor irritations fester into open sores without a way to drain the poison.

What I'm suggesting is a small group where grievances could be aired. It should he accessible to both pastor and people. He should be able to share his joys and his hurts. They should be able to listen and to act. Sometimes they should ask the congregation to act.

People with compliments or complaints could approach this committee with confidence. Someone needs to be responsible to let a pastor know that the people think he's doing a good job. Of course he's primarily interested in pleasing God. But it doesn't hurt to know that the people he serves appreciate him.

Complaints should be taken seriously. Sometimes the committee should supply missing information and satisfy the misunderstanding. The pastor could be informed of real or imagined slights. Sometimes the committee should tell the complainer he's out of order. They might even need to go to a chronic trouble-maker and tell him to get in or get out.

I'm not sure deacons can do this. In some churches, they're too much a part of the real or imagined power structure. A pastoral relations committee should maintain a low profile. They shouldn't get involved in power plays. The pastor can talk to the deacons or the church council about plans and programs. But I'm thinking about other kinds of things that need airing. Maybe the pulpit committee should be made permanent. That way there could be continuing contact. Maybe a personnel committee could do the job – but they'd have to be concerned about more than salaries and benefits.

Until we find some official way to deal with these problems, there will be self-appointed groups and individuals who want to attack or protect the preacher, according to their whims.

January 6, 1978

Bible Study

We're in trouble if we're depending on our Sunday Schools to do the Bible teaching. One-fourth of our members aren't even enrolled in Sunday School. Half of those enrolled don't attend.

George H. Davis

One-third of our Sunday School time is used for things other than Bible study. That leaves about forty minutes a week.

For every one hundred members, we have fewer than forty spending as much as forty minutes a week studying the Bible in Sunday School. And I'm probably being generous in my guesses.

Much of this time is spent playing hopscotch through the Bible. We're not going to remember much from a series of unrelated discussions, especially if we miss every third one. (Bible study isn't like soap operas: we can't miss a week and not miss anything.)

If we're going to get the job done, we've got to help and encourage people to spend time in personal and family study. But they need guidance and motivation. The Sunday School class should be a stimulus to further study rather than an end in itself. Some might want it to be the climax of a week's study. I wouldn't argue with that.

I'm not sure families study the Bible best when they spend time talking about the meaning of verses. But it's hard to believe we can teach without talking.

In Hebrew homes, the son would ask, "Daddy, why are we doing this?" And the father would tell what God had done for then. That may not be a bad pattern.

January 17, 1978

Church Renewal

While thumbing through some books on church renewal, I got to thinking about some of the phases we've gone through.

I remember the fifties and "a million more in '54." Baptists boomed in the post-war era (that's WW II, the *big* war). Some wags even suggested that if our growth continued at the rate we projected, there'd soon be more Baptists than people.

In the early sixties we discovered church renewal, well after others were finding ways of making membership more meaningful. I don't remember hearing of Dietrich Bonhoeffer while I was in seminary (1954-57). This German theologian had been executed by the Nazis in 1945. He, and others, refused to support Hitler's Third Reich. He questioned the "cheap grace" that permitted people to hold membership in a church without belonging to Christ.

He challenged us to think about the depth of our commitment. What kind of decision were we calling people to make? What difference did it make on Monday that you had claimed Christ on Sunday? Weren't there more important things than the size of our budgets and buildings? I don't know whether the slow down in our growth led to our interest in a deeper commitment, or whether our preoccupation with depth led to a shrinking of our breadth.

Now we're in the early stages of another emphasis on church growth, after it's old hat to many others. We're beginning to see signs of renewed growth and we're asking why and how. What's the formula for growing a church? How can *our* church grow? Do we really want to grow? What is growth?

by George

Will our emphasis on statistical growth mean we sacrifice depth? (We have never gotten very deep. Fewer than half of our members give any evidence of being disciples of Jesus.) Will "spirituality" be interpreted in terms of froth and foam, or will there be substance to it?

Toward the close of the eighteenth century, William Carey challenged English Baptists to "lengthen the cords and strengthen the stakes." (Isaiah 54:2) If the tent is to be enlarged, the tent stakes must be driven deeper or the tent will surely fall. I think I've seen this happen to a few churches. There was an influx of new people who weren't grounded in the faith. Tensions mounted until an eruption took place. Some left. Then the church went about the slow and painful process of rebuilding.

What led me to the renewal books in the first place was the search for an analogy. I'd heard the church compared to a theater where a play is in progress. Some see the congregation as the audience, the minister and choir as actors and God as the prompter. The writer of Hebrews 12 seems to think of God and the saints in heaven as the audience, the congregation as the performers, and the minister as the prompter.

I never did find it.

February 7, 1978

My wife

My wife – I think I'll keep her. We'll celebrate our twenty-fifth wedding anniversary the twenty-eighth of this month.

She was not my first girl but she has been my last. She's been a partner. She's listened to my preaching, laughed at my jokes, helped me be more tolerant, and grown with me.

She's the best thing that's happened to me since I began trying to follow Jesus. She's made me proud of her in so many ways. She's made me want to do better. She's endured hurt and disappointment without complaining.

She's the best wife I've ever had. She's been a help meet for me but she's more than that. She's a person in her own right. No one had to liberate her. Jesus Christ did that. She's a growing, changing person. And we're growing together.

A novel about colonial New England describes the husband/wife relationship:
Joel had decided to call the menfolks together and have Matt Hawes write another petition to the General Court; and Mima was glad and proud.
"They'll get so they look to you to tell 'em what to do," she said. "Men are easy led, Joel, if you lead them where they already want to go." She spoke happily. "We'll have a town here some day, and you're going to be the big man in it."
"Your father will always be the big man around here."
"You and him. You after him," she insisted. "You're a good man, Joel. Men listen to you."
He said laughingly: "You keep telling me how smart I am and you'll have me believing it." Then he added more seriously: "I wasn't much, you know, till you got hold of me. But you're so sure I'm going to work hard and do right that I have to do it to keep you from being disappointed."

"I guess that's the way with men," she agreed. "A woman's the root and a man's the tree. She's the ground he grows out of. That's a wife's job; to be good growing ground, so her man will be fine."

"What if she isn't? Say she's sour land, or sandy, or dry?"

"Then he'll be a stunted sort of man, or else he'll find another woman, that's all. A man don't get far without some woman loving him and always telling him he's wonderful."

He said, half to himself: "If I was a tree, I needed pruning pretty bad when you took hold of me, Mima." After a moment he added: "I still do, for the matter of that. I ain't all you keep telling me I am; but I mean to be. If you keep telling me, I'll get to be." There was deep tenderness in his tones. "You're good growing ground, Mima."

*Ben Ames Williams, Come Spring, Houghton Mifflin, Boston, 1940, p. 729.

February 21, 1978

Good Intentions Are Not Enough

Good intentions are not enough. When concerned citizens act, it should be on the basis of accurate information.

There are persistent calls for letters to the Federal Communications Commission to counteract a petition by Madelyn Murray O'Hair. According to the story, she presented a petition with 27,000 signatures to the FCC in an effort to stop religious broadcasting. A petition number is even given.

The truth is *no such petition has been filed*. Last month I attended a breakfast sponsored by Dallas/Ft. Worth (Texas) broadcasters. Honorable Robert E. Lee of the FCC was on a panel. He was asked about the supposed petition.

His response was enlightening. Lee said: (1) the Commission does not have the authority to stop religious broadcasting if they wanted to; (2) they do not want to; and (3) Mrs. O'Hair has not filed such a petition.

Commissioner Lee informed us that the FCC has received 7 million letters in opposition to the nonexistent petition. That amounts to about $1 million in postage plus time and paper. That's a terrible waste. I agree we need to act on some issues. But let's make sure we're acting on the basis of knowledge as well as emotion. Otherwise we'll wind up looking foolish as we fight imaginary enemies.

March 8, 1978

Spring Has Arrived

I was one of those who pooh-poohed the idea that last winter could be as bad as the winter before. Who ever heard of snow covering southern Illinois for two months?

by George

I'm not sure I would have made it without herbicide commercials. When the snow settled in like a squatter and the mercury hibernated, it warmed my heart to hear about weed-killers. Modown, Sencor, and Treflan manufacturers had no doubt planting time would come.

I used to feel herbicide endorsements were a hoax. Farmers from places I'd never heard of gave their testimonials. Then I saw "cousin" Dick Adams from Patoka on one commercial. I became a believer. I know Patoka is not a made-up place because I grew up two and one-half miles southwest of there.

I call Dick "cousin" because of what Ernie Adams told me. Ernie is a former Sunday School director for Illinois' Baptists. Now he works at the Sunday School Board in Nashville, Tennessee. When I was in Nashville last fall, Ernie told me about attending an Adams' family reunion near Patoka. He said he ran into my dad and asked what he was doing there. They got to talking and Ernie was surprised to learn that they were related. He returned to Nashville to tell my brother that they were "deputy second cousins-in-law."

Speaking of spring, I hope you'll consider investing in a church planter in northwestern Illinois. A church planter is not a box to plant shrubs or flowers in. He's a pastor who'd begin work in an area needing a witness. He'd plant and nurture a Baptist church. We'd help pay his salary until the church was self-supporting.

We're receiving money now, hoping to have enough to start paying a salary by early next year. It will take $1,000 per month and we'd like to have at least six month's salary on hand when we begin.

But I suspect giving ourselves may be more important than giving our money. I hope several of us will plan to spend a few days or weeks in the northwestern part of the state (at our own expense). We need to get acquainted with the area. We can encourage Christians there. We can see the need for Baptist churches. And, once a work is begun, we can strengthen it in various ways.

Why not consider Jo Daviess County for a week of camping or fishing? Visit Ulysses S. Grant's home in Galena. Fish in Apple River Canyon State Park for smallmouth bass. And if you get tired of listening to herbicide commercials next winter, you might plan a ski trip to northwestern Illinois.

March 22, 1978

(Untitled)

It looks like I got crowded out again.

April 21, 1978

White Mountain Ice Cream Freezer

I bought my wife a six-quart, White Mountain ice cream freezer for her birthday. As I sat there watching it work, I felt like a traitor. It wasn't buying her the ice cream freezer that made me feel guilty. I'm more practical than romantic. It wasn't the brand

George H. Davis

that made me uncomfortable. I've eaten ice cream from a White Mountain freezer for as long as I can remember.

The problem was this was our first *electric* freezer. When I was growing up, we froze ice cream like this: Put a fifty-pound block of ice in two gunny sacks – one inside the other. Lay the ice on the sidewalk and break it up with the side of a double-bit axe. Pour ice and salt alternately into the tub. Lay the gunny sacks on top of the freezer. When it cranks hard enough that the tub begins to scoot around, have someone sit on it.

I felt guilty because I wasn't making ice cream that way. I'd gotten some ice from the ice maker, some salt from the grocery (not the feed store), and I was watching the freezer crank itself!

Then I remembered. My dad's had an electric freezer for several years. Besides, where would I find a fifty-pound block of ice? And I don't even own a double-bit axe. And gunny sacks have gotten so expensive, I'm not sure I want to break up ice in them. And I didn't miss cranking all that much. The ice cream didn't seem to know the difference – it all disappeared.

And I got to wondering – am I wedded to old ways of doing things just because I've always done them that way? I saw a banner a few years ago showing the seven last words of the church, "We've never done it that way before."

Many old ways are good and shouldn't be abandoned just because they're old. Not everything new is good. But sometimes there are new ways of doing things that are just as good or even better than old ways. The real problem may be our suspicion of the new.

May 25, 1978

A. E. Prince

A. E. Prince is a remarkable man. Last month he celebrated the seventy-fourth anniversary of his ordination by visiting Barnhill Baptist Church where he was ordained May 29, 1904. He's making plans for a big celebration next year. He's been sharing anniversaries with the Barnhill church for the last few years. But next year's promises to be something special.

Dr. Prince delights to tell of an invitation to preach at Judson College in Elgin when he's 100. That's less than nine years away! He also delights in watching people watch him. In a recent letter he observed that some, like the natives of Malta watching Paul, seem to expect him to fall dead at any moment. But he's in good health. Eye surgery a few years ago helped improve his sight. Mrs. Prince drives for him.

Dr. Prince was born January 1, 1887 near old Victory church in Lamard Township, northwest of Fairfield. He was saved during a revival in Thackery, in Hamilton County, while his father was preaching. He joined New Hope Baptist Church, southwest of Thackery. His father was pastor there. On the fourth Sunday of May, 1897 Peter Prince baptized the waiting candidates. But his son did not have a change of clothes. He went to the wood lot where the baptism was in progress and sat on a log crying because he could not be baptized. His mother sat and cried with him. However, by the third Sunday of June, his parents managed to provide the extra clothing and he was baptized.*

His first church was Pleasant Hill, southwest of Mt. Erie. He also served Samaria, Unity (now Albion), Browns, Pleasant Grove, Barnhill, and Mill Shoals in our association. Other Illinois' churches include: Casey, Ewing, Charleston, Eldorado, Marion, Effingham, and Maplewood Park. He served as pastor in Texas, Louisiana, Missouri, New Zealand, and Hawaii. He was district missionary in Texas. He's been president of three colleges: Ewing, Hannibal - La Grange, and Honolulu Christian.

But, he's certainly not a has-been. He preaches almost every Sunday. Next Sunday, he'll be at Bloom. On August 13, he'll be at Keenes. He'll be at Sims September 10 for their centennial. But he's still looking forward to June 3, 1979. That's when he'll return to Barnhill for the diamond anniversary of his ordination.

*This incident is related in Dr. Prince's biography by Carvin C. Bryant, Born to Preach, Herald: Collinsville, 1967.

June 13, 1978

A Trip to Jo Daviess County

I take some pride in being born and raised in Illinois – though I had little to do with either. I've lived in southern Illinois all my life (except for three years of Seminary in Kentucky). I know a little about the area south of Interstate 70.

There are three areas in Illinois that are thought of as part of a tri-state area: (1) ours – with Evansville and Mt. Vernon, Indiana, Henderson and Owensboro, Kentucky, and southeastern Illinois. (2) Cairo, Illinois where you can take your choice of bridges and wind up in Kentucky or Missouri, depending on whether you cross the Ohio or Mississippi river. (3) Dubuque, Iowa and southwestern Wisconsin and northwestern Illinois.

Since we have been talking about supporting a church planter in Jo Daviess County, I wanted to get acquainted with the area. I had heard and read about Galena for several years but knew little about it. My family was gracious enough to go along with the idea of spending a week camping there. We roamed the antique shops in Galena, fished in Apple River, climbed Charles Mound, bought film in Stockton, and rode the ski lift at Chestnut Mountain Lodge. We attended church in Dubuque and bought cheese in Shullsburg, Wisconsin.

The county is rolling to hilly. You'd have to search to find a forty-acre field that's flat. Crops are stripped or contoured. There's corn and oats and hay. Dairy farming is big. Haying was in full swing when we were there. I had trouble figuring out what those big wagons with the high racks were for – until I saw a bale thrower in operation.

Galena itself is a tourist mecca. One of our kids asked if it was like Gatlinburg, Tennessee. I said, "Yes, only smaller." They boast twenty-five antique shops. But the real attraction is the stately, old houses. The most famous is a home presented U. S. Grant when he returned after the Civil War. It's now a state memorial. A number of homes are fine examples of 19th century architecture. Several of them are open to the public.

Galena is located on U. S. Route 20 about fifteen miles east of Dubuque, Iowa. Route 20 continues eastward to Freeport and Rockford. There are some beautiful scenic views along Route 20, especially near Elizabeth.

Most of the churches I saw were Catholic, Lutheran, or Methodist. There are some Presbyterian churches and we saw one Episcopal church. We saw a couple of Bible churches. There seems to be a need for some Baptist work in the area. Surveys are needed to determine more precise needs and prospects.

It's a long way up there. And we're a long way from being ready to support a church planter up there. But I sense a growing enthusiasm about the project. I hope you'll consider visiting the area. But remember to allow at least eight hours of driving time. Come by the office and I'll give you a Chamber of Commerce pitch. I'll even show you my chunk of lead ore (galena).

June 29, 1978

Which Way does the Channel Flow?

Associations are often looked on as channels of information from the denomination to the churches. The problem with this is that most state conventions and Southern Baptist Convention agencies have more resources than the associations do. I'm thinking of things like professional communications skills or the money to secure them. I'm not saying associations shouldn't attempt to communicate. I think we should do the best job possible. I think we should do all we can to improve our skills and equipment. But I doubt we'll match state conventions and SBC agencies.

Maybe the channel should flow from the churches through the association to the denomination. Most good programs don't originate in Nashville or Springfield and our leaders know that. Most begin in churches and are picked up by denominational leaders. Maybe it's important for them to know how people in the churches feel.

Ultimately, the job of all three denominational units is to help the churches do the work the Lord has given them. Clear communication is essential if we are to avoid suspicion and jealousy.

When Baptists have the opportunity to talk to each other, they'll usually come to an agreement. It's when we each want to protect our own little bailiwick that we run into conflict.

July 13, 1978

Friends

Does your world get smaller or larger when friends move?

I consider myself a rather shy person, but I've made several friends through the years. I haven't moved often –four times in twenty years. But my friends have moved almost that often, too. So I've been forced to find new ones.

by George

Everybody needs some friends. It's part of being human. Even the Lone Ranger needed Tonto. Our capacity for community may be a part of the image of God. The classic Black sermon on creation pictures God saying, "I'm lonely. I think I'll make me a man." God said it wasn't good for man to be alone. John said it was folly to claim to love God while hating our brother. Jesus taught that we cannot receive God's forgiveness until we build the bridge of forgiveness to another man.

Harvey Cox says we shouldn't feel guilty about choosing who our friends will be. If we try to get close to the paper boy, the mail man, the service station attendant, the grocery checker and carry-out boy, the meter man, the repairman, the trash man, etc., we won't get anything done for visiting with them. There's nothing necessarily wrong with driving past several neighbors to see a friend across town. We need someone we can be ourselves with.

Loyalty is one of the main ingredients of friendship. We're not blind to friends' faults, but we will defend them from outside attack. We take it personally. Our attitude is, "I <u>know</u> he's not perfect, but I sure don't need <u>you</u> to tell me his faults."

You may think a preacher has lots of friends. He <u>is</u> thrown with several people but he's probably not close to many. Sometimes he's afraid to let his humanity show. Some might use it against him. Some would be shocked at the sight of a tarnished halo. Some preachers prefer to remain on a pedestal. But most find a few close friends who accept them – warts and all.

It's hard losing friends. You feel abandoned when they move. You're glad for their success but you feel a touch of self-pity: "Poor little me. Here I am; left all alone." This may lead to depression. Church members may feel this when a pastor leaves.

When friends move, they don't stop being your friends, but it's hard to feel close when you're miles apart. Occasional reunions are good, but you need someone close by. It's not disloyalty to your old friends; it' s recognizing your continuing need for someone who knows you and loves you anyway.

Leonard Wright wrote, "As old wood is best to burn, old horse to ride, old books to read, and old wine to drink, so are old friends always most trusty to use." I don't know much about old wine, but I do trust old friends. Even so, sometimes you have to find new ones. When you do, your world gets larger in two ways: you have friends in more places and you have more friends.

August 4, 1978

Old and Stiff?

How do you keep from breaking instead of bending when you're old and stiff?

Now, mind you, I'm neither old nor stiff. But I <u>am</u> older and stiffer than I was twenty years ago. And I've noticed it's harder to bend.

Oh, I can still touch my toes but I'm tending to get set in my ways. Maybe that's not all bad. Experience should have taught me some things.

If I can remember all the good lessons I've learned and forget the others, I'll be the winner. Bob Dale says experience is not a bad teacher if you don't mind the school colors – black and blue!

George H. Davis

There's nothing like being around youth to keep you limbered up. Their activity and probing questions challenge you to defend yourself or change.

I've looked forward to this week at Camp with some pleasure and some pain – about like a boy looks forward to school opening.

August 22, 1978

Annual Meeting Highlights

I doubt anyone enjoyed the annual meeting more than Nellie Rudesill – unless it was Oakley Miller. Nellie celebrated her eightieth birthday Tuesday, September 19th. She's a confirmed church goer. She enjoys almost any kind of church service anywhere. She's faithful to attend annual associational meetings.

Brother Miller seemed to enjoy preaching Tuesday morning. And he helped others enjoy it, too. It was the most delightful sermon on the coming of Christ I've heard. I got the idea he's looking forward to it.

Harold Cameron, missions director for Illinois Baptists, captured what several mentioned when he said, "You've come a long way." He was referring to the harmony that prevailed and contrasting it with the arguments that used to be heard at annual meetings. Some remember them as occasions for strife and disputes.

I hope it's not because we no longer care enough about anything to raise a fuss. Some things are worth arguing about. Some are not. Wisdom is knowing the difference. Maybe we've learned to disagree without being disagreeable. I hope so.

We owe a great deal to pastors and missionaries who've endured some hard times and made the road smoother for all of us. Thanks to men like Kenneth G. Hall and Charles Holland and others.

Host pastor Lester Dean and the Crossville Church did a magnificent job entertaining us. From registration to the benediction they made us feel at home. And wasn't that noon meal something! I was at the tail end of the line and I never saw so much food – left. I was a little concerned there wouldn't be any apple pie left by the time I got ready for it. But there was.

I am conscious of your love and acceptance. You've shown it by giving me opportunities to teach and preach, by affirming my gifts and by providing an adequate salary. I'm grateful for the privilege of serving among you. You give me joy.

September 22, 1978

New Testament Churches?

Where are the New Testament churches? I suspect they vanished with New Testament times. I know we're quick to talk about being true to the New Testament pattern. We *say* the Bible is our sole authority. But I wonder. If all we had was the Bible, what kind of pattern would we follow?

We're better at repeating shibboleths than at understanding the substance of our faith. (Do you remember the story from the period of the Judges about the men from

by George

Ephraim who crossed the Jordan River to quarrel with Jephthah? They accused him of not notifying them when he went into battle against the Ammonites. He replied that he asked for help, but when none came he went on to defeat the Ammonites. Then he refused to let his critics return home. When any of them tried to sneak back across the Jordan, his guards would ask, "Are you an Ephraimite?" If he answered, "No," they would tell him to say "Shibboleth." But the men from Ephraim could not make the "sh" sound. They would say, "Sibboleth," and give themselves away. See Judges 12:1-6.)

Sometimes our main test for orthodoxy is saying the right words. We spend little time thinking about their meaning or saying what we mean with fresh, new words. We ask at ordinations, "What are the offices of the church?" I'm waiting for someone to say, "Well, let's see. There's the pastor, deacons, Sunday School director, clerk, treasurer, trustees, etc." Of course, we'd have to correct him, "It's pastor and deacons – the only ones mentioned in the New Testament." But which of us would want to operate without the other officers?

You see, the New Testament is not our only pattern. We take what we want from it, but ignore a number of other things: Paul would not allow women without a veil to pray in the churches. He also felt it was shameful for them to cut their hair (see 1 Corinthians 11:1-16). He would not allow women to speak or teach in the churches (see 1 Corinthians 14:32-35 and I Timothy 2:9-15). New Testament churches apparently had more than one pastor (elder): Paul sent for the elders of the church at Ephesus (Acts 20:17). He urged Titus to appoint elders in every town in Crete (Titus 1:5). By the way, that's not very Baptistic, is it? Paul saw Titus as a supervisor with authority to appoint elders. Of course, he saw himself in the same way. It's hard to think of Paul telling churches that they were autonomous and could do whatever they pleased. He seemed to feel that he was an overseer. But we ignore this and hold to our Baptist pattern.

Now, I have no objection to our taking much of our pattern from our society, but I think we should recognize where it comes from. Paul seems to urge Christian women to respect the customs of society. Though they were free in Christ, to be too brazen would bring shame on themselves and on the churches.

Let's stop our hypocrisy and recognize that we're living in the twentieth century, not in the first. Let our concern be in letting the spirit of Christ live in us today and not in trying to recreate earlier days. I have no problem with churches being autonomous, as long as they recognize Christ as head and other churches as sisters.

October 5, 1978

Pastors don't live on manna!

They buy food at the grocery store and gas at the service station just like you do. They pay the same paycheck-gouging prices you pay. And even if his salary is increased 7% to keep up with the cost of living, he's not getting a raise. He's just treading water. And the cost of living adjustment is usually for last year. He's always a year behind.

George H. Davis

Churches sometimes fail to think clearly about what's included in a pastor's salary. Obviously the cash salary is included. If a parsonage is furnished, the rental value should he included. But I've noticed that churches often overestimate the value of their parsonage. I've also noticed that pastors are often expected to make repairs on the parsonage. Normally a renter would not hesitate to tell his landlord about needed repairs. But when your landlord is also your employer, it's a sticky situation. Trustees don't always know what kind of shape the parsonage is in. After all, they don't live there!

Though a pastor doesn't pay taxes on a church-owned home, neither does he build up equity. If he decides to buy a home later, he may find he's up the creek without a down payment.

If utilities are furnished, their value should be counted as salary. Car allowance should not be considered as salary but as reimbursement for expense involved in doing his work. And I doubt you can operate a car for less than fifteen cents per mile.

Retirement and insurance benefits should be considered as fringe benefits. They're not cash received but are benefits. Many workers have retirement and insurance plans paid by their employer. Employees also have part of their Social Security paid by their employer. Pastors must pay as a self-employed person at almost 1/3 higher rates.

Convention and education allowances are not a part of salary. A pastor is expected to continue training and a church should bear the expense involved. They'll receive the benefit. Contrary to popular opinion, conventions are not vacations – they're hard work. But I believe pastors need to be involved in them. I also believe churches should encourage lay persons to attend state and national conventions. This may mean providing convention allowances for them, too.

Your pastor may not ask for a raise – he shouldn't have to! But our tendency is to get so tied up in our own concerns, we neglect others. I'll have to confess, I wasn't nearly so concerned about the associational missionary's salary before I became one. I hope you'll make sure your pastor is paid an adequate salary. If he isn't, he'll waste a lot of time and energy juggling his finances. You'll get just about what you pay for.

The Israelites called the food they ate in the wilderness manna, meaning "what is it?" Pastors may be asking, "Where is it?"

October 25, 1978

Missions

I hope our World Missions Conference left you asking, "How can our church get more involved in missions?" because I have some suggestions:

First; PRAY for missionaries. Pray for them by name. So often we pray, "God, bless all the missionaries all over the world." I once heard Bob Hastings say that it's spreading it kind of thin to pray for "all the lost people in the world." I think the same thing is true for the missionaries. We need to pray intelligently. We need to know something about their fields and needs. Home Missions, The Commission, World Mission Journal, and even the Illinois Baptist will help you keep in touch. Listen to the news with missionary ears. Think what this conflict or disaster may mean to missionaries in the area.

And pray FOR missionaries. Pray that the Lord will call out faithful people to serve him in places of great need. If we are to confront every person with the gospel of Christ, we must have more workers. Many will be preachers, but we also need people trained in medicine, education, agriculture, writing, broadcasting, and scores of other fields. I hope you'll pray for the missionaries you met last week and for others to help them.

Second; you can GIVE to missions. It starts with you as an individual. Quit asking, "How little can I give and still be thought respectable?" Begin asking how much you can give. The real bottleneck in missions giving is in our pocketbook. Then, begin to consider how much your church can share for mission work around the world. I believe giving on a percentage basis makes good stewardship. We give in proportion to our receipts. Give to associational missions. But I doubt even I could justify your giving more than 5% to the association. Give to the Baptist Children's Home. Again, I doubt the wisdom of giving more than 5%. And give through the Cooperative Program. It's Southern Baptists way of sharing with mission causes around the world. A church probably should give at least twice as much through the Cooperative Program as it does to the association or to the Children's Home. And keep increasing the percentage. Don't give me that old line about not enough of it getting to the mission field. If you really believe that, I'd like to talk to you.

Third; you can GO to the mission field. Keep in mind that every person is either a missionary or a mission field. I doubt God cares about our petty geographical boundaries. He sees people in need around our world. And we need to share that concern. Some of us may become career home or foreign missionaries. Others should serve as volunteers – both at home and overseas. The great majority will serve as Christian witnesses wherever they find themselves. Is it possible God wants you to practice your skill or trade in an area where Christian workers are desperately needed? You could work wherever there's a job and witness wherever there s a need. Oh, I know we have needs here. But, I also recognize there are many areas of much greater need.

November 22, 1978

Christmas and Family

Christmas and family are almost synonymous to me. I guess I enjoy the family get-togethers as much as anything we do over the holidays. I hope you also know this kind of joy.

Since you and I get to visit frequently, I feel like we've gotten to know each other. Since you don't see my family as often, let me bring you up-to-date. My wife, Leona, is teaching full time at Fairfield High School. That means she can't always go with me and I have to do the dishes once in a while.

Mark is a senior at Eastern Illinois University in Charleston. He's president of the Residence Hall Association and has just been chosen as a resident assistant in his

George H. Davis

dorm. He and Shelley Binder will be married in Peoria in June. He plans to do his practice teaching next fall.

After two years at Wabash Valley College, Jane is assistant director at the Wayne City Child Care Center. She lives at home but spends most of her time at work or in Edwards County, where she has a special interest.

Jim is a senior in high school and is involved in jazz band, the school paper and yearbook, Science Club, and football. Mike is a sophomore and plays in the band. He also plays football and tennis.

And our family is part of a larger family. Leona has a brother and a sister. They have five children. Her dad lives in West Frankfort. I have four brothers and a sister. My folks still live near Patoka (Illinois). Our family tries to get together at Christmas. We're kind of scattered and don't get together often, so when we do, we have some catching up to do.

We talk about what's going on in our lives now – our dreams and frustrations. We also relive our growing-up days. Almost every time, dad learns something new that we were afraid to tell him earlier. It used to be a tradition that we'd go tromping through the fields after dinner to see if we could scare up a rabbit. We weren't so interested in killing him as we were in visiting along the way. I don't know if we've gotten lazy or just wised up; any more we just visit at the dinner table.

I wonder if Joseph and Mary didn't visit with their families as they traveled toward Bethlehem. And I wonder if Joseph ever asked, "Which one of you boys has had the saw?" And they all answered in unison, "Not me, dad." I believe God enjoys family reunions. I think he likes to see people laughing and enjoying each other.

Our family has shared some hard times as well as some good ones, but we've seldom been alone. When someone needed help, a brother was there. We've maintained a real interest in each other's families. We enjoy sharing our dreams and accomplishments.

It's a real joy to know your love and acceptance in our fellowship here. I'm keenly aware of the reality of our family-type relationships.

December 19, 1978

Some Words We Can Do Without

I have a couple of nominations for the Unicorn Hunters of Lake Superior State College in Sault Sainte Marie, Michigan.

According to a United Press International story in The Evansville Press (January 2, 1979) they issue an "annual list of words and phrases without which, the group believes, the English language would be better off."

This year's list of misused and overused words was topped by "I feel," "Social Security," "what are you into?" and "energy crisis." They point out that "Social Security is neither social nor secure; nobody knows what constitutes an energy crisis, what to do about it or whether it exists; and 'I feel' is too often used to mean, 'I believe.'"

This national society of poets, writers, and others cautions that "beautiful" has lost almost all meaning. "Somewhere down the road" was banished from business usage but not from song lyrics while "the bottom line" was banished for everyone except accountants and financial vice presidents.

My own nominations are "Bible-believing church" and "born-again Christian." When we talk about "born-again Christians" are we inferring that you can be a Christian without being born again? Or, are we referring to a person who has had a radical conversion experience as an adult? What about those who commit their lives to Christ without going to jail?

It's a little like talking about a "widow woman." The "woman" in that phrase is unnecessary (one of the few times she is). I never saw a widow who wasn't a woman. Unless we mean to reduce those who trust Christ in their formative years to second—class citizenship in the Kingdom, let's quit talking about "born-again Christians." A person either is or is not a Christian. Tacking on "born again" does not make him more Christian.

I have a little clearer idea what a person means when he says "Bible-believing church." He usually means "a church that looks at the Bible and interprets it like I do." Why doesn't he just say so? Because that would sound like he's the only one who really believes the Bible.

Maybe I've lived a rather sheltered life, but I've yet to find a church that didn't claim to believe the Bible. I know Catholics give almost equal authority to tradition, but I also know there's a renewed interest in the Bible among Catholics. And don't tell me about a Church of Satan: we're talking about Christian churches. Of course, some churches have different views or interpretations of the Bible, just as individuals do. Can I claim to have the only true meaning, though? One of our distinctives as evangelicals is the right of the individual to read and interpret the Bible for himself and I'm not ready to give that up. So let's banish "Bible-believing church" and "born-again Christian" from our vocabulary. They reflect arrogance and foggy thinking. Like the unicorn, they live in fantasy, not in the real world.

January 11, 1979

The Preacher's Job

An old adage says the preacher's job is to comfort the disturbed and disturb the comfortable.

That may be an oversimplification, but it <u>is</u> worth thinking about. The preacher's primary task is to announce the good news that God accepts sinners. His acceptance does not depend on them getting their lives straightened up first. He accepts them as sinners. And even after they begin following Jesus, when they stumble and fall, He accepts them. If we learn anything from the Gospel of Mark, it is that Jesus' love for his disciples was patient and persistent through their failure to understand and believe. That's good news!

A common misunderstanding of the gospel among Christians is, "if you'll get your life straightened out, God will accept you." <u>That's</u> no gospel. That's <u>terrible</u> news! Who can hope for God's favor under these terms? Part of the preacher's job is to shatter this perversion by announcing to sinners, "God loves you <u>now</u>." As a boy,

George H. Davis

H. A. Ironside was attracted to a preacher he heard say, "God loves naughty boys." I doubt we've gotten that message across.

And it will be hard for people to believe it unless they sense that <u>we</u> love them now – warts and all. Announcing the gospel will not mean much until it's demonstrated. And that's the tough part of a preacher's job – or any Christians, for that matter. Because, by the way, it's not <u>just</u> the preacher's job to share the gospel.

Besides proclaiming God's acceptance to sinners, the preacher encourages the Christian who feels like he's failing. Often his fellow Christians shun him when he needs them most. They don't understand him and so they avoid him. He gets the idea that if you're a <u>real</u> Christian, you don't make mistakes and you don't have doubts. Heber Peacock points out that in Mark faith and doubt exist side by side in the disciple's life. Perhaps it's summed up in the father's prayer, "Lord, I believe; help my unbelief." (9:24)

The preacher sometimes disturbs the comfortable. That's not always his intention; sometimes it just turns out that way. Some ideas need to be challenged. They have accumulated around the gospel but are not part of it. Jesus challenged some of the accepted religious practices of his day. He turned over the moneychanger's tables and drove the sacrificial animals out of the Temple. On another occasion, He caused men to simply drop their rocks rather than punish a woman according to their understanding of the law.

What complicates the preacher's job is that he also sometimes needs comforting and sometimes disturbing. He, like Isaiah, is a sinful man living among sinful men. But he's called of God to deliver His message. He hears the message before he preaches it and once he is comforted or disturbed, he can share it. That's his job!

January 23, 1979

Prayer and Prayers

A person may pray beautiful prayers and not be a person of prayer. On occasion, I've been told I'd prayed a "beautiful prayer", but I've never felt l had a deep devotional life. Not that I haven't worked at it from tine to time.

I remember a teacher who would begin class on a cold, blustery day praying, "Lord, thank you for the warmth of your love." On a hot, sweltering day, he'd pray, "Lord, thank you for the refreshing breeze of your Spirit." (That was before we had air-conditioned classrooms.) I never doubted his spirituality. But I remember another teacher whose devotion cropped out in his classroom prayers. He was obviously a man of deep piety.

There s nothing wrong with choosing our words carefully as we pray. I remember hearing Bob Hastings say that we should keep our minds in gear while we're praying. He was suggesting that we pray intelligently and specifically. When we lead a group, we should express their prayer.

by George

Jesus warned about the danger of praying to be heard by men. When we do, he said we have been "paid in full" when they hear us. I wonder if he was warning against flowery public prayer when there's little private prayer. He taught his disciples, "When you pray, go into your room and shut the door and pray to your Father." (Matthew 6:6) We're tempted to slam the door so everyone will know we're praying. I doubt we'll have to try to impress people with our piety, if we have it. It will find a way of showing itself.

At its heart, prayer is adoration and praise. We desperately need to bask in the presence of God and allow him to warm our spirits. We're often so busy serving we have little time to sit at Jesus' feet. The Psalmist wrote,

As the heart pants for the flowing streams,
So my soul pants for you, O God. (42:1)

We more frequently pant because we're so activity-oriented.

I recently heard Hugo Culpepper refer to the years he spent in a Japanese concentration camp as "the best three years I ever had." He had been a missionary in China at the outbreak of World War II. Later he served in Argentina; then as a Home Mission Board executive. Now he's a seminary professor. He was allowed to take his Greek New Testament to prison with him. During the three years he read it through twelve times. He refers to that as the foundation of much that's happened to him since. Would you be surprised if I told you his son teaches New Testament?

Prayer and Bible study are probably two of the best channels for spiritual nourishment. It's our loss when we neglect them. Jesus didn't use prayer as an escape from the pressures of ministry, but found strength for ministry through fellowship with the Father.

February 8, 1979

Things I've Done

I don't feel like I had a deprived childhood, but there are some things I didn't do until I was grown:
talk on a private telephone line,
fly on a commercial airliner,
write with a ball point pen,
meet a black person,
watch television, or
see a deer.

On the other hand, there are some things I haven't done in the last twenty-five years:
run a mile,
milked a cow,
eaten a squab,
hung flypaper,
smoked a cigar,

George H. Davis

ridden on a train,
cranked a tractor,
eaten boiled wheat,
gone skinny dipping,
read by an Aladdin lamp,
taken a bath in a wash tub,
made butter in a Daisy churn,
chopped out a hideout in a weedpatch,
made a cave out of bales in a barnloft,
listened to a radio powered by a wet cell battery,
cleaned the clotheslines with a kerosene-soaked rag,
stayed all night with the stock at the county fair,
read the Bible through in the King James version,
spent more than three days in the hospital,
started the engine on a Maytag washer,
emptied the pan under the ice box,
helped grease a wagon wheel,
cranked a cream separator,
played in a straw stack,
had all the answers,
eaten suet pudding,
baptized outdoors,
harnessed a horse,
taken castor oil,
played marbles,
ridden a horse,
driven a team, or
washed a hog

And it's been at least twenty years since I've seen a church-changing revival.

February 21, 1979

I'd Like to See a Revival

I'd like to see a revival
- of conviction for sin so we'd abhor sin as God does rather than treat it as a harmless plaything. I wish we could see our sin as being as horrible as our neighbor's.
- of concern for people. We insulate ourselves against people and their appeals and become insensitive. I pray that God will help us to feel toward people as he does and help us to risk involvement in their lives.
- of love for God and our fellow Christians. I wish we could fall in love with God and each other all over again. We'd see how much we could do, not how little we could get by with.

- of dedication to holy living. I'm thinking about a real purity of spirit that seeks to live close to God rather than walk the border between heaven and hell, stepping first on one side of the line then the other.
- of interest in Bible study. I want to immerse myself in God's word and hear him speak to me in fresh ways. I want to come to his word with openness and expectancy.
- of willingness to spend time in prayer. I want to see prayer as a vital part of my work and worship so I'll give myself to it without reservation.

I want to commit myself to seek renewal in these areas of my life. Will you join me?

March 8, 1979

Youth Camp Loses Another Good Friend

When Jerry Kissner died earlier this month, our associational youth camp lost another good friend. Jerry had served as a counselor at camp the last three years. His wife, Sharon, helped cook two of those years.

We always assigned Jerry a cabin with some of the older boys. They loved and respected him and he loved them. It was an ideal combination. He also worked well with the younger counselors. He gave them freedom and supervision.

Jerry was a thirty-year-old farmer from south of Wayne City. A deacon in Olive Branch Baptist Church, he was killed in a tragic chain saw accident at his hone March 8.

Not since the death of Dewitt Kelley five years ago has youth camp suffered such a loss. Brother Kelley was pastor at Samaria Baptist Church, near Albion, then at Stewart Street Baptist Church in Carmi. He directed camp from 1968-73. He and three Stewart Street members were killed in a car accident on their way home from the Mid-Year meeting in 1974.

Jerry's approach to life was optimistic and joyous. He showed the same enthusiasm whether he was leading a Bible study cluster or playing ball. He took responsibility seriously. When I had to be gone from Camp one day last year, I asked Jerry to be in charge. He was concerned about every camper and counselor. His genuine love for people was evident as he gave himself to the task.

We'll miss Jerry's winning smile and warm handshake. He'd even wrap you in a loving bear hug if you'd let him. You see, Jerry wasn't ashamed to show you how he felt about you. He was quick to say "Thank you." I don't know anyone who enjoyed praising the Lord more than Jerry did. Now he's free to do it through eternity.

I was moved by Audene Smith's testimony at the state evangelism conference in Mt. Vernon this week.

Audene was born with cerebral palsy. She is deaf and mute, but she is not dumb. She has taught a Sunday school class for the deaf in her church (Pennsylvania Avenue Baptist in Urbana). And God taught me some things through her.

Tears welled up in my eyes as Audene signed her story. (A lady from her church interpreted for dummies like me.) She told of her struggle with disease and pain. She related her anguish that she should be so afflicted. She took us along on her halting journey of faith.

I would never have said it aloud, but I suppose I had felt such persons should stay out of sight and not embarrass themselves and others. Even now I'm ashamed to admit that. But God got through to me through Audene. Thank you, God.

March 22, 1979

Mother's Day

I guess I'm just hopelessly sentimental. I bought my wife a garden tiller for Mother's Day. That may not sound very sentimental to you until I explain it a bit.

I have tried for several years to convince her that it's easier to cultivate friends than it is to cultivate a garden. But all to no avail; she was winning. We put out a garden every year.

Ralph Bunting has plowed and disked our garden the last several years. Last winter he sold his tractor – without even asking me. Can you beat *that* for nerve?

I have to admit, my wife's a pretty good gardener until August – by then the weeds are beginning to take over and she's lost her enthusiasm. Then she urges me to get the boys out to try to reclaim the garden.

This spring she wondered aloud if there was a tiller *she* could use. I guess she had decided that would be easier than getting me into the garden. I allowed there might be and made a mental note.

Now I have to tell you I'm not the world's greatest rememberer of special occasions. I dread shopping for presents (especially personal ones). As a result, my wife does most of the remembering and gift buying around our house. But, how would it look to send her out to buy her own Mother's Day present? So, I shopped around for a tiller.

So you won't think I'm completely crass, let me tell you I found a nice card and stuck it to the tiller with a pretty ribbon. I even wrote her a poem. It's none of your business what I wrote!

It just seems like gifts should be practical and useful. (We had friends who bought each other a toilet seat and a mailbox for their birthdays one year.) That tiller is practical all right and I think she likes it. She's let me use it several times. Come to think of it, I don't think she's used it yet. But she's got me to spend more time in the garden. Maybe that's the real present. Maybe I can learn to enjoy gardening. But it's so hard to overcome childhood memories. And I don't remember gardening as one of my favorite pastimes as a child. But maybe she'll let me use her tiller and she'll finish up with the hoe.

I know gardening is good exercise and I need that. But I need it worse in the winter. Do you suppose I could have a winter garden?

May 23, 1979

Mark and Shelley

Mark and Shelley were married last Saturday. Mark is our oldest son. Shelley is the youngest daughter of Mr. and Mrs. LaVerne Binder of Peoria.

by George

I tried to speak for both sets of parents in brief, introductory remarks at the wedding. I'm indebted to Mark and Shelley and to Pastor Neumann of Redeemer Lutheran Church in Peoria for the opportunity to participate in the ceremony.

I knew I'd have to write out what I wanted to say or I probably wouldn't be able to say it. I worked through my tears as I wrote:

This is an awesome, wonderful time. It's a time for the old and the new, for completing and beginning, for giving and receiving, and for laughing and crying.

For the past several years, much of our lives have focused in you. We've watched you learn to walk and run and fall and get up to run again. We've dried your tears and shared your honors. Now our dreams have reached their climax in your choice of each other.

We've turned loose your lives bit by bit, and sometimes reluctantly. Now we share your joy at the beginning of your new family. Our tears will dry and we'll share your laughter. We release you, but you'll seldom be out of our thoughts and prayers.

We have raised you for this time. Now it's a time for testing our teaching. Of course, neither our teaching nor our example have been perfect. But, hopefully, we have taught you love and forgiveness. We have learned from our parents and they from theirs. But, ultimately, we have all learned from God himself.

Your love will be tested, but love is not afraid of testing. It will pass the daily tests as well as the major ones. We believe in you. We believe your love will not only endure, but that it will grow through the years. Our teaching will be tested in your lives. Where we have taught you right, it will show. Where we have not, we ask your forgiveness.

We do not ask you to live for us, but for yourselves and for God. We will share your joys and sorrows, for you are still our children. Yet, you are adults. As we have lived our own lives, we expect you to live your own. We will not abandon you, but this is the final chapter in your liberation. We will continue to share your hopes and dreams.

Our families are larger, not smaller, now. For in reality, our families join in you. Our homes will be richer because of yours. Your family is enlarged, too. We wish you all the happiness we've known and more.

We're proud of you. We love you.

June 13, 1979

WE DON'T NEED CHURCH TRAINING

Twenty-seven of our thirty churches report no Church Training program.

WE DON'T NEED CHURCH TRAINING… unless church members need training in Christian doctrine. Do we need to understand more of what the Bible says about God, man, Jesus, the church, or the Holy Spirit?

WE DON'T NEED CHURCH TRAINing… unless we want to train new members. Do they need to understand the decisions they've made? Do they need basic training in doctrine? Do they need to know anything about our church, its history, or how it operates?

WE DON'T NEED CHURCH training… unless we want to train Christians to witness. Do we need continuing training to refine witnessing skills? Do we need a balanced approach to sharing our faith?

George H. Davis

WE DON'T NEED CHUrch Training... unless we want to strengthen the family life of our members. Do families need help in dealing with crises? Do they need help in raising children? Do children need help in understanding and relating to their parents?

WE DON'T NEED Church Training... unless we want some opportunity for the whole family to study missions. Do we understand the need for missions? What about missions methods?

WE DON'T NEed Church Training... unless we need help in knowing how to study the Bible. Do we understand the nature of the Bible? What do we know about how we got the Bible? Should we interpret all the Bible the same way?

WE DON'T need Church Training . . . unless we want to train church officers and committees in their work. Do all our committees know what their job is? Who's responsible for training them?

WE DOn't need Church Training... unless our members need to know how our church functions. Do they know how decisions are made and who makes them? Do they know what the work of the deacons and pastor is? Do they understand our relationship to other churches? Do they understand our role in the Association, state convention, and Southern Baptist Convention?

WE don't need Church Training... unless we need to know something about Christian history. Can we learn anything from the great movements in church history? Where did Baptists come from? Where are we going?

We don't need Church Training... unless we're interested in training prospective workers. Where do we get new workers for Sunday School? Who's going to train them?

Well, Maybe we do need Church Training.

June 27, 1979

When is Calling a Pastor Like a Horse Race?

Pulpit committees will receive names of a number of prospective pastors. But it will soon become evident that several should be eliminated outright. Some are not qualified. Others simply would not fit the church. Some of the most available preachers may not be the most desirable.

No, I'm not suggesting they rely only on their judgment. They need to be much in prayer and closely attuned to God's leadership. But, if God gave us good sense, why should we use it everywhere except at church? I know he'll overrule our judgment at times, but these will be the exceptions. If we're to love the Lord with all our mind, then surely we're to use it in seeking his will.

In time, it will become apparent to the committee that a number of men might be acceptable. They'll begin to gather more information about them. The more they know, the more (or less) desirable some will seem.

Eventually, they'll begin to focus on one man. They'll talk seriously about their mutual hopes and expectations. After each learns more about the other, one party may decide they're not interested in pursuing it any further.

by George

I think visiting informally with a prospective pastor is as important as hearing him preach. Preaching is important but so are a number of other skills.

It's also important to be as honest as possible with a prospective pastor. If a committee expects him to level with them, they'll have to do the same. I think it's important for a committee to talk to other people about the preacher. I doubt they'll find out all they should by talking only to him. I'd also counsel a prospective pastor to talk to an outsider about the church.

When a committee is agreed (I think it should be unanimous), they are ready to bring the man to the church and recommend him. ONLY ONE PROSPECTIVE PASTOR SHOULD BE VOTED ON AT A TIME. If the church does not call him, or if he does not accept, the committee seeks another person.

If a number of names come before the church at once, there's the potential for a split. Some will want one, some another. They may choose up sides and play My Favorite Preacher. That's tragic. Even when one gets a majority, there's still a residue of resentment. Some may pout because their favorite was not called.

I've noticed that committees sometimes shrink from responsibility. They don't want to eliminate anyone. They want the church to decide. But the church elects a committee to do some of its work. If a church trusts a committee, they should function. If not, they should resign.

A church that insists on calling a pastor annually should vote whether to retain him or not. To insert others to vote on at the same time is to invite division.

Calling a preacher is like a horse race when there's more than one running. And the only sure bet is that the church won't win.

July 12, 1979

How to Support Your Pastor

Your pastor needs more than an adequate salary. We keep saying money isn't everything but we act like it is.

He needs <u>encouragement</u>. I don't know any vocation as subject to discouragement as the ministry. I'm talking about more than a passing, "That was a fine sermon this morning, pastor." I guess every pastor likes to hear that, but often it's said so half-heartedly. I'm thinking about listening to his dreams for the church and helping him pursue them. Now that's encouragement!

You need to <u>pray</u> for your pastor. He needs the prayer and you need the practice. He has more demands on his time than can be met. He'll have to decide what's important and what to let go. He faces most of the temptations you do and some you've never thought of. He needs grace and strength to resist putting his thoughts and desires ahead of the Lord's.

One of the greatest compliments you can pay anyone is to <u>listen</u> to them. I'm not talking about the glassy-eyed stare while the mind wanders over the fields that sometimes passes for listening on Sunday morning. I'm thinking about active listening. The kind where he stimulates you to think.

George H. Davis

Your pastor needs your <u>respect</u>. This doesn't mean putting him on a pedestal. In the September, 1979 issue of <u>Church Administration</u>, Browning Ware writes, "Two fools are necessary to put a minister on a pedestal, one to build it and another to stand on it." (p. 16) He deserves respect as a person and as a fellow Christian. There's a difference between respect and reverence. Reverence is for God, respect for man.

Sometimes he'll need <u>correcting</u>. I remember being told that even though I'd finagled a way to get the church to vote to do something I wanted, it wouldn't be done. I still respect the man who helped me see my foolishness. (It's easier to talk about those mistakes long past than those more recent.)

Your pastor needs to be <u>remembered</u>. Birthdays and anniversaries are important. I never realized how important until Leona and I celebrated our 25th wedding anniversary. Being thoughtful enough to send him a card or to plan a surprise party helps him know you really care about him. When he's constantly reaching out to show concern for others, it's nice when some of it comes back to him.

Remember, you are his <u>family</u>. Many pastors don't live close to their families. They've moved away from where they grew up. Their parents may not be close enough to help spoil the grandchildren and they surely need some help!

If your pastor's family is far away, you can become his family. I'll never forget an older, fellow minister calling one Thanksgiving morning to see if we were going to get to go home. He wanted to invite us over if we weren't. Holidays can be lonely away from home.

July 25, 1979

Information, Please?

Remember when we used to ring the telephone operator and when she answered, "Number, please?" we'd ask for "Information, please?" Then she'd connect us to the information operator. (Now we call it directory assistance.)

I believe we have a system with some of that old, personal touch. The associational office is an information center. You can call with questions about literature, programs, services available, and a number of other things.

No, we don't have all the answers, but we do know where to find many of them. Annuals from the association, state convention, and Southern Baptist Convention contain an amazing amount of information. While most pastors have these, many laypersons don't.

A <u>Directory of Southern Baptist Churches</u> lists the churches in every state. The <u>Missionary Album</u> has pictures and biographical information about Southern Baptist foreign missionaries.

And preachers – I have an ever-renewing list. Now, mind you, the most available may not be the most desirable. But, I can help churches get information about some good men. I'm not interested in telling any church who they should or should not call. I am interested in helping them with the process they use in finding a pastor.

by George

I think I can help churches and individuals understand how Baptist churches operate. Some of it I've learned the hard way. You can learn a lot in the school of hard knocks if you don't mind the school colors – black and blue!

We're also building a library of training materials for pastors, deacons, Sunday School teachers, and others.

There's no such thing as a stupid question. If you don't know the answer, it's a good question. So, if you have a question, call "Information, please?"

August 10, 1979

I Believe in the Church

The church is a divine/human organism. It was established and is sustained by God. It is made up of human beings who seek to follow his leadership.

During the 1960's there were many critics of the church. Some said she was too concerned with keeping the machinery oiled, not enough with ministering to human need. Others said she was too much of a political organization. Still others said she was irrelevant; that she didn't count in the real world.

I believe the church has weathered this storm of criticism and has been forced to reexamine her mission in the world. There was some merit to these charges. The church has listened to her critics and has dug her roots deeper into God's purpose.

The church needn't fear her critics. Sometimes in trying to protect the church, we tend to smother it – like putting a jar over a candle to keep it from being blown out. But the winds can only bring more oxygen to keep the flame burning more brightly. It's God's business to keep the flame burning. Ours is to light up the dark corners of the world.

I guess I believe in the church because I believe in people. I believe people have the capacity to know and respond to God. Not that we ever do that perfectly, but you can never write another person off completely. Even the person or group that seems most closed to God's leadership (as I see it) can rebound with amazing insights into his will.

God has a way of breaking through our prejudices and destroying our molds. Sometimes He has to let the sheet down three times as He did with Peter.

The church is probably her own worst enemy. I believe it was Gandhi who said, "I'd be a Christian if it weren't for Christians." But God is amazingly patient with his people. He continually calls us to repentance and faith. These are not just steps in initiating the Christian walk. They are the way of life for the Christian.

I guess ultimately I believe in the church because I believe in God. He stays with us. He holds His model before us. We can be ready to give up until we catch a fresh glimpse of Jesus. In Him we find our faith and strength renewed.

Through the ages God has used unlikely instruments for his purposes. Someone has said, "God has hit some mighty straight licks with some mighty crooked sticks." That's no excuse for being less than we ought to be but it is encouragement to turn more and more of our lives over to God.

George H. Davis

I might have chosen another way but God has chosen his church. I'm glad because that's you and me.

August 29, 1979

Where It Counts

Over the past ten years our churches have experienced healthy growth in giving to world missions through the Cooperative Program; from $41,610 in 1970 to $98,910 this year.

But I'm more impressed with the fact that we gave 9.7% or our <u>total</u> receipts last year, compared with 9.2% in 1970. Now, that's not much increase, but it's going in the right direction.

We did much better in gifts for associational missions; from $9,724 in 1970 to $36,235 last year. But the percentages are even more impressive; 2.1% of total receipts in 1970 to 3.6% last year.

The gaping need in missions is for BOLDNESS in praying and giving. How bold will <u>you</u> be? Will you increase your giving by a least 1% of your income (say from 10% to 11%)? How bold will your <u>church</u> be? Will you increase her giving through the Cooperative Program by a least 1% of the undesignated receipts?

October 9, 1979

Who am I?

I'm a rather serious-minded person, but I still have fun. I'm generally known as a man of few words. Sometimes this gets me into trouble. I don't always use enough words to explain myself fully. I may appear to be hard-nosed (and with my nose, that's <u>hard</u>). I may seem to be laying down an ultimatum. But I don't expect everyone to agree with me. I do expect the freedom to argue for my position.

I sometimes appear to be rather distant, but I have some warm relationships. I probably function better in small groups or with people I already know. It's still hard for me to meet new people. I meet many people, but I guess I tend to hold them at arm's length before accepting them.

Every time I see the bumper sticker asking "Have you hugged your kid today?" I feel a little guilty. I'm not a very demonstrative person. I find it hard to express my emotions in acceptable ways. I believe I love my kids, even if I don't hug them often. I'm not quite like the fellow whose wife frequently asks, "Do you love me?" Tired of her persistent need of reassurance, he responded, "I told you I loved you forty years ago and if I ever change my mind, I'll let you know." I am able to convey my feelings to my wife, though sometimes clumsily. And I think my kids know of my love and concern for them though it may be expressed indirectly.

I have some rather definite opinions about many things but I'm willing to listen to others in most areas. I've been over enough road to have formed many ideas which have become more or less set. Like Riley of the old "Life of Riley" radio show, "My head's made up." But I don't know it all. I have much to learn in many areas. I've learned how little I know about some things.

I enjoy life and sometimes I'm able to laugh at myself. When I begin to take myself too seriously, I'm in trouble. I have to remind myself of my own fallibility. I'm sometimes wrong, though it's seldom easy to admit it.

I'm stubborn. I believe everyone should be a little stubborn in wanting to see his ideas carried out. If he's not, no one else will be. The alternative is to be wishy-washy. Many good ideas die because no one pushes them. The secret is to know which ones are worth pushing.

I guess I'm a rather complex person. With all my preconceptions and hang-ups, I want to examine issues and to make up my mind on the basis of known facts. I guess labels are necessary, but they're also dangerous. A person is not a computer who always reacts in predictable ways. God has given us memory, feelings, conscience, and the ability to reason. He expects us to use these gifts in making decisions.

Well, that's about as much of me as I can stand to show you right now. By the way, who are you?

October 25, 1979

SUNDAY SPECIALS

Christmas is coming and so is Sunday shopping. Some stores will begin to open Sundays until Christmas for the "convenience" of Christmas shoppers. In some areas, stores are open seven days a week year round. I don't like it! With a little planning we can buy what we need in six days.

I object to Sunday specials – items that are on sale Sunday only. A store that is that hard up for Sunday business had better close!

A pizza ad in a southern Illinois newspaper caught my attention:

EARN MONEY
FOR
YOUR CHURCH!

We'll donate 10% of what you spend with us after church Sunday.

All you have to do is get a receipt when you pay for your Sunday check. Then give the receipt to your Pastor who will then get 10% back for your church at the end of each month.

George H. Davis

Their motives may have been pure but it sounded to me like a bribe.

A grocer told his pastor he was going to begin opening his store on Sunday. "What time will you open?" asked the pastor.

"Seven o'clock," was the reply.

"Will you get down on your knees in the middle of your store at 6:30 and ask God to bless your business that day?" asked the pastor.

"No. I can't do that," the grocer replied.

"Then you'd better not do something you can't ask the Lord to bless," concluded the pastor.

The next time you get ready to go shopping on Sunday, why don't you ask God to bless you and your witness as you go. Or, when you go out to eat, ask God to bless not only the food but also those who prepared and served it.

One positive way a Christian witnesses is by his conduct on the Lord's Day. Going to church doesn't sanctify everything you do after that. The whole day is the Lord's Day. According to the scriptures, it's a day for rest, worship, and doing good. It's time we quit thinking of Sunday shopping as a harmless pastime.

November 7, 1979

The New Pilgrims

If you've been born from above, you have a heavenly citizenship. If you were born in the United States, you're a citizen of this country.

Which citizenship is most important? Which makes the most demands? Which takes priority?

As a citizen of this land you're expected to obey our laws, vote for representative officials, and pay taxes.

What are your responsibilities as a citizen of heaven? Your first responsibility is to recognize that it's a higher citizenship. As a citizen of heaven you can't be limited to any one country. God made the whole world. Jesus commissioned his followers to disciple the world. To assume that my responsibility ends at my national boundary is to regard my heavenly citizenship too lightly.

Paul referred to the church as a colony of heaven (Philippians 3:20). George Webber points out three things about a colony. (1) It is utterly dependent on the homeland if it is to be sustained in a hostile world. The early pilgrims on the New England coast had to have supplies and new personnel along with encouragement from the homeland. (2) "There was an unmistakable unity which surrounded the lives of the colonists. If a child contracted smallpox, the lives of everyone were in danger. If the Indians attacked, all had to come to the defense of the colony." (3) The only reason for the colony's existence was its work in the world. Though they built a stockade for protection, their work was in farming the land and fishing the streams. They were to subdue the wilderness and bring it under the lordship of the colony's king. (God's Colony in Man's World, p. 45)

Webber goes on to point out that "our work as colonists is made possible only because the territory assigned to us has already been claimed by our Lord." The

by George

enemy has already been defeated but he has not yet admitted it. So, we must protect ourselves in the world. But, when we withdraw into the stockade, we are actually preparing for our work in the world. "It is our sins in the world which we confess to God when we gather in the church. It is the concerns of our life in the world for which we intercede." (pp. 49-50)

We have to have buildings. But buildings sometimes become barriers to going out to become what we should.

If God created the whole world, can we afford to narrow our concern?

What does this mean for us day by day?

1. I'll be a world citizen. If my work, or travel, or mission service shall move me about, I'll seek to continue my Christian witness.
2. I'll watch and read the news through Christian eyes. This means I'll read the Bible as I read my newspaper. I'll balance the pessimism in the news with the assurance of victory in the scriptures. I'll think what world situations (political or economic turmoil or disasters) mean to Christians.
3. I recognize that I'm a brother to Christians around the world and I'll seek to join hand and heart with them. I'll pray for them.
4. I'll give all I can and encourage my church to give all it can to mission causes outside our community.

The new pilgrims can hardly afford to be provincial. I'm proud to be a citizen of the United States, but I'm also grateful for my heavenly citizenship. It means, no matter where I am, I'm at home. My concern is to be where God wants me to be doing what he wants me to.

November 21, 1979

What Is A Para-Church Group?

Much is being written and said about para-church groups. Most of it has been critical.

It has been pointed out that when trouble comes people tend to turn to churches for help. Television preachers are little help when your world comes apart. You need another human being you can relate to when you try to put the pieces back together.

Some of the criticism centers in the charge that para-church groups ask for your support but offer little in return. They are attractive because they demand little in commitment and offer a feeling of respectability. They stage a very professional show. Few churches are able to compete with the millions poured into these productions

According to Baptist Press, Virginia Baptists have urged "para-church groups to pay taxes on their business enterprises that compete in the marketplace." They called for the public disclosure of sources and expenditure of funds.

Some have parlayed religion into quite a comfortable living. The Bible recognizes the right of a preacher to live by the gospel (see 1 Timothy 5:17-18). But, does that include luxury?

George H. Davis

There's some fuzzy thinking about who the para-church groups are. According to The World Book Dictionary (1971) para is a prefix meaning beside or near. A para-church group is a group that exists along side the church. It is not the church.

Jesus loved the church and gave himself for it. He left his work to the church. Para-church groups may be an indictment of the church and its failure to carry out its Lord's commission. Sometimes, though, they seem to offer simplistic solutions to complex problems.

Churches, nor Christians, exist in isolation. A part of being a Christian, or a church, is being in fellowship. I doubt the Lord ever intended for there to be "Lone Ranger" Christians or "independent" Baptist churches.

Associations are churches in fellowship on mission. Churches, both in the first and twentieth centuries, are related to one another. John wrote to the churches in Asia. A part of being a church is being in fellowship (association). Associations have traditionally existed for fellowship and as a platform for doctrinal discussion. They have developed programs to assist churches. They do some things individual churches could not do.

But associations are natural extensions of churches. They are not organizations along side or in place of churches. They are an expression of relationships within the body of Christ.

State and national conventions are also extensions of churches. They exist "to assist in establishing and developing Baptist churches" (IBSA constitution). They serve the churches. Denominational boards and commissions help churches in specific areas. I also see ministerial alliances as a natural outgrowth of Christian fellowship in a community.

Denominational bodies on every level are controlled by the churches. Messengers set budgets and hear reports of their elected workers. They must be satisfied with the work being done on their behalf. They cannot just be yes men who smilingly approve everything presented.

Admittedly, denominational workers sometimes treat agencies as their own. We sometimes forget that we exist by and for the churches. When we do, we need to be reminded.

But, let's be clear who para-church groups are. I don't think associations or state and national conventions are included. I think they're an integral part of what it is to be a church

December 6, 1979

A Year Of Learning

This has been a year of learning for me. It began in January when my wife's stepmother fell, breaking her knee, and had to be hospitalized. She had been caring for Leona's father, who had been bedfast for about a year. (Cancer was slowly draining his strength.)

This meant Leona had to go immediately to care for her father until other arrangements could be made. (She has a sister in Chicago and a brother in Texas, but we are closest to West Frankfort -- the family home.) She finally found someone to stay during the week and we (Leona and I) took turns going down weekends. By this time, her step-mother was back home in a wheel chair.

I don't know how much experience you've had caring for invalids. It's not very glamorous. It's lonely and depressing and frustrating. Trying to prepare meals and being away from my own family were the hardest things for me.

We knew it had to he done. There was no question nor complaint about that. We were grateful we could do it. I didn't feel it was fair for my wife to carry the whole load, so we tried to share it. She got caught in a snow storm one weekend and couldn't get home. I'm not very good at baching under the best circumstances and that was the weekend our power went out.

By March it became apparent the lady who was staying during the week wasn't working out. We decided to bring them here to stay with us. They still needed someone to care for them during the day while Leona was at school. Yvonne Lathrop was a life saver. She cared for and learned to love them.

By summer, Leona's stepmother was able to assume more of Grandpa's care. By fall we felt safe in leaving them home when we went to work.

Grandpa was tough but cancer gradually sapped his strength. He died like he argued -- giving up only grudgingly.

Here are some things I've learned out of these experiences:

1. The care of your family can sometimes keep you from attending church. Sometimes they need full-time care. I see this as a higher priority.
2. I also learned how much you miss the fellowship when you have to miss church, You can hear good music and preaching on television but you still miss the fellowship.
3. I was reminded that we often forget the person with a long-term illness. There's nothing noticeable to remind us. They're not hospitalized and we have a hard time maintaining our concern for a prolonged period.
4. I was reminded, too, how important even a casual visit is. Besides his pastor, I suppose the person most faithful in visiting Grandpa was a man named Buster (I don't even remember his last name). He'd come every few days and spend 30 to 40 minutes. They'd talk of anything and everything. Grandpa looked forward to seeing him.
5. Families are flexible. When we brought Grandpa and Ruby to live with us, we knew there'd be adjustments. He had spent about eight years with us when the kids were small. Now they were willing to help in his care. This meant staying home sometimes. You can do what has to be done.

You learn some things in school. Some things you learn only by living. You decide to study some subjects. Others are thrust upon you. The important thing is to remember what you've learned and live by it.

I'm not sure I'm ready for this year to end for I've still much to learn. As I think about another year beginning, I'm reminded of M. Louise Haskins "The Gate of the Year:"

And I said to the man who stood at the gate of the year: "Give me a light, that I may tread safely into the unknown!" And he replied "Go out into the darkness and

George H. Davis

put your hand into the hand of God. That shall be to you better than light and safer than any known way."

December 19, 1979

Five Fabulous Fridays

A few years ago we had a Sunday School attendance campaign called Five Fabulous Sundays. We made much of how seldom we have five Sundays in February and tried to sign people up to attend Sunday School all five of them.

I have a suggestion for a new campaign -- Five Fabulous Fridays! Doesn't that sound even better than Sundays?

But a good campaign needs more than a name. What's it all about? You can't get people to Sunday School or church on Friday, can you? What happens on Friday? Well, for many people, it's payday. And I think that's almost as spiritual as Sunday School. Most people would rather miss Sunday School than payday. It will be easier to sign them up. I know we're getting a late start, but I think we can still encourage people to show up to pick up their paychecks every Friday this month.

Am I kidding? Only partly.

Why are we more interested in getting people to attend a Bible study session than in picking up their paycheck? Oh, I know it's the business of the church to encourage people to participate in Bible study. But, doesn't the church have anything to say about where and how a person works? Aren't we interested in how he earns and spends his money? Or, is it only what he gives to the church we're interested in?

Almost twenty years ago, Bob Hastings wrote <u>My Money and God</u>. He asked three important questions: (1) How do I earn my money? (2) How do I give my money? and (3) How do I spend my money?

I believe the first and third questions are just as important as the second. I think God is concerned with how we earn our money and <u>that</u> we earn it. A lazy goof-off tither does not honor God. A lazy preacher is not as pleasing to God as a hard working ditch-digger.

Neither do we please God by a giving him one-tenth and spending the rest on ourselves. We work not only to support our family but also to give to help others. Sometimes tithers are selfish and materialistic. Some have even suggested that tithing is a way to get rich.

We sometimes think of the ministry as the greatest way to serve God. I think we need to learn to look on every vocation as a way to serve God and man. Every job ought to be God-honoring and helpful to man. I see the call to be a Christian as God's highest call. How we fulfill that call depends on our gifts and interests. I suspect we please God more by our faithfulness than by the kind of work we do.

One problem in any campaign is how to tell if it's successful. Now, it's a pretty good bet people will pick up their paychecks. But, whether they've earned them and whether they spend them wisely may be another question. It's hard to measure when we've helped people to be good stewards in their work and in their spending habits. I guess that's why we count noses and nickels at church. It's easier.

But, is success our only criteria? Aren't we obligated to be faithful? And if I read the Bible right, our attitude toward money is as important as how much we give to the church. Don't misunderstand -- I've been in church-supported work the last twenty-three years. I've given my life to serve God through the church. I believe in the church. I'm glad to be in a church-related vocation.

But I think we've shortchanged people into believing that the church is only interested in their presence and offering on Sunday. We <u>do</u> have a bigger message than that.

Anyone for Five Fabulous Fridays?

February 8, 1980

It's a Nice Place to Visit...

The White House is a nice place to visit but I wouldn't want to live there. My wife and I were among twenty-six Southern Baptist Radio/Television Commission trustees and their wives invited to the White House two weeks ago. The Commission voted last October to give a Christian Service Award to President Carter. Since he felt he could not attend the awards dinner in Ft. Worth February 28, he invited us to Washington. The presentation was videotaped to be shown at the dinner.

It was our first trip to Washington. We got there Monday morning, February 11. We had the afternoon free for sight seeing. Fortunately we ran into trustee Jim Elliott from Washington state. He and his wife had been there since Friday. Someone from their church had been there all the previous week and had shown them around. That made them experts.

Jim took us touring. It didn't take us long to find a fellow hustling tours. He asked how long we had and laid out our route. He took us in a van to various places and told us, "I'll pick you up in forty (or twenty, or sixty) minutes." We spent the afternoon skimming the surface of some of the main tourist attractions: the Bureau of Printing and Engraving (where they print money), the Air and Space Museum, the National Archives, and the Museum of History and Technology.

Tuesday morning began with all of us together for breakfast and a briefing on our trip to the White House. Jimmy Allen, our new Radio TV Commission president, has been rather close to Jimmy Carter over the years. However, he had nothing to do with the award being given. That was the trustee's decision. He was very helpful in preparing us for the White House visit though.

Fifty-five of us (including Dr. and Mrs. Allen and Robert O'Daniel from Baptist Press) boarded the bus at 11 o'clock. As we pulled into the White House drive, John Woods, pastor of First Baptist Church in Paducah, said, "I know how it is. I live in a parsonage, too." Someone asked him if he had more than a four-year lease.

We went to the Executive wing. We were early and the President was running a little late. It seems everyone wants to see him. After a brief wait, we were ushered into the cabinet room and the President came in shortly. He was very warm and gracious in welcoming and greeting us.

George H. Davis

After receiving the award and responding to the presentation, the President asked if he might greet and shake hands with each of us. There being no objection, he proceeded. As he made his way around the room, he missed one couple. As he came back she got a kiss. Some of the other wives wished they'd been missed, too.

The President went back to the oval office and Bob Maddox took some of us on a mini-tour of the White House. He's the Georgia Baptist pastor who joined the White House staff as a speech writer. He's now a liaison for religious affairs.

We went to Kennedy Center for the Performing Arts for lunch. My wife and I took off on our own then to do a little more touring before we boarded an evening flight home.

Some observations-

1. Allow plenty of time when you visit Washington. One fellow said, "It's a good thing they built all these buildings or we wouldn't have anything to see when we come here." Well, there's lots to see. Get some help. If you contact your congressman ahead of time, he may be able to arrange special passes to Congress and the White House.
2. Take plenty of money. Travel of any kind is getting expensive. They seem to feel everyone in Washington is on an expense account. We did find a very reasonable seafood restaurant Tuesday evening.
3. Take your kids. I know this sounds contradictory to the previous paragraph, but you can find reasonable accommodations. Kids need to see Washington. There's enough variety to interest everyone.
4. If you have any hope of ever seeing the President, be careful what goes on your record. The first assurance we had we were going was when we got a call asking for our birthdates, birthplaces, and Social Security numbers. Secret Service men were not in evidence at the White House, but they apparently had done some checking.
5. Pray for the President. He has tremendous responsibilities. Bob Maddox told us Mr. Carter is in his office by 5:30 or a quarter to six each morning. He maintains a heavy schedule. I don't envy him.

The White House is a nice place to visit but I wouldn't want to live.

February 26, 1980

"Go home and go to bed."

I had spent the day training Vacation Bible School workers. That night I was to begin a Bible study which would continue through the week. As I talked through the day I could feel my throat getting raw. I decided to run to the doctor between my afternoon and evening sessions. He threw me for a loop.

Judson Phillips looked at my throat and told me to go home and go to bed. I explained to him, as tactfully as I could that I couldn't. I had a Bible study session scheduled and I had to go on with it. Then he threatened me.

"Would you rather go to the hospital?" he posed. I knew he wasn't kidding. I went home and went to bed.

by George

That's been years ago, but I learned an important lesson. I'm not omnipotent nor indispensible. I don't remember now whether we rescheduled the Bible study or whether they went on without me. (I guess it really won't matter in eternity.)

Whenever I catch myself in an exaggerated idea of my importance or thinking how much God needs me, I think back on that experience. It's painful, but it's also helpful.

How do I know when I'm taking myself too seriously?

- I'm in trouble when I feel I have to put my two cents worth into every conversation as if people were dying to hear my opinion. When I think I've got to have the last word, I'm forgetting that it is my word and that it's fallible. Only God's word is final and infallible.
- When I pose as an authority on every subject I'm only kidding myself. Other people know better. They hear me say things that don't mesh with their experience. They recognize that I'm out on my bailiwick and have made a fool of myself. They probably recognize that before I do.
- I may feel the backlash when I try to straighten everyone else out. When I do this, I'm assuming I'm always right and no one else is. The truth is, I'm right once in a while and I'm wrong once in a while. So is everyone else. We certainly ought to help each other, but hopefully, we can do it as equals -- not as superior / inferior.
- When I assume an infallible position, I'm playing god. I say playing because it's obvious to everyone else I'm not really god.
- I wear myself out when I think if I don't do it, it won't get done. I have more work than I can do. I can enlist and train others to do some of it. But that involves risk. I put my neck into someone else's hands. If they goof, I get choked.
- I have to trust myself to another person. It also means I trust the other person. If I'm Superman, that's hard to do because I have superhuman qualities and no one else does -- I can do incredible feats but I doubt anyone else can.
- If I can't do it, maybe it shouldn't be done -- or, maybe someone else can do it better.
- I've presumed too much when I forget I'm disposable. The world was here long before I made my grand entrance and likely will survive long after I'm forgotten. I need to ponder the searching question God humbled Job with: "Where were you when I made the world?" (38:4a)

Dr. Phillips helped me recognize my humanity. I may need to be reminded from time to time, but there's usually someone around who'll do that.

March 10, 1980

The Highest Call

We've supposed that the highest call anyone receives is to foreign missions. The next rung down the ladder is generally thought to be to home missions--especially among Indians or a language group. The call to be a pastor has been thought to be the next step down and at the bottom is the layman.

George H. Davis

I believe the call to be a Christian is the highest anyone receives. The direction we take in following Christ is of secondary importance. I doubt God is more pleased by my faithfulness as a preacher than by yours as a lay person. What's important is our faithfulness, regardless of our vocation.

I believe in a call to Christian service. I'm committed to serve God through his church. But this doesn't place me in a different category than the person who serves God as a school teacher or as a farmer.

In a classic study, H. Richard Niebuhr suggests four elements in a call to the ministry:

1. The call to be a Christian
2. The inner call of God
3. The providential call in which God gives talents for ministry
4. The church call to minister in some particular congregation

(The Purpose of the Church and Its Ministry, Harper, 1956, pp. 63-66)

Some have one or more of these elements but without all four, ministry is crippled. Some limp along trying to serve God in answer to an inward call. How much fuller the ministry when we have outward confirmation of what we feel inwardly! When some part of the body of Christ recognizes and responds to our testimony to a call, we are freed to exercise that ministry.

During the examination preceding ordination, a preacher is often asked, "What would you do if this council decides not to recommend your ordination?"

We expect him to answer, 'Well, I'd go ahead and preach because that's what God has called me to do."

That answer is only partly right. One must be true to what he believes to be God's call, but he may be mistaken. The affirmation of a council and a church should not be ignored. We need to pay attention to how others see us. After all, it's very difficult to serve God if the people among whom we serve do not accept us.

Somehow we've gotten the idea that preachers must be drafted--they must never volunteer. I remember my own struggle with this.

I felt God wanted me to preach and gladly accepted that as his call. But then I remembered hearing others talk about fighting the call for several months or years. I decided I must have been mistaken about my call because I didn't have an experience like that. I felt God wanted me to preach and I wanted to.

Finally a wise teacher asked, "George, who gave you the desire to preach? Couldn't God work with your will and not just against it?"

Later I discovered, "If a man desire the office of a bishop, he desireth a good work." (1 Timothy 3:1) I can only say, "Amen!"

March 21, 1980

What is Man?

Nowhere is our theology more confused than in our understanding of man. We talk on and on without agreeing on our definitions. We make unsafe assumptions. We suppose only our interpretation of scripture is correct.

Is man, by nature, a sinner? Of course. We all agree he is. Or, do we?

Man, left to himself, sins. But, the real question is, "Why?" Does he sin because he can't help it, or because he chooses to sin? If it's human nature to sin, can man he held responsible? Didn't God make him that way?

I don't believe humanness = sinfulness. The Bible speaks about man being created in God's image and likeness. I think part of that is the freedom to choose and responsibility for those choices.

God has not determined the course of man's life. He <u>has</u> determined that if we follow him we enjoy life and if we rebel against him we suffer death. But the choice is ours. (I recognize that God's choice of us is behind our choice to follow him. However, since I don't enjoy God's perspective, I'm looking from the human point of view.)

I have no problem with God's foreknowledge and predestination. I don't understand all about God's election but then a God you can understand is no God.

Man sins when he chooses another way than God's. He may try to refuse responsibility and sink to the animal level. However, he is more than an animal and is responsible to his creator for his humanity.

He may try to rise above his humanity and live by his own rules--as if he were God. The serpent's suggestion to Eve was "you will be like God" if you forget his silly rules and live by your own. When man tries to be God, he acts like the devil.

The essence of sin is rejecting our humanity, not living it out. It's no good to shrug, "I'm only human." God knows what we are because He made us. He made us for fellowship with Himself. It's when we break that fellowship we're in trouble.

The wonder of our humanity is that God adopts us as His children. So we're not only sons of men, we're also children of God. This is possible because Jesus shares our humanity. The Son of God became a son of man that the sons of men might become sons of God.

Of course Jesus is divine but he's also fully human. I don't understand how this can be. I only know that's the testimony of scripture. One reason he came to earth was to be our example. The Bible says he faced every temptation we do and lived victoriously. He also came to bring us forgiveness for our failings.

One of the problems is that the Bible is not a textbook of systematic theology. Nowhere do we find a chapter on the doctrine of man. We have to read and attempt to understand the whole message. Sometimes statements appear to be in conflict. That means we must search even harder for the truth.

I don't see the whole Bible as having equal weight. Some parts are heavier than others. E.g., I wouldn't take Job 14:7-12 or Ecclesiastes 3:18-22 as the last word on life after death.

The words of Jesus are more important than those of Job. The Baptist Faith and Message statement on the Bible concludes: "The criterion by which the Bible is to he interpreted is Jesus Christ." He is God's last Word.

When we look at the message of the whole Bible, we begin to get a picture of man. It's not completely clear because we're sinful men trying to come to some conclusions about other sinners. We're involved in the study so it's not completely unbiased. We're fallible, so we may be wrong. But it's imperative we have some notion about man and ourselves.

George H. Davis

The way we see man influences not only our understanding of salvation but also our view of the church.

Since I believe God ordained that we learn from each other, I believe it's important that we talk to each other about our understandings. It's not enough just to castigate each other as liberals or fundamentalists.

> *What is man, that you think of him; mere man, that you care for him?*
> *Yet you made him inferior only to yourself; you crowned him with glory and honor.*
> *You appointed him ruler over everything you made; you placed him over all creation.*
> *Psalm 8:4-6 TEV*

April 9, 1980

How Do You Observe Associational Emphasis Week?

We're getting so many special days and weeks it's hard to keep track of them all. There's National Pickle Week and Grandparent's Day--both terribly important to pickle pickers and grandparents.

Church calendars have Soil Stewardship Week and Jewish Fellowship Week--both of which affect Christians in rural and urban settings.

You won't be surprised when I tell you my favorite is Associational Emphasis Week. The suggested date for this year is May 19-25.

Unlike the weeks of prayer for state, home, and foreign missions, we're not attempting to raise money for associational missions. (That's not to say we'll never promote an offering for a special project during AEW. But, you'd have to approve it before we do.) Associational work is underwritten by churches giving a percentage of their undesignated receipts, just as they do through the Cooperative Program.

Like the state, home, and foreign missions emphasis, I hope this will be a week of prayer. I hope you'll pray for me as I try to lead in planning and coordinating our work. Pray for me as I work with and encourage your pastor.

An excellent byproduct of AEW would be a Pastor Appreciation Day in your church. You may wish to observe it on your pastor's birthday or his anniversary with you. If you need some ideas, call me and I'll give you an earful.

I've suggested a plan for praying for Jack Landham, our church planter in Jo Daviess County. I suspect that our prayer will be as important as our money.

You'll think of many ways to remind yourself to pray for Jack on the day assigned to your church. Any kind of group from your church that meets on that day should pray for him. You can also pray as a family for his family.

Pray for our associational workers. They're busy, dedicated people. They're active in their churches. They're committed to helping you do your work.

Some say we ought to support associational workers by attending their meetings. I prefer to think these workers and their meetings support you and your churches.

Churches don't exist to support an association. Associations should strengthen churches. If we're not, we need to change our ways.

Churches are in association. Dale Clemens, pastor at Meadow Heights Baptist Church in Collinsville, has pointed out that it's as silly to talk about independent Baptist churches as it is to talk about married bachelors.

Baptist churches are interdependent. We are in association—in fellowship. We cannot ignore each other any more than we can ignore members of our family. We are part of each other.

We need to pray for each other. Our fellowship is not what it should be until we can pray for one another. When we do, our fellowship will be deepened and strengthened. Isn't that a glorious cycle!

I'm praying for you.

April 23, 1980

I Remember Grandpa

As a boy I remember attending the Davis family reunions at the Mt. Vernon City Park. About all I was interested in then was getting a boat so I could go out on the lake. The reminiscing of the old folks and the constant "Now which one are you?" bored and embarrassed me.

I'd really like to attend the Richardson family reunion June 8. (Hester Richardson was Grandpa's mother.) But I'm supposed to be in St. Louis for the Directors of Missions Conference preceding the Southern Baptist Convention.

Grandpa Davis was a farmer. When I was small we lived just one-half mile from Grandpa's. I'd run off to their house and sometimes they'd let me sleep on a cot behind the heating stove. Later they moved to town and we moved into their house.

When he moved into town, Grandpa never got far away from the farm. Patoka is really more farm than town. When the grain elevator is the tallest building in town, that tells you something. There was seldom a day he wasn't out at the farm. Even after he should have quit driving, he'd make the two and one-half mile trip. Folks got so they'd watch out for him.

I remember Grandpa's hands. They were often scarred and scabbed because he had skinned a knuckle making me a toy boat. He'd use a hammer and wood chisel or a saw. Sometimes he'd hollow out a 2 x 4. Other times he'd use a thinner board to make a paddle-wheeler.

I don't remember whether we ever got him to help us make rubber guns or not. If we did, I'm sure it was when Grandma wasn't looking. Those guns would shoot rubber bands made from inner tubes and were capable of raising quite a whelp. (You've got to explain so many things to kids nowadays. Some of them never heard of rubber guns. And all they know about inner tubes is sliding down a snowy hill on one or taking one to a swimming hole.)

I remember Grandpa's love for music. He was always humming and drumming his fingers. Well, you couldn't really call it humming as we think of it. I think he could breathe and hum all at the same time--in and out, like you'd play a harmonica.

George H. Davis

It was sort of a hiccuppy hum. And the drumming wasn't exactly drumming--at least not like a snare drum or a bass. I guess it was more like at bongo, but I'm not sure he'd ever seen one. His drumming and humming sometimes got on Grandma's nerves. "Oscar," she'd say in a rather firm voice. His mind was probably a thousand miles away but he'd interrupt his music, temporarily.

He was always singing—mostly songs I never heard anyone else sing, before or since. I think he made some of them up. He'd sing about Andy Gump. Do you remember him from the funny paper? He was the guy with no chin.

I remember once when Grandpa was leading singing at church. He had us sing the third stanzas only of all the songs. He thought they'd been neglected too long.

I remember his appetite for Zane Grey books. I think he must have read them all. He kept the librarian busy scouring up new ones. He had a great love for the West. As a young man he'd gone to Idaho for his health. He had been very sick with tuberculosis. He never forgot what those trips did for him. He'd spend hours of an evening reliving those days with Zane Grey's characters.

I remember his sense of humor. One of his favorite expressions was, "I'll bet a hen." That was his way of nailing down an argument. One day he said this to one of Grandma's brothers who was visiting. It turned out Grandpa was wrong and Grandma made him pay off. No amount of explaining that it was just an expression would satisfy her. Uncle Dick went home with the hen.

He had some rather definite political ideas. "I wouldn't mind voting for a Democrat, if I could find a good one," he'd say with a smile.

I'd go with him to his Land Bank meeting. He'd call me his bookkeeper. I'd write or draw or scribble or squirm while he took care of business.

When we first got married, my wife would tell me she was going to fatten me up. "Grandma never fattened Grandpa up," I'd remind her. But it wasn't because she couldn't cook. I tell my friends it's hard work that keeps me slender. I can't understand why they laugh.

I guess it's a sign of old age, but I miss Grandpa now more than ever. There are so many things I'd like to know. Every boy should be close enough so Grandpa could help raise him.

June 3, 1980

Convention Resolutions

Southern Baptists are in danger of talking ourselves to death. At least, that's the impression you get if you take the forty-eight resolutions presented at last week's Convention seriously. At least two concerned abortion. Two dealt with prayer in public schools and two with the Bible.

The Resolutions Committee tried to distill them and came up with twenty-six recommended statements. We spent over two hours debating, amending, debating, and adopting them. It makes you wonder if it's worth the man hours involved. Perhaps as few as 7500 messengers voted on the resolutions. 7500 X 2 hours @ $3.10/ hour (minimum wage) = $46,500. Did we do that much good?

by George

I was pleased with some of the resolutions and unhappy with some, but that's not the point. Is the whole resolution process worthwhile?

I've sat in ministerial alliances when we voted we didn't like under-age drinking, gambling, etc. I've yet to see law enforcement officials tremble in their boots over our resolves. I think they know our bark is worse than our bite. Maybe they also realize some of us are doing what others of us are voting against. I recently heard Baptists described as people who don't drink--in front of each other.

I'm not against taking a stand. I just wonder if conventions are the appropriate place. I'm not against lobbying. But it needs to he done where the legislators are, not just wherever we happen to get together.

It seemed to me we were most divided in St. Louis when we debated the resolutions. In fact, there was little debate except on the resolutions. We seemed to get along on everything else.

Resolutions often deal with emotionally charged issues. I doubt we change anybody's mind with our brilliant insights. Like Riley of the old radio show, "My (our) head's made up." Debate is of little value in deciding emotional issues.

Many of the same issues surface year after year in our resolutions. Fortunately, the Committee is doing some comparing and weeding out so we don't just repeat ourselves. They surely have their hands full.

Where the Convention meets also seems to affect our mood, too. Issues seem to differ in different areas. Mixed bathing is a problem in some areas.

I'm not afraid of controversy if it's over things we can do something about. But I'm reminded that the association is the primary place for doctrinal discussion. It's there we know each other and have a foundation of fellowship. It's hard to debate with someone you don't trust. It's hard to trust someone you don't know.

The national Convention exists "for the promotion of Christian missions at home and abroad and any other objects such as Christian education, benevolent enterprises, and social services which it may deem proper and advisable for the furtherance of the kingdom of God." It's hard to see how some of the resolutions fit into that statement from our constitution.

If it's not too late, I'd like to offer a resolution to end resolutions:

WHEREAS, We meet annually and express ourselves on a number of issues few of us are experts on, and

WHEREAS, Few people who are in a position to really change things pay much attention to us, and

WHEREAS, We frequently get emotionally involved in the discussion of volatile issues and forget the spirit of Christ toward those who differ with us

Therefore be it RESOLVED, That we quit offering resolutions except to thank the host city or to express appreciation for some person's exceptional service, and

Be it further RESOLVED, That we use the time saved by not arguing over resolutions to get better acquainted and to explore ways we can work together.

Be it further RESOLVED, That anyone offering a controversial resolution be required to read all the resolutions passed by the Southern Baptist Convention over the past twenty years.

George H. Davis

Now that I think about it, maybe I won't offer this resolution after all. It might pass!

June 18, 1980

Why Am I Leaving?

I suppose you've heard several definitions of mixed emotions. One that comes to mind is of the vacationing preacher who skipped church to play golf. He got a hole in one but couldn't tell anyone about it.

Moving has never been easy for me. Charles Chandler describes it as a bittersweet experience. Everett Lemay says, "You put your roots down one at a time, and jerk them up all at once." You don't stay seven years in a place without forming close friendships. I think I can go into any of our churches and know most of the people. Some I've gotten real close to—we've worked together in Camp, searched for workers, planned programs, and shared our concerns.

I'm not leaving out of any deep sense of dissatisfaction or discouragement. I'm not being run off nor frozen out. I'm leaving because I believe it's what God wants me to do. I believe he led me here and now I believe he's leading me away.

I believe he wants me to grow. He wants me to develop new skills and interests. I've served all my life in southern Illinois. I've enjoyed it. I've learned many things. You've given me the opportunity to get some real experience in associational work. You've let me write and have encouraged me. I'm deeply grateful for that.

Except for seven years at Altamont (Effingham area), I've served churches south of Route 40. For years this was the dividing line that Southern Baptists rarely crossed. Now I'm going to an area where no church is yet thirty-five years old. It's also an area where several new churches are needed.

I'll be working with twenty-two churches and three missions in eight counties-- from Arcola to Loda (north of Paxton) and from Bloomington/Normal to Danville. I'll be doing much the same kind of work I've done here.

One big difference is their work with college students. They have 70,000 students on five campuses. I'll be directing the work of two full-time workers with these students. That'll be a challenge. Keith Stanford reminded me that if we had 70,000 ethnics or military personnel or newcomers in an association, we'd gear up to reach them, Why not put a like effort into reaching college students?

I've been excited about that work since I first heard about it early this year. I trust it's not just a longing after greener pastures. I'm reminded that what appears to be greener grass is sometimes Astroturf! Findlye Edge points out that one way we can know God's call is in what we get excited about. Another way is in what we can think of a number of ways to approach the work. Still another clue is that we can't stop talking about it.

I'll be using some of the skills I've learned here to develop communications in East Central. I think there's an even greater need since their churches are so scattered.

They have a strong pastoral support program. I want to plug into that and contribute to it. The mix of small/large churches and vocational/bi-vocational pastors is about the same as here. One of my real joys here has been in attempting to serve as a pastor to pastors.

You can't ignore the universities when you minister in Bloomington/Normal or Champaign/Urbana. They have a way of influencing not only their area but the whole state. But, we're not moving so the boys can attend the University of Illinois. They may wind up going there, but for the present at least, they're plugged into Eastern.

It's not easy to leave friends like you. You've meant so much to me. You've been patient and supportive. You've accepted me for what I am and helped me grow. You've meant much to our family as they've grown up. We'll be leaving our daughter with you. She'll be married to Gary Ehrhart of Keenes August 8. (That's why we can't move until the middle of August.) Take care of her.

When you come to Champaign for the state tournament, look us up. We'll even put up one or two. When you're visiting someone in Carle Clinic, give us a call. Maybe we can visit. Above all, pray for us. We'll need a generous helping of God's grace to do this work.

Best of all, why not come over on moving day and lend a hand?

July 7, 1980

The Observer/On Mission
East Central Illinois Baptist Association
September 1980 – December 1996

Hi! I'm George Davis

Hi!

I'm George Davis--your new director of missions. But, I don't want to stay new forever! I'm looking forward to meeting more and more of you and getting better acquainted. I enjoy being treated as a guest at first but I hope we'll soon be feeling at home with each other.

Our house is beginning to look like a home--thanks to my wife's persistence. By the way, I'd like you to meet my family. Leona (my wife) and I have only our youngest son at home full time. He's Mike, a senior at Centennial High School in Champaign. Our middle son, Jim, is a sophomore at Eastern Illinois University in Charleston. Our only daughter Jane, is married to a farmer/machinist, Gary Ehrhart of Wayne City, Illinois. Our oldest son, Mark, is married and lives in Peoria. He works in a chemical laboratory and his wife, Shelley (a Peoria girl) works in Caterpillar's office.

We owe a special word of appreciation to several people who've made our move easier. Yvonne Lathrop of Fairfield brought lunch over for us one day while we were packing. Her husband, Glen, spent one evening helping me get some things collected. Nina Dickey of Fairfield had us out for lunch on loading day. Delbert and Osie Winget of Champaign invited us to spend the night with them when we got to town. Then they spent most of the next day helping us get started unpacking. Jim Torry of Champaign stopped by to help associational secretary Norma Clark bring order out of chaos after moving the office to the Baptist Student Center in Urbana.

Which reminds me--the associational office has moved to the second floor of the BSC at 1008 South Lincoln. Our phone is (217)384-1664. Norma works Mondays, Wednesdays, and Fridays. I'm in and out. It's better to call if you want to see me. For a while, Norma will probably be able to tell you more than I can.

I'm living in the associational parsonage at 1903 Broadmoor in Champaign and our phone there is still (217)352-5386.

I'm more interested in helping you than in getting you to help me. I want the association to encourage and support pastors and churches as they seek to fulfill their ministry. We can do this by training workers, providing opportunities for fellowship and growth, and leaning to love and pray for each other. We need each other. Just as Christians grow and develop in the fellowship of a church, churches are strengthened in the fellowship of an association.

Please don't hesitate to call on me if you feel I can help. And I'll be calling on you to get acquainted and to offer my support.

September 1980

by George

FLABBERGASTED!

That's the only word to describe my feeling on finding four persons I had known in previous pastorates when I preached at Tuscola recently.

I knew Morris and Joyce Weaver and their family were members at Hillcrest Baptist Church in Tuscola. They had been members at Second Baptist in Herrin when I was pastor there (1964-69). They moved to central Illinois but we had kept in touch with them. Morris had stopped by to see us when we lived in Grayville. We had stopped by to see them when they were in Sadorus. We got acquainted with Joyce's parents in Wayne County.

Joyce had called to see if I could supply for them on September 21 so I was not surprised to see them. But when Dick Stilley introduced himself, I was surprised! I had known Dick before either of us were married. He and his family were members at Liberty Baptist Church east of Benton. I was a student at Southern Illinois University in the early '50s and was their pastor. Now we both have families that are rapidly growing up.

We spent the day with the Weavers and they mentioned Jim Coatney. "Not Jim Coatney from Louisville?" we asked. "Yes, that Jim Coatney," they assured us.

I never was Jim's pastor, but during Seminary (in the mid '50s) I served a church north of Louisville, Illinois and we had an apartment in town. We spent weekends and summers there. Jim's aunt was a member at Second Little Prairie and I met Jim through her. His dad was a state trooper and they belonged to First Baptist in Louisville.

After a quarter of a century, I saw these two men in the same church several miles away from where I had known them. I was flabbergasted.

I'm not sure about the lessons out of all this. For one thing, it reminds me how short twenty-five years really is. It can seem like an eternity when you're living through it, but looking back it's only a moment.

There's also a real joy in seeing people grow in their Christian commitment. Sometimes you have to stay around a while to experience this. It's a tragedy that most pastors never know this joy.

October 1980

I"m Not A Speeder

I'm not a speeder. I try to drive within the limit.

But, recently I got a ticket for going 56 in a 45 miles per hour zone. I wasn't in a hurry. I was just careless.

I can think of all kinds of excuses. I had just gotten off the Interstate and was used to driving 55. But, my wife had just suggested I slow down.

I could say it was unfair for the patrolman to catch me coming down a hill. But the sign didn't say "45 except when going downhill."

I could observe that traffic was light and I had my car under control. But, the sign said

George H. Davis

```
┌─────────┐
│  SPEED  │
│  LIMIT  │
│   45    │
└─────────┘
```

I say I'm not a speeder, but I got caught speeding.

I try not to make a practice of sinning, but I do sin.

I could make all kinds of excuses to justify my sin, but it wouldn't make much difference. I am a sinner.

I guess I'm a speeder, too

November 1980

Secretaries Are Missionaries, Too!

I got a call the other day wanting to know if their mission money was going to missionaries or just to secretaries.

I told the caller, "Both."

After I hung up, I thought of a better answer. (Don't I always?) Aren't secretaries missionaries, too?

A secretary can help a missionary do a better job. If she takes care of the office and paper work, he is freed for what he needs to do. Without a secretary he may get bogged down in detail and not get his work done.

If I hadn't had a secretary, I wouldn't have gotten that call. I had gone to lunch and Norma was working over.

I've been around long enough to have met many of the people our missions contributions support and I believe in what God is doing through them. I believe they're worthy of our support--both financial and prayer.

The next time you hear somebody criticizing Southern Baptist's mission program, ask them for specifics. It's not enough to charge that seminary professors are liberals. That's grandstanding--playing to the crowd. That's the rabble rousing kind of charge that some (rabble) like to hear.

Get specifics: which professors are liberal? How are they liberal? I'm not ready to say all our programs are perfect. But, I'm tired of irresponsible pot shots.

December 1980

The Rusty Slide

One of our neighbors has a swing set in his back yard. It's nothing fancy--two swings and a slide. It's not new but it is in working order.

The thing that has struck me about it is that I've never seen anybody playing on it. In fact, I've never seen any kids in their back yard.

by George

Swings are not much for going places--you just cover the same ground over and over again. They *are* great for building confidence in young children. They build their muscles and learn how high they can swing. The more daring jump out when the swing is at its highest peak. The more imaginative "bail out" as in paratroopers.

Swings are also relaxing for grown ups. They no longer have to prove their prowess but can lounge leisurely. (The ultimate luxury is a porch swing. The problem is so few houses have porches anymore.)

It's sad to watch a swing set rust--undisturbed. I remember how we used to take bread wrappers (they were made of waxed paper then) and sit on them going down the slide. That made them slicker so we could slide faster.

I wonder what is gathering dust and rust around your place? Good things no longer needed. It's easy for a home, a church, or a life to get cluttered up with outgrown toys.

January 1981

The Bottom Line

Sometimes a church is chosen as an example because "they baptized 150 people last year." Then the clincher is added, "That's the bottom line isn't it? Isn't that what we're all about?"

Is it?

I agree baptism is important. It is a significant way of confessing our faith and identifying with God's people. It is the most visible way we have of counting converts.

But, is counting converts our primary purpose? Doesn't Jesus commission us to *make disciples*? Doesn't he call us to *follow him*?

It seems to me the bottom line is whether we're *becoming Christlike* in our attitudes and actions. Are we leading converts into Christlikeness?

I'm committed to the church. But it's the church as the body of Christ, not just as organized religion. I'm unwilling just to initiate members, collect dues, and pass out paid up memberships. I think the Lord expects more of us.

I recognize how hard it is to measure Christlikeness. But part of our problem may be in wanting to measure everything. We certainly need his Spirit without measure.

To the degree we have party spirit, or envy, or strife, or jealousy we can be pretty sure we don't have the Spirit of our Lord. I'm afraid the bottom line shows a deficit.

March 1981

On Becoming a Deacon...

My church has asked me to become a deacon.

How does it feel after sixteen years as a pastor and eight years as a director of missions to become a deacon?

George H. Davis

I feel *humbled*. Some of the finest men I've known have been deacons. I'd risk my life to them. They have been the kind of men who could disagree with me and defend me at the same time. They've cared enough to confront me when I was out of line. I'm humbled to think that someone would see me as a part of that kind of group.

I am *flattered*. I've never felt the work of deacons and pastors was that different. We're both in the business of caring for people. I've seen my role as director of missions in the caring vein, too--as a pastor to pastors.

I was not asked to be and did not volunteer to be ordained again. It's not that I consider ordination to the ministry higher than that to the deaconate. The primary difference I see is that the pastor works in a broader area and devotes his full time to his work.

I am *gratified*. I see myself as a caring person. Though my strengths may be more in carefully analyzing programs, I've tried not to lose sight of people. I'm glad someone sees me as people-oriented enough to entrust their ministry to me.

I've been uneasy about my church membership. I've never fully appreciated those who only wanted to be card carrying members. But in some ways, this is the kind of member I've been. I'm gone about as much as I'm there. (Oh, I do send my money, but I'm convinced that's not the greatest gift. My church really needs me--my time and energy.)

Being involved in Deacon Family Ministry will provide me a needed avenue of service. I can find time to visit families just like other deacons do. I doubt I'm any busier than most of them.

I have a deep respect for my fellow deacons. I feel they've accepted me as a full partner in ministry. This means, in part, that I'm accountable to them. I feel that more strongly now than I ever did as a pastor. I'm glad for the growth potential in that kind of partnership.

March 1981

You Won't Be Disappointed

Have you ever noticed that things generally live up to your expectations? If you expect a meeting (or a service) to be good, it usually is. If you expect it to bomb, it usually does.

Is this because you have unusually keen insight? I doubt it. I suspect it's because you rarely exceed your expectations. What you get out of a meeting (or a service) depends as much on your attitude as upon its structure and content. How else can you account for such divergent appraisals of the same meeting?

My wife and I recently attended Home Mission Board orientation for new missionaries. I knew a full week would be too long to spend there and sure enough, it was. But there were some serendipities. Webster defines serendipity as "the gift of finding valuable or agreeable things not sought after." (I wonder if it's a cousin to what the Bible calls grace?)

One of the unsought joys of the week was getting acquainted with 64 other missionaries. Eight were from other countries. We came from 22 states and are going to 27. Some were former foreign missionaries or children of foreign missionaries; others were converts of foreign missionaries. Some had years of experience; others were still in seminary. Some were going into seaman's ministry; some will start churches; some will work with unwed mothers or others in need. Some will work with Arabs or Southeast Asians in Tennessee; some with deaf in Illinois. Some will lead associations in rural areas; others in metropolitan areas.

After the commissioning service at Prays Mill Baptist Church in Douglasville, Georgia, the church had dinner on the grounds. They were wonderfully thoughtful hosts.

One of our group overheard a youngster observe, "It's a good thing we're feeding these missionaries like this. This may be the last good meal they'll get." I hate to disappoint her, but I suspect that suffering through a week of sitting may be as much sacrifice as I'll make for a while.

May 1981

Just Suppose

Long ago and far away a loving father wrote some guidelines for his children's behavior. They were collected from his experience and knowledge of his family. They represented his accumulated wisdom.

His children and their children read and revered his words and raised their children by them. As much-used copies of the guidelines began to deteriorate, other copies were lovingly made. Generation after generation found them to be a perfect treasure of heavenly wisdom.

Centuries later some of his offspring got to arguing over how the guidelines came into being. They grew bitter as they accused each other of not believing the treasured words. The main concern seemed to be in proving certain views concerning their origin. There was little enthusiasm or energy left for ordering their lives by the father's words.

June 1981

Generic Christians

I had not encountered generic groceries until we moved to Champaign. I'd heard about generic drugs, but not milk, or margarine, or applesauce. But, I don't do much grocery shopping.

I don't have any feeling one way or another about generic groceries, but I do react to people who want to "just be Christians" and avoid any denominational labels.

I'm a Christian before I'm a Baptist, but I _am_ a Baptist--a Southern Baptist, if you please. It's not that I think we have a franchise on heaven. I'm aware of some of our shortcomings and I know we have blind spots. I recognize that there are a variety of ways of working together. I just happen to prefer ours. We combine maximum

George H. Davis

freedom with the fellowship base to get things done. We relate to each other as equals--brothers.

I know we can rely too heavily on brand names. They sometimes have a better reputation than their present product deserves, and vice versa. But, it's up to the major brands to do most of the research and development. They introduce new products--some of which will ultimately be copied by generics.

When I buy a brand name, I know who to hold responsible. Who knows who makes the generic? As Baptists, we have built in accountability; first, to the Lord, and, then to each other. Our boards and agencies answer to those who created them and finance them. Not everyone can serve on these boards, but those who do represent us. Let's wear the name Southern Baptists gladly.

July 1981

First Anniversary Thoughts

I'll soon complete my first year in East Central Illinois. It's been a year of adjustment for our family. By now I think it's unanimous--this is our home. We still have friends in other areas but we're making friends here.

It's been a year of challenge. I was not accustomed to operating on such a tight associational budget. But, thanks to your support, we're managing.

It's also been a year of learning and setting direction. We've laid the foundation in campus ministry. We have some exciting programs on the drawing board--some that we're designing. I'm looking forward to the years to come.

August 1981

The Call to Preach

In a classic study H. Richard Niebuhr suggests four elements in a call to the ministry:
The call to be a Christian
The inner call of God
The providential call in which God gives talents for ministry
The church call to minister in some particular congregation
(The Purpose of the Church and Its Ministry, Harper 1956, pp. 63-66)

Some have one or more of these elements but without all four, ministry is crippled. Some limp along trying to serve God in answer to an inward call. How much fuller the ministry when we have outward confirmation of what we feel inwardly! When some part of the body of Christ recognizes and responds to our testimony to a call we are freed to exercise that ministry.

During the examination preceding ordination, a preacher is often asked, "What would you do if this council decides not to recommend your ordination?"

We expect him to answer, "Well, I'd go right ahead and preach because that's what God had called me to do."

That answer is only partly right. One must be true to what he believes to be God's call, but he may be mistaken. The affirmation of a council and a church should not be ignored. We need to pay attention to how others see us. After all, it's very difficult to serve God if the people among whom we serve do not accept us.

September 1981

The Old, Wooden Horse Trough

We had an old, wooden horse trough at "the other place." That's what we called the place where I spent my first few years. When Grandpa and Grandma Davis moved to town, we moved one-half mile east to their house.

We had hired hands living at "the other place" when I was young. (I sort of resent that term now. They were more than hands. They were persons. But, we were only using then current terms.)

Back to the horse trough--it was made out of heavy staves held together by steel bands. In its later years we poured a concrete bottom in it to try to stop the leaking. We'd fill the cracks with black pitch.

It was really wonderful. I suppose it was about ten feet across. When we'd been fishing, we'd sometimes bring some to stock the tank. I don't think they ever lived very long.

In the winter we'd put a coal-fired heater in the middle of the trough to keep it from freezing.

The old trough is gone now. So is the windmill that kept it full. It was replaced first by a metal tank and more recently by an ingenious device made of plastic and fiberglass. We still had to keep the metal tank from freezing over in the winter. This new critter keeps the water covered so it won't freeze. You just have to teach the cows to push the lid down to get to the water.

That old trough with its stately tower of steel made a grand sight. But the new waterer is better. And I wonder if it wouldn't keep fish alive longer. I expect it stays cooler in the summer.

Do we sometimes cling to outworn methods and equipment when something better is available? Someone has suggested that the seven last words of the church are, "We never did it that way before."

November 1981

Long Handles

How tastes change!

I played hooky one day rather than wear long underwear to school. I rode the bus to school but then walked up town and down the railroad track. It was a l-o-n-g day. I got back to school in time to ride the bus home.

I don't remember why I made such a fuss that day because I wore them other times. We had the one-piece style with the button-over (not the drop-down) flap.

The real humiliation was undressing for PE. I always imagined I would be the only one wearing long underwear.

Then I remember the warm day in early spring when my brothers and I pulled off our long handles to go swimming. I think we'd been fishing and evidently they weren't biting. Anyway, we decided it was too nice a day to waste, so in we plunged. I guess it was the fact that our hair didn't get dry before we got home that made a lasting impression on me.

When I got my first pair of thermal underwear (for hunting), my kids were soon sneaking out of the house with the shirt on. Now it seems to be cool (or tough, or whatever the current word is) for both boys and girls to wear thermal shirts under an unbuttoned flannel shirt. Men and women wear insulated tops as jackets or vests.

Trying to keep up with trends can strip your gears.

I guess it has always been so.

"Silent Night" was written for two voices and a guitar. The church organ in Oberndorf, Austria had broken down and wouldn't be repaired for the Christmas Eve service. An assistant priest, Father Joseph Mohr, wrote the text and asked the acting organist, Franz Gruber, to compose the tune. It has become a standard. Yet, we seldom hear it sung with guitar accompaniment.

I've heard people rant about keeping drums and guitars out of church.

I'm becoming a country music fan. Isn't the whole world? At least I can understand the words--sometimes to my embarrassment. A friend of our family just had his first song recorded by a major star. I'll tell you about it, if you'll ask.

I guess we get more emotional about music than any other aspect of worship. It's one part we can participate in.

Now, I sometimes wear my thermal drawers for protection under wool trousers.

My, how times change. Or, is it me?

December 1981

The Race

Junior Wickersham and I had a race and I lost. In doing so I qualified as the slowest boy in high school.

The coach had us outside running and noticed that Junior and I kept coming in well behind the others. So he decided to have a run off to see who was really slowest.

Though I was no more than average height, I was quite a bit taller than Junior. In fact, he was kind of scrawny. But he outran me.

I guess that confirmed my limits in sports. There's no great demand for a player of average height who's s-l-o-w.

I've always enjoyed sports but never excelled. When I realized I wasn't a sprinter, I fancied myself a distance man. We'd never heard of cross country, but we used to run the mile from our house to the gravel road--or at least part of it.

by George

Junior was killed in an accident a few months after our race. I had been sitting beside him in the back of a pick up. We were on our way back to town to pick up Cokes for a class party. The driver lost control on loose gravel and plowed into the ditch. As the truck swerved back onto the road, it turned over pinning Junior under the cab. The door handle caught him in the temple.

I remember my dad's gratitude for our safety when my stepbrother and I got home that night.

Maybe being slow on my feet has shaped me in other ways. I've generally been a good student. I usually have lots of patience in making machines work. I've even learned to work with people. It hasn't been easy to overcome timidity and some feelings of inferiority.

In sports speed and size are important. In life other things are equally useful.

January 1982

Shame

I grew up with a kind of reverence for the University of Illinois. My parents met as students here. I remember thumbing through some of Mom's textbooks and looking curiously at Dad's insect collections as I grew up. I read with interest the Alumni Association newsletter which came to our home.

I remember Dad telling about Red Grange's exciting broken field running. I followed the career of Dike Eddleman from Centralia (just fifteen miles from home) to the University. I remember at least one Rose Bowl victory.

In recent years Illinois sports have been erratic at best. Last year there was the controversy about quarterback Dave Wilson. The Big Ten denied Illinois revenue from televising football games for one year.

The state legislature, sensitive to the moans over the loss of $500,000, authorized a special lottery to benefit the U of I. Details have been worked out and it begins this month. Proceeds from the first two weeks of the Pick Four game of the Illinois Lottery will go to the U of I Athletic Association.

I'm deeply disappointed at the willingness of the University to accept such funds. While I recognize that gambling has been legalized in Illinois, that doesn't make it right. Neither does the plea of a good cause justify destructive ways of raising money.

Whatever mistakes the U of I made in handling the Dave Wilson case, they pale into insignificance compared to our willingness to use the proceeds of a lottery to attempt to develop our sports team.

I sometimes feel our teams need a shot in the arm (or somewhere) but I doubt that whatever we realize from this lottery will prove to be the magic elixir. I doubt you can buy better teams. I know you can't buy better persons and I think that's ultimately our goal.

I have no quarrel with those who wish to donate to the Athletic Association. But to hold out the chance of a prize for a price constitutes gambling. I don't think that's the way to develop character—either the fans' or the players'.

George H. Davis

I think it's a shameful way to finance a sports program.

February 1982

A White Rose Day

Mother's Day has been a white rose day for almost as long as I can remember. I grew up in a tradition of wearing a red rose on Mother's Day, or a white one if your mother was dead. Mine died when I was eight.

She had come from New Hampshire to Urbana to attend the University of Illinois. Her dad's brother taught engineering here and she stayed with him. He lived just two blocks from where my office is now.

Dad came here from south central Illinois to study agriculture. He roomed about five blocks from the office. So I'm back where my parents met and married.

I think about Mom now and then and miss her, but I'm not much for playing "What if she'd lived?" God has been able to work for good in my life and I'm grateful.

I'm thankful for a father who kept four boys together when that must have seemed impossible at times. I'm also thankful for a stepmother who stepped in and helped raise five boys (four already there and one she brought) and one girl. I know it wasn't easy, but she stayed with it.

Our family is close--not geographically, but emotionally. So Mother's Day isn't just a time to grieve; it's also a time to laugh.

May 1982

Rainmakers Meet

ECIBA's annual Pastor/Staff family picnic drew thirty-eight persons to Lake of the Woods at Mahomet on May 20. They represented twelve families. That's four times as many as showed up last year.

After about a month with little rain, the Champaign area received 2.72 inches that evening. Fortunately, we ate under a shelter and were able to leave between showers.

The RA track meet had just been completed the previous Saturday when the area received at least ½ inch of rain. Awards ceremonies were moved indoors, at Unity High School, near Tolono.

We might be willing to schedule another outdoor activity during July or August if the price was right! I'm joking, of course. We'd meet just for the joy of getting wet. After all, we're Baptists, aren't we?

June 1982

We've Got Trouble

One of our favorite pastimes seems to be trying to figure out what's ruining our kids. Through the years there have been a number of suggestions—pool, movies, television, rock music, etc.

by George

It's interesting that we look for corrupting influences outside ourselves. It's also interesting that every generation sees the next as going to the dogs.

As I remember, the Music Man was primarily interested in selling band instruments and uniforms. I wonder about the current generation of doomsayers.

July 1982

Not Enough Burners or Too Many Pans?

Most stoves have four burners--two in front and two in back.

I guess I've got a limited number of burners, too. I can keep a few things cooking pretty well up front but that means I've got to push other things to the back burners. When they get full, some things get pushed off the heat. They soon stop cooking.

I think that's what's happened to me this summer. We lost the use of both our cars through accidents last month. It's hard to keep from being preoccupied about people and property involved in accidents. After you know the people are ok, you start working on getting around. Going from a two-car family to an eight-footed family is quite a shock!

But friends and insurance (in that order) are a real help. We're beginning to work toward solutions.

Pastor Kim also crowded into my life in July. I have deep respect for him but he brought his own set of expectations and experiences. I'm slowly learning to work on my own priorities.

Maybe I'll soon be able to find a place, at least on the back burner, for some things that got pushed aside. Then, as routine returns, I'll have the emotional energy to get some projects cooking again.

Thanks for your prayerful support.

August 1982

The Difference

Have you ever tried to find out how a popular television preacher is spending your money? Would you allow your church to operate without reporting to its members?

It's not so much a matter of trust as it is of good stewardship. God holds us responsible not only for how we earn, give, and spend our money. He also expects us to see that our church is a good steward of its money.

One of the basic differences between churches and parachurch groups is accountability. You may be able to get a financial statement from a "super church," but I don't think that's enough. I want to have a voice in deciding how the money's spent and not just be told, after the fact, that it went for good causes. I have that privilege in my church.

September 1982

George H. Davis

Imagination?

On this morning's news, I heard about a person who received burns to their eyes with Visine. The eye drops apparently had hydrochloric acid added to them.

Shortly after the Tylenol tampering story broke, there was a Visine scare. However, the irritant turned out to be something else.

This latest copy cat certainly doesn't get an "A" for originality. But, neither do most churches. We're slow to experiment in either worship or ministry. We doggedly follow the tried and true paths.

I suspect the biggest room in most our churches is the room for imagination. I frequently say, "The best ideas haven't been thought of yet." (If I say that too often, it's not very imaginative, is it?)

Almost ten years ago, the Foreign Mission Board published a booklet on graphic design called <u>Imagineering</u>. I like that idea--dream about what can be, then engineering it! Make it happen!

Not every new idea is a good one. But, neither are all old ideas. James Russell Lowell counsels us

"Nor attempt the Future's portal with the Past's blood-rusted key." (from The Present Crisis).

But even his language now sounds somewhat stilted. It doesn't grab men on the move.

October 1982

Can Anybody Modify a Fuzzbuster?

Radar detection devices have become popular with those who want to outwit police. Insistent on speeding and tired of trying to spot "a bear in the bushes" they've resorted to an electric alarm to notify them when they're being watched.

What this country really needs is a device to notify us when God is watching.

We seem to have developed the attitude that anything's alright as long as you don't get caught. We tend to carry this over to God. Whatever we can hide from Him is ok.

If somebody would just begin marketing a device that would tell us when God's watching--an Almighty Alert. We could put on our best behavior when there's a "Big Bear in the Air." Then, as soon as we got out of range, we could go back to normal. After all, God surely doesn't expect us to be perfect, does he?

Have we lost a sense of an all-knowing God? Do we feel we worship a God you can con? A God who doesn't really understand what's going on nowadays? Or doesn't care?

Or, worse yet, have we lost faith in a loving Father? A Father who knows all about us and still loves us? I suspect it's a greater tragedy to forget God's willingness to forgive than to feel we can hide from Him.

November 1982

by George

I Owe Them

Two men had a great influence on my early ministry—Kenneth G. Hall and Bluford M. Sloan.

Brother Hall was associational missionary when I became a student pastor at Second Little Prairie Baptist Church, near Louisville, Illinois. When I graduated from Seminary, he recommended me to First Baptist Church in Altamont.

Because of his encouragement, I served as an associational Vacation Bible School worker, Training Union worker, and moderator. He was my model.

He left Louisville Association before I did. When he left, I began trying to fill his shoes in teaching some Seminary Extension classes. Over the years, I've taught about fifteen courses--hardly a fraction of the number he taught.

When I moved to Herrin, I served as associational coordinator when our missionary retired. Later, when I moved to Fairfield, I found myself trying to step in the tracks Brother Hall had left as Mt. Erie Association's first full-time Superintendent of Missions. I gradually learned of the giant steps he took. By the time I arrived, there was no longer much doubt about the value of a person to lead out in associational work. But his path had not been easy.

Bluford was state Training Union Director. He asked me to be a consultant for southeastern Illinois. I worked with Bible Drills and Speaker's Tournaments. I helped plan and promote our first state Family Life Conference.

Bluford encouraged me to go to Ridgecrest several years to learn how to help churches do a better job of training. He sent me to Nashville to learn about new programs and then sent me out to lead conferences in other churches and associations. He gave me several opportunities for growth and leadership development.

I owe a great deal to these men. In someone else's words, neither of them "Never done me nothin' but good."

I paid tribute to Brother Hall when I was in Greater Wabash (formally Mt. Erie) Association. Bluford's death last fall reminded me of my debt to him.

I guess one of my goals is to be the kind of encourager to someone else these men have been to me. They never asked to be repaid, but I think they expected me to pass it on.

January 1983

XXX

What do you think of when you see XXX?

You may see a winning line up in a game of ticktacktoe, or part of a diagram for a football play. You may want to add to it and think of flour or baked goods. Or, you'll think of only one X—the unknown, as in 5X=9.

You may think I'm trying to cover three spots, since X marks the spot. Or, you may think of a jug of moonshine, though that's a little out of my bailiwick. Surely no one reading this column would think of a very vulgar movie.

George H. Davis

If you have a good memory, you may think of kisses. Remember when we sealed our letters with kisses?

That brings me to what XXX means to me. Thirty years ago the 28th of this month I married a coal miner's daughter from West Frankfort. She's been the joy of my life. She's challenged me with her devotion and encouraged me with her enthusiasm. She's been by my side in joy and sorrow. She's made the good times better and the bad one's bearable.

She always wanted to be a preacher's wife and is kind enough to refer to me as her favorite preacher. She struggled with her role when I changed mine. After twenty years as a pastor, I became a Director of Missions. Her role changed, too, but she didn't complain.

She must be what the Lord had in mind when he promised man a help meet. She's suitable; she fits well. That's how Webster defines the adjective, meet.

She's the finest lady I know

February 1983

I was Speechless

I don't think of myself as an outgoing, aggressive talker but I recently found myself completely at a loss for words.

We were having our annual Champaign/Urbana cluster service. The Garden Hills, Temple, and Pennsylvania Avenue choirs had joined for some stirring music and Norm Langston had spoken convincingly about faith/action as the foundation for life.

As the service was closing, John Thomason called my wife and I to the front. He presented us with an anniversary cake and a corsage and boutonniere and called on Charles Chandler. He presented us with a farm scene painted by Linda Myler.

The painting was especially meaningful because Leona has taken lessons from Linda. She's also in our Sunday School class. She even got the right kind of cow in the picture--a white face.

To say we were surprised would be a gross understatement. We were flabbergasted. They'd even arranged for our oldest son and his wife to come over from Peoria. (They'd been here for the weekend and had returned Saturday night to be in their church Sunday morning.)

After almost three years, I thought I knew my brothers in ministry. I didn't really think they were that sneaky and conniving. But I love them anyway.

Our thirtieth anniversary will be a memorable one. Thanks, guys and C/U churches.

We're going to miss John and Polly and their family. They've made some unique contributions to our fellowship. Their moving to Mississippi just means we'll have friends in more places.

March 1983

by George

Ordinary People/Extraordinary Opportunities

We'll get better acquainted with some missionaries through our World Missions Conferences. I have a hunch we'll find them to be ordinary people like you and me.

They're not saints nor martyrs. They're real people. They're growing and learning. They're fallible. We're all made from the same pattern. We're all children of God, seeking to serve him.

Missionaries have been given extraordinary opportunities for service. They've been called to work where doors are open and adversity is real (see 1 Corinthians 16:9). They're being supported by loving people.

How did they get such opportunities? Likely by making the most of those they had. Then they were given more.

Jesus told a story about a man who refused to accept responsibility for the one talent he had. It was taken from him and given to a man who already had ten. "For everyone who has will be given more, and he will have an abundance. Whoever does not have (or does not use what he has), even what he has will be taken from him." Matthew 25:29

I suppose the lesson for us is to be faithful where we are with what we have.

Missionaries don't want to be worshipped. They're human. They have been given extraordinary opportunities for service because they were faithful in insignificant things and places.

April 1983

I Believe in Words

"One picture is worth a thousand words," according to the old Chinese proverb.

That may be true but I want to be a bit more careful how I spend my thousand. It had better be a pretty good picture.

I believe in words. It's not that I don't like pictures. I do. Pictures are great. They show up and show off. They illustrate brilliantly. They can clear up confusion.

But I believe in words. They're like old friends. They stimulate and convey warmth. They can stir the imagination.

Words don't have to be big or fancy to move me. Sometimes simple ones are better. I like to read or hear words used well. I shudder when words are misused or abused.

I enjoy reading. Sometimes I laugh as I read. Sometimes I cry. My farm background helps me identify with James Herriott's descriptions of his veterinary visits to Yorkshire farmers. I'm inspired by the joy Peter Jenkins finds in his walk across America.

Words kindle ideas. Ideas move men. Don't pity the poor preacher who has only his words to move a congregation. Was ever a higher compliment paid words than when John described the Son of God as Word? The Word uses words.

George H. Davis

Remember, the one who said, "One picture is worth a thousand words," didn't paint a picture; he used words.

July 1983

Swimming in the Salt Water Pit

I've never been to Great Salt Lake in Utah or to the Dead Sea but I do remember swimming in a salt pit. Around some oil wells there used to be salt water pits. I guess that's where they dumped the salt water the wells produced.

When I was growing up there was such a pit two or three miles east of our house. My brothers and I went there once or twice.

It was easy to swim in the salt water. It was no trick to float. If you tried to dive, you tended to pop back up like a cork. It was fun--fun as long as you stayed in the water, that is.

When you got out and started drying off, the salt didn't evaporate. It caked on your skin. You couldn't see it, but you could feel it as it began to itch.

The first business when you got home was to take a bath in fresh water. (We didn't have a shower yet.) You felt like you'd itch to death if you didn't get the salt washed off.

Some things provide a fascinating diversion but leave you itching to get rid of the residue that clings to you.

August 1983

We Are Family

I enjoy family--parents, children, grandchildren, brothers and sister, aunts, and cousins.

I'm learning more about my family. That's important to me because that's part of who I am. I've learned that grandpa Davis' grandpa Richardson was a farmer/preacher in southern Illinois.

You're another part of who I am. Family is blood lines. The cross is our family tree. We are family because of Calvary. Our association is a family of churches. We're not only related, we care for each other. We seek each other's welfare.

We don't rejoice at a sister church's trouble but at her good fortune. We are family.

September 1983

Legalists Have Less Fun

Nothing takes the joy out of life so fast as feeling you're responsible for keeping everybody else in line. It's a heavy responsibility. You have to stay on guard all the time.

by George

You not only have to monitor the language but also the grammar of television personalities. You have to keep track of not only your kids, but your neighbor's, too.

Probably the legalist's greatest challenge comes on the highway. You have to check not only speed but also traffic laws.

Grandpa Charnock's law says, "You never really learn to swear until you learn to drive" (Murphy's Law, Book ~~Four~~ Three by Arthur Block, Price/Stern/Sloan: Los Angeles, 1982, p. 69).

Keeping other people straight is really a full time job. In fact, it's better if you can just observe others disobeying the law. Trying to drive and watch at the same time may overload your circuit. You might even find yourself bending the law. That's inexcusable for a legalist! You have to be scrupulously straight.

I suppose the hardest thing to keep an eye on is your attitude. It's easy to get the feeling you're better than those lawbreakers.

The only remedy for legalism I know is to admit you're a lawbreaker, too. There is joy in forgiveness. But, to get there you have to admit your failure.

October 1983

Preaching Along Route 45

As I was driving home several weeks ago, I got to thinking. I tried to remember towns along U.S. Route 45 where I had preached. As I headed north I recalled preaching in:
- Enfield when Earl Philips was pastor.
- Mill Shoals in a revival with Bob Sledge and once at a community Thanksgiving service.
- Fairfield at both First and North Side. I held a revival at North Side when Norris Price was there. I was a member at First and supplied there several times. I also thought of a revival with Archie Akers at Pleasant Grove, southeast of town and supplying at Mt. Zion, northeast of town. I also preached at Elm River, east of town, when Terry Buchanan was pastor.
- Geff (Jeffersonville). I think I preached when North Side had a mission there. I remember missing an appointment when I didn't realize the pastor was expecting me.
- Cisne on several occasions.
- Flora during a revival at Oak Street where I got to visit with my youth Sunday School teacher and 4-H Club leader, Carroll Majonnier. Mike Sanders was pastor.
- Louisville during a revival with Clebert Weger. I also thought about my seminary pastorate--Second Little Prairie, just north of town.
- Watson. I couldn't help detouring a couple of miles to revisit the church where I preached a revival when Francis Sparling was pastor.
- Effingham where I spoke at Immanuel during a World Missions Conference. I can't remember preaching at First but I did teach some Seminary Extension classes there. I also thought of a revival at Jackson Township (Little Prairie),

George H. Davis

southwest of town, a couple of years ago.
- Neoga, both at the old theater building and then at the new building when Cecil Fuson was pastor.
- Tuscola where I ran into Fred Stilley from the Benton area, Jim Coatney from Louisville, and Morris and Joyce Weaver from Herrin.
- Tolono in a revival with Truman Smith this spring.
- Champaign/Urbana where my first ministry function was the wedding of Larry Askew and Pat Davis at Temple during the late '60s. Larry was a student at Southern Illinois University and part-time minister of music at Second Baptist in Herrin, where I served. Now, in the '80s I've supplied at Pennsylvania Avenue, Garden Hills, and Temple, and last Sunday at Northside Mission.
- Thomasboro where I also supplied last Sunday.
- Rantoul where I'd supplied for Paul Dann.
- Paxton where I'd visited with Dave and Dianne (Davidson) Healy. Dianne grew up in my first full-time pastorate, Altamont.
- Kankakee. I have a vague recollection of riding the Illinois Central from Carbondale to Kankakee one weekend to preach as a college student. (If that wasn't such a long time ago, I might remember better.)
- Chicago where I spoke in several churches during a World Missions Conference when Preston Denton was Director of Missions.

Well, that's over thirty years of preaching relived, and I'm not home yet.

November 1983

Of Windmills And Power Stations

I observed two power sources as I drove across the Association recently. One was an old windmill standing forlornly in a corn field. I wondered about its history. Was there once a barn nearby? Was this a pasture a generation ago?

Just across the field I saw an electric power substation. It was located along a country road for easy access. The electricity was distributed to neighboring farms to heat homes, cook meals, pump water, drive power tools, etc.

I like windmills. We had two when I was growing up. Grandpa had another one at his place at the edge of town. I liked to loosen the chain that let the fin follow the breeze. That turned the fan into the wind and started the water pumping.

There was something satisfying about watching the wind do your work. I remember pumping water by hand for 60 cows when the wind died.

There's little demand for windmills now. For a while they were grabbed up for TV or CB antenna towers. Windmills as a source of electric power have not made it--at least, not in our area. (I remember Harry Perkins of Vernon producing his own electricity from a windmill 40 years ago. He stored it in wet cell batteries. But, Harry was something of an oddity.)

For all my fascination with windmills, it's hard to beat the convenience of flipping a switch to pump water.

by George

I wonder if we're not too tied to romantic, old ways of providing the Living Water to thirsty men. Can we find ways of using electronic switches to share our faith? I think we can and will.

I think we can overcome the negative influence of religious hucksters and use television in a wholesome, positive way. I believe people are ready for an alternative to trash.

There's nothing quite so lonely looking as the skeleton of a windmill standing useless in the wind, unless it's a church refusing to plug into the electronic age.

December 1983

Urbanizing The "Farmer"

George means farmer, but I'm not.

I was raised on a farm in south central Illinois. My folks still live there. They raised five boys and a girl. None of us farms.

While I'm not a farmer, I'm not an urbanite either. Until Champaign, the only time I'd lived in a town of more than 10,000 was while I was in school.

Just how little I've been urbanized was demonstrated recently. I took my car to a garage in downtown Champaign. I called the Metropolitan Transit District to ask what bus I could catch to work and where to catch it. "Red South at Neil and Church," I was told. Looking at my watch, I thought I could catch the 9:14.

I got to the corner in plenty of time--in time to see Red South pulling away. Then it dawned on me that there are two bus stops at that corner. I had waited at the wrong one.

February 1984

Spring Sprang!

Like an unwelcome guest, winter came early and stayed late in central Illinois. On the first day of winter we got eight inches of snow. And, who can forget the day before Christmas? You can almost make up a negative temperature and wind velocity and anyone who was out that day will believe you.

We had several nice days in February then more winter. Three weeks after the calendar said it was spring, the first crocuses were just beginning to show their faces.

About that time my wife and I drove to Fort Worth, Texas. It was a two-day trip but it jumped us three weeks ahead in seasons. As we drove down I-57, we noticed red bud trees blooming in southern Illinois.

As we crossed Arkansas, we noticed dogwood in bloom. Entering Texas we saw the orange blossoms of Indian paint brushes and their state flower--blue bonnets. Roses were blooming in Fort Worth.

It was as if someone had pushed the fast forward button. I halfway expected to start raking leaves by the time we returned home. But, sure enough, when we got back, they had hit the rewind button. We were still waiting for spring.

George H. Davis

Now, three weeks later, we're trying to get those early spring chores done. Though sometimes tardy, spring does come.

There are seasons in the life of a church. We have times of sowing and times of reaping. Sometimes we want to reap before we've sown.

I'm learning you don't smell the roses without a great deal of pruning, mulching, fertilizing, and care. You may even suffer some loss. Should it be any different encouraging people to bloom?

May 1984

Alone Again; The Two Of Us

For the first time in several years, my wife and I have no one to wait up for. Our youngest son, Mike, moved out tonight into an apartment he's sharing with two other guys.

Actually, our baby's 21, and he'll be back this fall while he finishes his senior year at the University of Illinois. I'm not sure whether this trial period is for him or us!

It seems like we've been leaving the porch light on and waiting up for one or more of our kids for most of our lives. To be honest, Leona has been a better waiter-upper than I. I've often waited with my head on a pillow and when my head hits a pillow it's usually not long until there's a pile of sawdust nearby.

Now we've no reason to leave the porch light on. I know we're going to enjoy being alone again, but there's also a touch of sadness in seeing our kids move out. They've brought us a great deal of joy and some concern. I know that will continue.

I've been telling parents for years that the point of raising kids is to raise them-- to turn them loose. I've known that was easier said than done.

Tonight I remembered other bittersweet moments over the past several years. I recalled walking down a dorm hall to head home after moving a son back in for another year at Eastern Illinois University. I wasn't prepared for the lump that filled my throat. I'd puffed carrying boxes up the stairs. Somehow, I didn't expect a touch of sadness.

I guess that's part of life. Joy is never unmixed with sadness and sorrow can turn to joy. Part of the growing comes in recognizing the feelings and learning from them.

June 1984

Bill

I walked into Bill's room and found him sleeping soundly. He was more gaunt than I remembered him ten days ago--more jaundiced.

I spoke his name softly but firmly. He did not respond. His breathing seemed labored. I wanted to turn and leave.

I hadn't expected to find him looking so weak and vulnerable. I had seen the look before, too often.

I wasn't sure I wanted to face him but I called his name again. In a moment he awoke and was alert. His mind was clearly more alive than his body.

We visited for a while. We talked of friends and weather and work. We talked about his progress, or lack of it; about what he needed.

We prayed together. There was great gratitude in his heart and voice. He seemed overwhelmed that someone would care for him.

I left feeling richer. Rather than being depressed over his condition, I was uplifted by his grace. His appreciation warmed and moved me.

I find myself wishing I could have known Bill in his more productive years. Yet, I wonder if he's ever touched anyone more deeply than he did then with his courage and determination.

July 1984

Reflecting On Experience

I don't know whether it was getting my first pair of glasses, or the amazement at how much better I could read with them. Maybe it was the realization that I was the oldest person at our Share and Care retreat.

I got a letter last week from a lady who stayed with my brothers and me after our mother died. At eight, I was the oldest. She has stayed in touch with us through the years. My children delight to call her, "Dad's baby sitter."

She referred to a column I had written four years ago remembering my grandpa Davis. She also remembered him fondly and remarked how much like him I am. I was touched.

I guess it's slowly dawning on me. I'm not just a man who happens to have grandchildren. I'm a grandpa.

I'm enjoying my grandkids. It's fun watching Brittany do her unique little duck walk and hearing Cody try to say zucchini. I don't know whether I was too busy to delight in my own children or whether age has dulled my memory of the cute tricks they must have done, too.

Experience (that sounds better than age doesn't it?) has its benefits. I don't want to be young again. Sometimes I wish for more energy or agility.

But age also brings its changes. I've noticed that my wife and I now prefer separate hymnals. But, we haven't got to separate beds yet.

September 1984

Don't Get Your Wires Crossed

I was the first one to arrive for a revival service at Hillcrest Baptist Church in Tuscola. I'd been careful to look at a revival flyer to see what time the service started. I'd rather be twenty minutes early than one minute late.

George H. Davis

One thing I'd neglected to note from the flyer was when the revival services ended. It was Thursday night. The last services were on Wednesday. I was the only one to show up for revival services. I foolt so feelishl

I wish I could tell you that was the only stupid thing I've ever done, but honesty will not allow me. I've done my share of stupid things and may have started on yours. But that doesn't make me stupid.

One or two or a dozen lapses into stupidity do not prove a permanent condition. If we can accept our lapses and see the humor in them, we can have healthy growth. A key ingredient in a sense of humor is the ability to laugh at ourselves. It's when we take ourselves so seriously we can't tolerate any lapses that we get into trouble.

I redeemed the evening by dropping in on Pastor Cliff Perry. I shared my embarrassment with him. He even treated me to some cider and string cheese.

It reminded me of an incident several years ago. I had overhauled the engine of my Volkswagen bug. I got everything put back together but it wasn't running right. I drove over to see Nile Deputy, VW mechanic par excellence. He took one look and asked, "Do you have your spark plug wires crossed?"

Now it's hard to cross your spark plug wires when you only have four cylinders. In fact, Nile was surprised it would run that way. But when he switched them it ran much better. I told him I was hoping it would be something simple, but not <u>that</u> simple.

"Oh, I won't tell anybody--unless I see them," he promised me. He was as good as his word. He charged me a cup of coffee for his work. At the coffee shop a fellow came in and sat down beside him. "What do you think of a preacher, who thinks he is a mechanic, who gets his spark plug wires crossed and drives all the way from Fairfield to Mt. Carmel to get them uncrossed?" he asked his friend. He didn't tell anybody--until he saw them.

As I drove away, Nile called out, "Don't get your wires crossed?"

I'm sure Cliff is much too nice to ever say anything like that.

November 1984

A Limited God or Little Faith?

Our forefathers debated whether the atonement was limited to the elect or whether Christ died for all men. I doubt we'd be able to generate much interest in that question now.

Perhaps our debate should be over whether or not God is limited. I'm not thinking so much about the theological controversy as the practical one. After all, what is our theology? Is it what we say we believe, or what we practice? I know our ideals must always be higher than our achievement. But we often act as if God were far removed from us, or powerless to intervene in our sophisticated day.

The Psalmist says Israel "limited the Holy One of Israel. They remembered not his hand (power)" (78:41-42). Matthew says Jesus "did not many mighty works there (in Nazareth) because of their unbelief" (13:58).

by George

We can close ourselves to God and limit his work in our lives. Our very familiarity with God may lead us to presume upon his grace.

Two recent experiences have encouraged me. On separate occasions I've heard persons say, "If God wants to have (do) this, he'll have to work it out. There's no way humanly to accomplish it."

It's not a choice between activism and rust. I believe God expects us to do all we humanly can to serve him. But we need to recognize that all we can do is sometimes not enough. To rely on our own understanding and ability often leaves us with a piddling little mess.

Jesus said the disciples were unable to cure a demonized boy because of their unbelief (see Matthew 13:19-20). But God honored the prayer of the boy's father when he cried out, "Lord, I believe; help my unbelief" (Mark 9:24).

How do you explain this? Why did God honor the father's faltering faith but not the disciples'? Could it be that the father was deeply conscious of his weakness and failure and that the disciples assumed they had God's power? Could this be the difference--confession versus presumption?

God voluntarily limited himself in the person of Jesus. He took a finite, fragile body. He refused to call upon legions of angels to rescue him from arrest and death. But it was in defeat that he was victorious. God raised him up.

Isn't it only as we confess our desperate need of God that his unlimited love and power are available to us?

December 1984

A Right Or A Privilege?

Why is it that our <u>right</u> to own a gun is so vigorously defended while the <u>privilege</u> of driving a car may be revoked?

We treat driving as a privilege to be licensed and regulated. If we drive irresponsibly, we may lose that privilege. Secretary of State Jim Edgar says that driving is not a constitutional right every citizen can expect and which the state cannot deny. He keeps reminding us that the state has the responsibility to keep unsafe drivers off the highways. I agree.

But why do we so fiercely defend our right to bear arms? Oh, I know what the Second Amendment to the United States Constitution says. It's the only amendment which gives the reason for its existence.

"A well-regulated militia, being necessary to the security of a free State, the right of the people to keep and bear arms, shall not be infringed."

This 1791 amendment assumes citizen-soldiers. They were expected to furnish their own personal weapons. Since every citizen was expected to be ready to join the fracas, every person must be allowed to own and carry a gun.

Can you imagine a soldier today showing up with a gun he brought from home? What do you suppose his sergeant would say?

The need to guarantee every citizen the right to own a gun is past. If he's drafted, his country will furnish weapons. At home, we expect police to protect us. The

George H. Davis

alternative is to arm everyone and expect anarchy. And we're nearly there! I'm not convinced that a gun in every home or every hand is the answer.

We're suffering now from attempts of individuals and groups to take the law into their own hands. Frankly, I fear them about as much as I do criminals.

Maybe it's time to repeal the Second Amendment. I think I'd rather see that happen than adding an amendment supposedly guaranteeing the right of children to pray at school.

January 1985

An Old Family Recipe

When we were newlyweds, my mother-in-law gave us a new General Electric waffle iron. With it we got a recipe booklet. We're on our third or fourth waffle iron but we're still using the Quick Plain Waffle recipe from that booklet.

Since I'm the official breakfast cook at our house, I soon fell heir to the job of making waffles. When our kids were growing up, they could put them away faster than I could make them. I soon learned to double the recipe.

Recently, I cut the recipe in half. And I got to wondering. Do I adjust to change that easily in other areas of my life? As a young man I learned to tie my tie in a Windsor knot, or a double Windsor. Now, I hear that's out of style. But I'm not changing--at least, not yet.

I find myself critical of the Baptist Hymnal (1975 edition). I tell myself it's the warped bindings I don't like. But I wonder if it's not some of the new songs, too. (By the way, the "old songs" are not old; they're the ones we grew up singing.)

Fast foods tend to turn me off. As a kid I thought a hamburger and chocolate shake in a restaurant was heaven. Now my thoughts turn in another direction.

I don't have a computer yet. Oh, I'm curious but I'm not sure I'm willing to learn a new language. I've never played a video game, except for a very primitive one we bought our kids when they were small.

I've never washed my car in a do-it-yourself car wash. Automatic, yes. Do-it-yourself, no.

I guess we're all slow to change in some areas. We may adopt new ways in our cars or offices. But the church seems to be the last bastion of tradition. Someone has suggested that the seven last words of the church are: "We've never done it that way before."

So, if you're in the neighborhood, come by for breakfast. I'll stir up some waffles. If I turn my back, my wife might even throw in a few blueberries. Or, I might just turn the kitchen over to the real cook. Then we might have biscuits or muffins.

February 1985

Is Saturn Our Savior?

It's an understatement to say that there's considerable interest in the location of General Motor's new Saturn plant. Communities across the country have put considerable time and energy into attracting the new car plant with its 6,000 plus jobs.

I'm fortunate to never have been without work. In fact, I've usually got more around me than I'll get done. But I do have friends who are looking for a job. I also know some who've taken a second job so they can continue farming.

Can we expect business to deliver us? Are more jobs our primary need? I know it's easy for me to undervalue more jobs since I already have one. But would 6,000, or even 12,000, new jobs make life in any of our communities substantially better? Can we expect industry to bail us out? Does more money mean better living?

I have nothing against money. I've learned to spend it rather handily. But I'm reminded that our expectation of deliverance by the state lottery has not really improved our lives. Few of us are better off. I suspect we're worse off if we're expecting to win a living rather than work for it. The lottery has not given us lower taxes, has it?

While we're talking about government, I have grave doubts we can expect it to deliver us from moral failure. I have no doubt that we have serious moral problems in our society. But passing new laws to insure that other people live by our standards could be counter-productive. We might find ourselves in the minority.

I suspect we'll have to look within and to God for real help. I know we're money-spending, moral (or immoral) beings. But I believe deliverance will not come in the form of money nor morals. Only as we are new beings at heart will our lives be better.

I'm reluctant to pin my hopes on government or business as savior. They're so fickle. If business starts losing money, it may abandon me. If a majority turns its back on my interests, I can no longer depend on the government for help.

March 1985

Let The Bible Speak For Itself

How many times did Peter deny Jesus?

According to Mark's account (14:66-72), he denied Jesus once before the cock crew the first time and then two more times before the second alarm. Matthew (26:69-75) and Luke (22:56-62) tell of three denials but do not mention the cock crowing a second time.

Who is right? Well, I suspect they're all right. They all say that Peter denied Jesus after being warned of the danger. They also note that the crowing of the rooster was a bitter reminder to Peter of his Lord's warning.

Some literalists suggest five or six denials. They want to harmonize the accounts and reason that Peter must have denied Jesus three times before the cock crew the first time and at least twice before the second crowing.

Is this kind of violence to the Scriptures really necessary? Why can't we just let them speak for themselves? Does every account have to agree in every detail? If I understand their emphasis, the gospel writers were more concerned with the denials than with the number of times a rooster crowed. After all, once a rooster gets started crowing, you can't turn him off like you would an alarm clock.

It seems to me that if we allow different accounts of events in Scripture to contain variations in detail, we have a stronger witness. If witnesses agree in every detail, it's not only unusual, it's suspicious--maybe one is copying from the other. If they agree on everything, we don't need more than one.

The strength of Scripture comes from the fact that witnesses don't always tell the story in exactly the same way. They usually agree on the main thrust but sometimes vary on details. That doesn't mean God is lying. It simply means that the event was seen through different eyes. As the stories were passed on and recorded, minor variations occurred. To attempt to homogenize them so they all agree in every jot and tittle is to rob them of authenticity. It's the same spirit that would pour us all into one mold and have us all believe and behave in exactly the same way.

April 1985

The Wrong Question

Attacks on Baptists colleges and universities prompted an anguished father to plead, "Where can I send my children where their faith won't be destroyed?" Several of us wanted to chime in with the name of our favorite school, but I doubt that would have helped.

Reflection tells me he was asking the wrong question. He should have asked, "How can I help my children have a faith that will grow when challenged?"

Ours is not a Pollyanna world. As much as we'd like to shield our children from its stresses and disappointments, we can't. That is, we can't unless we want to keep them children always. If we can allow them to grow up we must allow them to face challenges.

One aspect of education is challenge. Old ways of thinking and bodies of knowledge are challenged. Some of what we have learned may have to be unlearned. New concepts take the place of old ones.

Should it be any different with Christian education? The only way my faith doesn't need to grow and develop is if it's fully mature now.

For most of us learning and growing is a lifelong struggle. The challenges and adversity we face provide the opportunity for growth. Oh, it's not automatic. Make no mistake about that. But one of the ways we grow is by dealing with difficulty.

Our emphasis should be on helping our children to have a healthy, inquiring faith. We can't answer all their questions with neat little answers tied up with a bow. We don't even know all the questions they'll face. Our world is changing and they'll live to face questions we haven't even dreamed of.

Our best hope is to teach them to think and to pray and to seek to grow. I know that's not easy because it calls for some maturity on our part and some trust. Sometimes when our faith is fragile we want to give others easy answers because we're not willing to struggle with the problems.

May 1985

by George

A Tale Of Two Conventions

"It was the best of times. It was the worst of times." That's the way Charles Dickens opened A Tale of Two Cities.

It wasn't quite that good or quite that bad, but this year's Southern Baptist Convention in Dallas challenged those extremes. I was alternately encouraged and discouraged.

I was encouraged by the electoral process. Though charges of collecting ballots from messengers leaving and redistributing them to new arrivals were made, they came after the election of officers. The majority attending the Convention clearly wanted Charles Stanley to serve a second term as President. It was even clearer they wanted Winfred Moore as First Vice President.

I was encouraged by the formation of the Special Committee. They will "seek to determine the sources of the controversies in our Convention, and make findings and recommendations regarding these controversies...." The Committee seems to have balance and the confidence of all parties. It is expected to report in Atlanta in 1986 though it may be continued until 1987.

I was discouraged by the growing political nature of our Convention. We're becoming more and more like the national political conventions. We pack the hall for key votes then many leave. By Thursday afternoon everyone who wanted to could find a seat in the main hall.

Again, we tend to show our approval by applauding when a motion we favor passes. I guess there's a place for applause during the Convention but I'm not sure it's during the business sessions. We've quit saying, "Amen" during sermons and substitute applause. I think I can learn to live with that but simple voting should be enough during business.

I guess my problem is, I'm old enough to remember hearing Carl Bates scold messengers in St. Louis in 1971 for applauding. He reminded us, "You're at the Southern Baptist Convention, not the ball game." (Several had taken in a Cardinal game the night before.) We seem to be short on people like him who command respect. Where have all the Baptist statesmen gone?

I am discouraged by our loss of trust of one another. Everyone is suspicious of the other. This is partly the result of our size. We can no longer assume a common background.

I'm encouraged by the increasing number of lay persons showing an interest in the Convention. It takes a while for a newcomer to figure out what's going on, but I think it's a healthy sign when more lay persons attend. Charles Chandler's idea of chartering buses and finding moderately-priced motels is a way to encourage lay participation.

June 1985

Bears And Bushes

I get some of my best sermon ideas listening to other preachers. I can take what they say, improve on it, make it mine, and preach it.

George H. Davis

I recently heard John Hessel refer to "Bears and Bushes." He didn't preach the whole sermon--he just teased us with it. (John is a "Together We Build" consultant for Southern Baptist's Stewardship Commission.)

I'm not sure how he developed his thesis: You need to be able to tell the difference between bears and bushes. Here's my attempt: 1) Some bushes look like bears. 2) There are bears behind some bushes. 3) Most bushes are only bushes.

We've all watched enough television to know that bears can be dangerous. We're warned not to try to feed the bears in National Parks. They may take more than we offer.

Sometimes when our church is considering a new venture, we worry about the dangers lurking in the unknown. We wonder what's around the corner. We want to try to prepare for the future and not lunge blindly ahead.

It's not hard to tell the difference between a bear and a bush up close and in the daylight. But, we often have to make our identification at a distance and sometimes in the shadows.

The line between faith and folly sometimes seems thin. Faith follows God without knowing all the answers. It knows the Guide. Folly foolishly presumes upon God's grace.

Bears can hurt you. Bushes can seldom do more than scratch. It's important to know the difference.

Now all I need is a text and a poem.

July 1985

The Deacon Who Didn't . . .

Last year I completed a three-year term as a deacon at my church.

I began with the rather naive hope that I'd become a good deacon. I finished disappointed with myself and a little burned out. I hadn't lived up to expectations--mine or others.

Oh, I wasn't turned out. I finished the term. I remained respectable. But I didn't do all that was expected of me. Some of the expectations were unrealistic. They had more to do with promotion than ministry. But I also knew that I wasn't ministering to the families assigned to me.

Maybe I became a deacon for the same reason I became a Lion. I enjoyed the meetings--eating and visiting. I didn't enjoy selling candy on the street corner to raise money for the blind.

I gained new appreciation for deacons who quietly went about ministering to persons in need. Often the church was unaware of needs they lovingly met. Much of their work was not spotlighted. Their real power came from their role as servants.

I guess the most disappointing thing I learned about myself was that I'd rather not be a servant.

August 1985

by George

Is Growth Essential?

"Yes, but…"

That's what I find myself saying as I read church growth books. They insist every church can and should be getting larger. While recognizing qualitative as well as quantitative growth, they invariably focus on numbers. The goal is to be bigger than last year.

Church growth experts have helped us focus on conversion growth. We're often satisfied with transfer members and internal growth. (That's what Charles Chaney and Ron Lewis [Design for Church Growth, Broadman, 1977] call it when children of faithful members are led to faith in Christ and added to the body.)

Somehow we must redirect our efforts to reach outsiders. We're not very successful in getting in touch with them, let alone winning them to the Lord. It's easy to forget that Jesus chose his disciples in the commercial district of Galilee rather than in the environs of the Temple. The men he chose knew they had no credentials to present to God. We want to limit our rolls to the respectable.

At the same time we need to develop the church into a redeeming community, not just a community of the redeemed. We need to be the kind of family that lifts and helps and instills hope in those who come to us. If we treat them as if they have a long way to go before they come up to our standards, we'll lose them. We're also likely to lose our church in the process.

Mission expert Orlando Costas says that growth may simply mean that the church is getting fat! He insists the issue is not whether a church is growing but whether it is faithful to its mission in its setting. Willis Bennett assumes, "Not all churches can be expected to grow numerically. Population mobility and decline, and other demographic factors may be of a prohibitive nature." (Effective Urban Ministry, Broadman, 1983, p. 108)

To make business standards the yardstick by which we measure churches is to fail to understand the spiritual dimension of growth. Pastors are sometimes under pressure to produce. They are expected to grow a church, then go to a larger church and do it again. This pressure may be self-imposed.

The problem with putting the primary emphasis on numbers is that we do only what will bring people in. Little attention is paid to their growth and development. So what if forty percent of them leave because of slander and gossip by other members.

Sometimes we're too faithful to New Testament patterns. The Galatian church was in danger of devouring one another, presumably with careless words. Paul feared "quarreling, jealousy, anger, selfishness, slander, gossip, conceit, and disorder" in the Corinthian church. (See 2 Cor. 12:20 RSV) He warned Timothy about those who had "a morbid craving for controversy and disputes about words, which produce envy, dissension, slander, base suspicions, and wrangling among men." (1 Tim. 6:4b-5a RSV)

Somehow we have to grow in Christlikeness while we're seeking to bring others to him. I'm not against growth; I'm for balance.

September 1985

George H. Davis

When People Don't Like You

Sooner or later most of us will find ourselves in a situation where some people won't seem to like us. The reasons may be as varied as the situations: they've heard certain things about us, they don't like the way we look, or they disagree with something we've done.

For most of us it's a shock initially to learn that anyone would not like someone as kind and generous as we are. Everyone can explain his own actions. It's other people's we have difficulty figuring out. Each of us can give a perfectly good, logical explanation that any reasonable person would accept. The problem is, we don't always operate on reason. Our prejudices color our judgment.

I have some difficulty with the glib statement that we are to love the person but not his ways. It's always been a little difficult for me to separate the person from his deeds. I believe we're responsible for our actions. This is part of the image of God in us. We answer to God and to each other. I know there are times when we don't want to be responsible to each other but I don't think we have that choice. God has made us part of a family. Our relationships are part of who we are. We cannot escape that.

One of the first things we can do when challenged is to <u>reexamine our attitudes and actions</u>. Others may attribute wrong motives to us but we should seek to understand what led us to behave in the way we did. Those answers don't come easily but they're worth searching for.

In geometry we learned that a straight line is the shortest distance between two points. That's also true in human relations. <u>Going straight to the person with whom we differ</u> can cut through a web of tangled, second-hand reports.

Another thing that can help is to <u>remember our common humanity</u>. None of us is always right. On any issue we're probably partly right and partly wrong. So is our opponent. Few issues are clearly black or white. Most are shades of gray.

Finally, we can <u>pray for those who disagree with us</u>. I say finally but it shouldn't be the last thing we do. It's hard to pray without asking God to help them see we are right. But we should learn to listen as well as talk to God. He has some very important things to tell us.

I guess the ultimate temptation is to project these steps on someone else and ask if they are behaving properly. It's so hard for us to be hard on ourselves.

October 1985

Grandpa George, God, and Cowboy Boots

"Grandpa George, would you talk to God and see if he'd bring me some cowboy boots?" my grandson asked as he visited early this month.

I was flattered that he thinks God would listen to me. I was concerned about what he'd think about me and/or God if he <u>didn't</u> have any cowboy boots. I was also frightened what his next request would be if God <u>did</u> have cowboy boots.

by George

I guess it makes as much sense to ask God for what you want as it does to ask Santa Claus. The danger is that we treat God like a Santa--that we spend all our time asking him for things and none listening to what he wants from us.

There's time to teach a three-year-old the difference between God and grandpa and to tell him <u>he</u> can talk to God <u>and</u> listen to him. In the meantime, Grandma and I went shopping.

November 1985

At What Price Democracy?

While family and friends are still in shock over the death of servicemen headed home for Christmas, the media is asking disturbing questions about the cause. Skeletons in the closet of the charter company are being dismembered. The whole charter system is being dissected.

If I had a son among the victims, I believe I'd wish they'd leave me and my family alone for a while, rather than dredge up all they could. I think I'd prefer that the disturbing questions be asked later and perhaps quietly. I'd have enough trouble handling my grief without adding confusion and accusations.

I'm not suggesting disturbing questions shouldn't he asked. What I'm questioning is the timing and the willingness to let every disgruntled ex-employee spew his venom publicly. Aren't grieving families entitled to at least a few moments of privacy? What happened to the idea of sitting in silence in the presence of one overcome by grief?

But before we blame mass media, let's look at our record as churches. Budget discussion seems to bring out every unhappy member. Questions are raised about things unrelated to the budget. Persons who feel they have been slighted find a way to get the church's ear. People drop insinuations they couldn't get away with in a political forum.

No, I'm not against full and free discussion. I'm for responsible discussion.

Churches are not <u>just</u> democracies. At their best, they're <u>theo</u>cracies--societies where <u>God</u> has his way. Though we rule by majority, sometimes we go awry. The majority is not always right.

We need to find ways of handling discussion without being destructive. We're fond of quoting great-aunt Chrystalbell's advice, "If you can't say something nice, don't say anything." But when we start talking about money at church, that's ignored. Discussion seems to focus on what's wrong. We pick over minor items and ignore major ones. Some have chosen to avoid such scenes by staying home.

Yes, I know there's a time for confrontation, even if it's unpleasant. But I'm not sure that a business meeting is the time. Perhaps it should be done privately or in a small group. I'd like to see budget discussion handled more positively. I'm all for questions seeking information. I'm against questioning that tears down. It doesn't take much skill to tear down; it takes craftsmanship to build.

Maybe budget planning committees could hold open hearings where interested persons could present ideas. The problem with this, in the public sector, is that people do not attend hearings. They gripe to people who are not making the decisions.

George H. Davis

I believe in democracy, but before that, I believe in God and brotherhood. We need to "love the brotherhood" (1 Peter 2:17) more than we love to express our negative feelings.

December 1985

"I make a motion . . ."

It hardly takes a ground swell to get a Baptist church to vote to do some thing or another. It usually takes one person with an idea to make a motion. Normally, after a minimum of silence (we're allergic to silence), it's seconded and carried--unless it calls for spending a definite amount of money.

Sometimes motions are made by well-meaning but poorly informed members. They've heard of something being done somewhere and think we ought to be doing it here, too. This is based on the assumption that what's good anywhere must be good here. Once a motion is made, most members will not oppose it. They don't speak or vote against it. They just don't vote. So the motion carries 15 to 2 with 19 abstentions. That's what I call under-whelming approval.

Some motions ought to be forgotten even though they managed to make it through a business meeting. An alternative might be to refer them to an existing group to study the proposal. But, if we do that, let's be honest enough to bring a report back to the church. Some good motions die, not from lack of a second but, from lack of assignment. No matter how much an action is needed, it probably won't get done unless someone is made responsible. We need to learn to expect a report from them.

All of this leads me to propose a new officer for our churches. We could call him (or her) our Undone Actions Officer. It would be his (or her) responsibility to pick up all the motions that have fallen through the cracks and assign responsibility or blame for them. He would work alongside the Chief Executive Officer. Most of our churches have not identified our CEO but we have one. He's (or she's) the one who gets things done. The UAO would function much like the CEO except that he would be limited to working on actions that have been approved by the church but have gone undone for a period of three months.

We're well known for passing resolutions. This usually means we don't want to do anything but criticize or praise. It's a whole lot easier to pass a resolution than to do something positively helpful or to put an end to something harmful. And we feel better once we have "resolved" the problem.

I'm not suggesting the UAO handle resolutions. After all, his title is Undone <u>Actions</u> Officer, not resolutions. I'm not sure actions and resolutions have anything in common.

I think I'll propose adding an UAO to our roster of workers. The vote would probably carry. <u>That's</u> what scares me.

January 1986

by George

Remember When?

I'm approaching the age when nostalgia becomes an appealing pastime. I have a lot of pleasant, funny memories. It's so easy to focus on the past, even to take up residence there. In fact, nostalgia seems to be on the way to becoming a national pastime. Look at the antique market; consider the prices for old books, the craze over old pictures. How else do you account for Garrison Keillor's success with tales of Lake Wobegon, his imaginary home town in Minnesota? Many of us grew up in our own Lake Wobegon and he strikes a responsive chord with small town America. Through him, we relive our childhood.

While there may be some healthy aspects in being able to laugh about our past, there are some definite dangers in longing for the return of the good old days. To begin with, they never were that good. We tend to remember the good and blot out everything else. But for the Christian, there's also some tension between faith and forever facing backward. Faith is forward facing; it's walking confidently into the future.

The writer of Hebrews warns us of the dangers of lingering at the elementary level of faith. He encourages us to go on to maturity. Abraham is cited as an example, "By faith he sojourned in the land of promise, as in a foreign land, living in tents with Isaac and Jacob, heirs with him of the same promise. For he <u>looked forward</u> to the city which has foundations, whose builder and maker is God" (11:9-10).

I guess we all long for simpler days when decisions were either black or white, not shades of gray. We'd like to go back to when faith was easier and there were no nagging, unanswered questions. Is it that youth has to have answers, even if they're wrong, or that age becomes skeptical of solutions?

I'm not so worried about faith that's mixed with doubt as I am with that which retreats from the struggle. Faith is wrestling in the dark with the Unknown in search of a blessing and recognizing that a permanent limp may be a blessing, not a curse.

February 1986

Good News America, God Loves You?

I have some uneasiness about how we understand and interpret the theme for our spring revivals. Old Testament Israel could have used the slogan--Good News Israel, God Loves You. By that they would have meant, God loves you more than anyone else. You are his favorite among all the nations on earth. He has favored you with his blessing and his truth. Israel, you're it!

I sense some of that attitude among Christians in our country and am appalled by it. I hear it said that America is God's last hope. I suspect the truth is, that <u>God</u> is <u>our</u> last hope.

Old Testament prophets constantly battled Israel's pride. One of her greatest, Moses reminded his people:

> It was not because you were more in number than any other people that the Lord set his love upon you and chose you, for you were the fewest of all peoples;

but it is because the Lord loves you, and is keeping the oath which he swore to your fathers, that the Lord has brought you out with a mighty hand, and redeemed you from the house of bondage. (Deuteronomy 7:7-8).

One greater than Moses wept over Jerusalem and lamented,

> How often would I have gathered your children together as a hen gathers her brood under her wings, and you would not! Behold, your house is forsaken and desolate. (Matthew 23:37b-38).

Moses affirmed that God's blessing was given solely because of his unmerited love and his purpose to bless others through Israel. Jesus warned that Israel had refused God's call over and over and they were destined for desolation.

There's such a short distance between purpose and pride. It's wonderful that a people have a sense of God's call and a willingness to be used in his work. It's tragic when a people become puffed up and think they're better and more deserving of God's blessing than any other.

God <u>does</u> love America. He loves us in our arrogance and sinfulness and wants to save us from ourselves. He wants to deliver us from our bondage to things and our slavery to self. But the Bible says God loves the <u>world</u>. He wants us to be witnesses to his love--trophies of his grace.

If we're willing to own up to our desperate need of God's love and forgiveness, there's hope. If we cling to our Yankee pride and piously pity those who were not fortunate enough to be born in America, we're headed for God's trash heap.

During the Civil War, Lincoln was asked if he believed that Providence was on the Union's side. He replied that he was more concerned to be on God's side than he was whether God was on his side. Can we get back to that? Can we believe that God loves Latin America and Central America as much as he does the United States of America? Can we accept his love for Russia? If we can escape our self-centeredness, there may be hope that we can be God's people, used for <u>His</u> purpose.

March 1986

I Lost A Friend

I don't know why news of JoAnn's death touched me so deeply. Years ago she had asked me to help in Bible School in their country church. I went two or three years. She was one of the most gifted, willing workers there. I knew she was not well but she pushed herself on. She often came when she didn't feel like it but her spirit was always bright. She had a way of making you feel better, just being around her. She was no Gloomy Gus.

JoAnn was only 58. I say only because I'm 54. Maybe that's one reason why her death hit so close. It made me realize that someone my age could die. I knew that but her death reminded me again. I remembered a nostalgic line from a Burl Ives song, "They're tearing down buildings I watched them build." I guess that's some of what I felt.

Her death gave me a growing sense of my own vulnerability. I'm not expecting to die, but then, I guess few of us do.

But I think there was something else, too. It's not easy for me to respect everyone. That may shock you, but I'm afraid it's true. I had deep respect for JoAnn and her husband. They were honest, hard-working folks. They were quiet and didn't call a lot of attention to themselves, but they were dependable. They were capable and willing to use their abilities for others. Their lives were centered in their church. They were solid citizens--known and respected in their community.

Though I never stopped at their house, I always felt like I wanted to. They made me feel like I was a friend. I guess that's another reason JoAnn's death hit me so hard. I felt like I'd lost a friend!

Maybe it's the feeling of friendship that I miss. It's good to be respected but it feels a lot better to be called on as a friend who can help. I'd like to think that's the way JoAnn saw me.

Maybe there's some anger. Anger that such a gracious lady should be sick for so long and die so young. I remember how proud she was of her grandchildren. I know she enjoyed them but I'm afraid her joy was cut short. She didn't get to see them grow to maturity. As a grandparent I cry out, "THAT'S NOT FAIR!"

Yet, the JoAnn I knew had struggled with illness and <u>won</u>! She had not allowed it to make her spirit sick. She had won!

April 1986

Our Chickens Come Home To Roost

For at least a generation, young preachers have been exposed to the possibility of interpreting the early chapters of Genesis symbolically. To read them as news may severely limit our capacity for learning the truth they're telling. Yet, we have been reluctant to trust lay persons with this possibility. As a result, many Christians seem to believe that unless you understand the whole Bible literally, you don't believe it.

When you compare the Biblical accounts to other ancient Near Eastern stories, the message is clear. God is sovereign and holy. He stands in stark contrast with weak and capricious so-called gods. Man, the crown of God's creation, becomes sinner when he disobeys the Creator. Made for God's fellowship, we are responsible for our distance from Him.

These theological truths seem far more significant than any "scientific" truth I can learn from Genesis. In fact, its difficult to make the world view of the Old Testament jibe with modern scientific thought. Rather than becoming defensive about that, I think it makes more sense to recognize that the Bible is more interested in why the earth began than in how. Its focus seems to be on who God is and how man can know him.

Truth is not diminished when it's spoken in parables—it's enhanced. I believe the greatest truths can only be comprehended by comparison. Our understanding of God is greatly enhanced when Jesus compares Him to a father. I think we get our best pictures of God in metaphors.

Even our language is ambiguous. Perry Yoder points out (<u>Toward Understanding the Bible</u>, Faith and Life Press, Newton, Kansas, 1978) that "words do not have meaning, but are used to express or convey meaning" (p. 16). Words do not have the one-to-one correspondence with meaning that symbols do. A red traffic light always means stop. But a word can have several meanings. "Sail" can mean the act of sailing. Or, it can refer to the object which catches the wind to propel the boat forward in the water. Also, one idea can be expressed by different words, as in "bachelor" and "unmarried man." Yoder continues, "It is our task, then, as audience, to determine what sense the author wished his or her words to have" (p. 17). It's not enough just to say, "It means what it says." Otherwise, why would the Ethiopian eunich reply to Philip, "'How can I understand unless someone explains it to me?'"(Acts 8:31 TEV).

For me, the truth of the Bible is not diminished when I recognize that it may be contained in symbolic language. I want to focus, not on the pictures, but on the Truth they teach. I don't want to tell you that you can't interpret the Bible literally. But, for me, its truth is so much larger when I allow it to flow naturally.

June 1986

I Don't Want To Join

There are two groups that I'm not anxious to join, yet they're among the fastest growing groups in our population. Senior adults are rapidly becoming a force to be reckoned with in our society. It's estimated there will be 31.8 million persons 65 years of age and older in the United States by 1990. By 2000, the estimate is 35 million.

To make matters worse, Southern Baptists generally consider those 55 and over Senior Adults. We celebrated Senior Adult Day in our church last spring by giving each Senior a flower. One of the ushers asked if I wasn't qualified for one. I quickly let him know that I was *not*! Then I realized that I *will* qualify this fall. Whew! Talk about making your day!

I like the way a local financial institution advertises, "55 or *better*." One problem I see is that most restaurants don't recognize you as a Senior until you're 62 or 65. I'm not sure I'm ready to be called a senior adult unless I get a discount. But, considering the alternative, I prefer to become a Senior. After all, many of my friends are already there.

The other group that's experiencing a boom is single adults. Young people seem to be waiting longer to marry. Married people are becoming single, through divorce or the death of their spouse. I'm told that almost 40% of the adult population in our country is single. Frankly, I prefer not to join that group, considering the alternative. I have no sympathy with Thomas Hardy's "Epitaph on a Pessimist":

I'm Smith of Stoke, and sixty-odd,
   I've lived without a dame
From youth-time on; and would to God
   My dad had done the same.

(Pocket Book of Quotations, Henry Davidoff, ed., New York, 1952) I marvel that my wife's been able to put up with me these 33 years, but I sure don't want to change that now.

July 1986

by George

Brotherly Love?

F. C. and M. C. were brothers but they had little love for each other. It seemed they were constantly arguing and accusing each other of dirty tricks. Each felt the other was trying to gain the upper hand and neither trusted the other.

As for the father, he was proud of both of his sons, but their bitter wrangling hurt him deeply. Sometimes he grew weary as each son claimed his father's favor. The truth was, he didn't have a favorite--he loved them both. He worried that they seemed to spend their energy fighting and had little left for his work.

Each son had a stubborn pride about him. Each felt he was a little better than the other--a little more like his father. Actually, neither of them resembled the father very much. They had been so busy pushing each other, they'd neglected to spend much time with their father and neither knew him well. Each claimed he was the true son of his father, but neither had the father's spirit. It was that lack that concerned their father. He desperately wanted the boys to grow up. They were so much alike and had the potential of growing in his likeness, but their bitter spirit was poisoning any growth.

They fought over the normal things--who was biggest and who best represented the family. They were both guilty of twisting and distorting the other's words and trying to make the other look ludicrous. Each seemed to enjoy putting the other down. They each worried who was going to control the father's possessions. Each wanted to leave the mark of his personality on what he controlled. Each often overlooked his father's wishes. Observers sometimes wondered why the father didn't give his considerable resources to someone else--someone who carried more of the father's spirit.

At times the father must have wanted to let the boys fight it out and to turn to their cousins to get his work done. But he loved them both so much it was hard to give up on them. He even sent a group to talk to the boys to try to bring them together. But, from the way they talked about each other, you'd never believe they belonged to the same family. At times their father must have stood back and thought, "I wonder whose boys those are?"

Who are these battling brothers? Well, you may have met them. They're called Fundamental Conservative and Moderate Conservative.

"Then he (Joseph) sent his brothers away, and as they departed, he said to them, 'Do not quarrel on the way.'" Genesis 45:24

August 1986

I Wasn't Fed!

I went to one of the finest restaurants in town. They have a name for fine food and excellent service. I looked over the menu and consulted my palate, then ordered and waited with growing expectancy.

But to my dismay, the waiter simply set the food on the table in front of me. He didn't <u>feed</u> me. He made no effort to place the food into my mouth. Surely he didn't expect me to cut up my own food and chew it up, I thought. Well, if that's the way he's going to act, I certainly won't be back here again. And, tip? Forget it!

Is that any more ludicrous than complaining that I wasn't fed at church? A few television preachers tell their listeners, "If you're going to a church and still not being fed, go where you'll get fed." Well, I can't swallow the regurgitations of some TV preacher who wants to tell me what the Bible says. I prefer to feed myself and trust the Spirit of God to nourish me. I don't want anyone digesting my food for me. I'm not a baby. I can feed myself.

I expect my pastor to have studied and prayed and to have a word from God for me. But I don't want him doing my thinking for me. I expect to test his word by my experience and understanding of God's Word. I don't expect him to be infallible; only faithful to what he believes to be God's leadership.

I expect to prepare myself for worship and learning. I will study and pray and will listen actively. I will try to process what the pastor's saying and decide what it means for me. What should I do about the truth he's preaching? I suspect that God may have a slightly different message for each worshiper. But, if I come without preparation and am unwilling to exert any effort, I'll likely go away unfed.

I'm suggesting that if you feel like you're not being fed at church, the first place to look is within. Are you participating in worship, or are you a spectator? If you just want to be entertained, you'd probably better stay home and watch television. If you want secondhand religion, I recommend the TV variety. But, if you're willing to wrestle with tough problems, a local fellowship of disciples is your best choice.

September 1986

I Was Warmed

Despite our first chilly weather, I was warmed at our annual meeting this week. I felt good about our strengthened emphasis on worship at each session. Jim Justice did a superb job of planning and leading us. The Bible studies also were helpful as they focused on families in the Bible.

It's always a joy to recognize new pastors and other ministers. Rick Tribble of Danville, Bethel attended his first associational meeting in East Central. It was good to see him and Dot at each session. Michael Layell also attended his first annual meeting here. He's a Southern Seminary student working with Ron Sanders at Illinois State.

Speaking of campus ministers, I was surprised when Ron and Harrel Morgan, at the University of Illinois, gave me a plaque remembering my six years of supervision of their work. Ron has been at ISU five years and Harrel at U of I nine. I was warmed by their thoughtfulness and appreciation.

I also enjoyed honoring Ron on his fifth anniversary. A former student of his, Jill Morris, paid tribute to him as an encourager. I presented him a five-year "pin." Actually, it was a brass horse blanket pin.

I guess it was a sense of God's presence and a spirit of brotherhood that warmed me most. Perhaps taking more time to recognize God's presence was a key to feeling it. I also have a growing recognition that we all don't have to agree on every detail to behave as brothers (and sisters). We can respect each other and enjoy fellowship without being clones. I sense some genuine caring and concern for one another and am grateful for it. It's not found everywhere and I don't want to take it for granted. It takes time to develop a real sense of companionship and I appreciate those who are willing to make that kind of commitment.

I need warmth and you have given it. I want to be able to reciprocate. Thank you for being such gracious people. May God continue to lead us as we seek to become His people.

October 1986

"You Made My Day"

That's the way Pastor Don Houdasheldt described his feelings to the congregation at homecoming services at Patoka Baptist Church. My brother, John, and I had been there all week in revival. They had a goal of 110 for Sunday School and reached 139.

John and I reveled in being home. We've stayed close through the years and enjoy each other's company. He's Minister of Music at Hillsboro Heights Baptist Church in Huntsville, Alabama.

One of the good things about going home is that people are surprised; they don't expect much of you. It was fun renewing acquaintances. We often had to ask people to help us with their names. I didn't recognize a cousin and was I embarrassed! We explained that our memory was good, just short.

I know you can't go home again in the sense of regressing into the past, but it was good for me to touch home base. I visited an abandoned cemetery where Grandpa Davis' family is buried. Though it's less than a mile from home, I remember being there only once before.

As I age and enter new fields of interest, it's important for me to remember who I am and from where I have come. Perhaps the roots need to reach down and dig in as the limbs stretch out.

It was good to spend the week in the house where I was raised. The same two (or is it three?) steps still betray one trying to sneak in late. As I was growing up, I never could get upstairs without my folks hearing me. Sometimes I'd take two or three steps at a time, but I'd always hit a squeaky step. It seemed to say, "Be sure your sin will find you out."

It was good to remember folks at my home church who had influenced me for good and God. I remembered Pearl Britt, who taught me as a Junior boy. For some time I had a New Testament she had given me.

I remembered Gene Dodds. He was our pastor, but he also was our Royal Ambassador leader. He took several of us to RA Camp at Lake Sallateeska. It was there I claimed Christ. Gene baptized me in the old baptistry under the platform floor. You had to move the pulpit and the rug and raise the doors to get to it.

George H. Davis

I remembered Carroll Majonnier who, with Dad, led our 4-H Club. He also taught our Young People's class. I remembered Aunt Eva Wasem sitting beside me during a worship service and helping me pick out the bass part as she sang along with me. I'll never forget her interest.

I remembered receiving a check for $5 or $10 from my home church while I was in college. Treasurer Ted Nattier enclosed a note explaining someone had given him the money and asked that it be sent on to me. Though it doesn't sound like much now, I remember it being very welcome.

I remember Pastor Billy Mitchell coming to Carbondale to take me to Louisville to enroll in seminary. I hadn't planned very far ahead and it was his urging that swayed me.

I'll always be grateful for these people and their encouragement. I hope I can pass it along to others.

November 1986

I Was Insulted!

On a recent trip to Springfield, I stopped at a Denny's restaurant. I glanced over the menu and settled on a Senior Citizen's lunch. What disturbed me was that when I placed my order, the waitress didn't even ask for proof of my age!

How could she know I was old enough to qualify for a Senior's meal? I certainly don't look like an old man. You'd think that she'd at least have the courtesy to ask if I was 55. She surely wasn't looking for a big tip.

This started me to wondering: do we pay enough personal attention to people at church, or do we see them as just another "customer"? People like to be noticed. They like for us to recognize things that are significant in their lives--things like birthdays, promotions, the birth of children or grandchildren, and retirement. How can we let them know we recognize them as the individual they are and not just as a cog in a wheel?

I suppose it starts with us being willing to spend some time getting to know people as individuals. We hardly can recognize their accomplishments if we spend no time together. Then we must care about them. This needs to be a genuine concern for them, not just for the "tips" they will leave us.

In our increasingly urbanized society, it's not easy to notice the individual. We're thrown together with scores of people daily. In self-defense, we tend to insulate ourselves. We create pigeon holes and classify people according to some predetermined prejudice. But people are not pigeons and they don't like to be treated as if they were.

If you want to make a person's day, mention something special you've noticed about them. Don't insult them by not noticing how young they look or how good a job they're doing.

December 1986

by George

Why Change?

I'm not inclined to change too quickly. I like to take my time, look at the evidence, and make up my mind. Sometimes this irritates my wife, who can decide rather quickly. It may irritate others too, who are not so fast to let me know.

After six years, I've decided to change the name of our newsletter. <u>The Observer</u> seemed so detached and neutral. I wanted something warmer--something with a punch. I thought of several possibilities and talked with our Program Council about them. They encouraged me.

A widely-accepted description of an association is "churches in fellowship on mission in their setting." I felt <u>On Mission</u> captures what we are trying to do together. I plan to use the sub-heading 'in east central Illinois."

I value the opportunity to communicate through our monthly newsletter. I think it's a valuable medium and give considerable attention to it. I'm interested in improving it so that we tell our story more effectively. A newsletter is of little value if it's not read. I want to make it hard not to read <u>On Mission</u>. Of course, I'm interested in your feedback. I'm also interested in major events or emphases in your church. You have some meetings which others might enjoy. And if we're to be "in fellowship," we need to get better acquainted. That involves spending time together--both in print and in person.

I want the newsletter to be readable, attractive, and informative. I'll try to keep you informed about what we're doing together if you'll help me know what we're doing separately.

Change is not always easy, nor is it always good. But growth involves change. I don't have to change my name, but I do need to grow into the Name. If I'm called a Christian, I can only rest in Christ-like attitudes and actions. With all others I must be restless.

Change for its own sake is not so appealing to me as moving toward a goal. If I can see what I'm trying to do, I have less difficulty adjusting.

I hope you'll change with me, not because I say so, but because it strikes a responsive chord within you. If it doesn't, please let me know. We are on mission <u>together</u>.

January 1987

I Needed John

John Ivers, a long-time member at Temple Baptist Church, died last week. I'll miss him. From the time I came to Champaign, John and I hit it off well. We had mutual friends in Fairfield, Mill Shoals, and Barnhill. He checked me out before I arrived. I enjoyed visiting with him every time we got together.

But the thing I'll remember John for is that, a few years ago, he told me that I was his favorite preacher. It may sound selfish, but I needed to hear that. I knew John had heard better preachers but I enjoyed the compliment. I believe it was Keith

George H. Davis

Miller who said that each of us needs five people whose faces light up when we enter the room. I'll miss John because he boosted my sagging ego.

I enjoy preaching but I also enjoy not having to preach three times every week. Looking back, I see that as a heavy load. I remember becoming ill on Sunday afternoons as a young preacher. I had no sermon and found an alibi for not preaching. It's still humiliating to think about it. Nothing has improved my preaching so much as not having to preach every week to the same congregation. Any preacher ought to be able to come up with a few good sermons a year.

Part at my philosophy of preaching is that the preacher should use simple language. Highfalutin language has no place in the pulpit. Sermons should be understood by children. A sermon should touch the heart more than the head. Of course, a preacher should use sound reasoning, but more decisions are made on the basis of feeling than thinking.

I recognize that people respond to different kinds of preaching. Not everyone thinks of me as his/her favorite preacher. But I was moved when one of John's grandsons told me he was glad I came to the memorial service. He said he remembered his grandpa saying I was his favorite preacher. I know there was much more to John Ivers than I ever knew, but he surely knew how to cheer a preacher's heart.

I suspect Miller is right. If our life is to be rich and full, we need friends who value us. I've been blessed by people who have encouraged me. They've helped me accept new challenges and learn new ways.

The King James' version of Psalm 18:24 begins, "A man that hath friends must shew himself friendly." I'm not sure that means you have to be an extrovert—I'm certainly not! But I think you have to pay attention to people and put value on them. You have to believe individuals are important and are not to be run over or abused. Jesus' Golden Rule says, "As you wish that men would do to you, do so to them" (Luke 6:31).

I need to learn from John to pay attention to people—to listen to children. John's pastor, Marion Bennett, told of a youngster interviewing John about the Great Depression. It had been a school assignment and at first he had trouble thinking of anyone he knew who could remember that far back. Then he thought of John and apparently his experience led him to believe John would pay attention to him and take him seriously. He did and after the visit, John remarked, "That's a bright young man." Well, John, you were a real encourager and I'll miss you.

February 1987

What Does a Director of Missions Do?

Last fall I conducted a survey about what is expected of Directors of Missions. I sent a questionnaire to all our pastors and Mission Board members. I also sent it to most state convention staff persons and to all the DoMs in Illinois. The response was overwhelming. I received 87 replies to 103 surveys--84.5%. They answered 96.1% of the questions, so I feel I gathered a representative response.

by George

What do you expect from a DoM? The two most widely agreed upon answers were: (1) suggest areas where new churches are needed and (2) be a source of information about the denomination. The first response makes me wonder if it's not a carryover from an earlier era or a "pioneer mission" mentality. We used to expect associational missionaries (as we knew them) to be out starting new churches. In recent years we've drawn in and placed more emphasis of seeing existing churches prosper. We've also faced the reality that you have to work with present churches and pastors in starting new work. We probably need to recognize that growth must be <u>both</u> quantitative and qualitative--we need more churches as well as better churches.

While DoMs and pastors felt the associational leader should spend a major portion of his time in the office, others were not so sure. Board members and state workers opposed this. It may be that pastors and DoMs know more about the amount of office work to be done, but there's a rather strong expectation that the DoM be a field worker, too.

I was surprised that there seemed to be some reluctance to use the term pastor for the relationship between a DoM and pastors in the association. Some feared that this could lead to a hierarchy--the local church pastor (bishop) and his pastor (archbishop). I recognize that I can't be a pastor to someone who doesn't want me, but I can be available. However, some see a threat; they think of the DoM as a powerful person.

J.C. Bradley, in <u>A Baptist Association: Churches on Mission Together</u> (Convention Press, 1984), describes the DoM's role as three dimensional. He/she is a: (1) mission strategist, (2) minister to the churches and church leaders, and (3) general leader of the association. He sees the second role as interpersonal, not organizational. That should allay some tears of a Baptist hierarchy.

Most persons seemed to be comfortable having a DoM mediate when there are difficulties between a pastor and church members. However, some Mission Board members were cautious--they wanted to be sure such service had been requested.

Pastors and other DoMs seemed to expect a DoM to take the initiative in contacting a search committee when a church is seeking a pastor. They also expect him to recommend some prospective pastors. Mission Board members and state workers were a little more cautious in their approval of these activities. Some suggested that two or more names be given at a time. This has been my policy for some time.

I was pleased to see that the DoM is seen as being in the front line of denominational activities. This places a heavy responsibility on a person to keep informed, but I welcome such opportunities. I'm proud to be a Southern Baptist. In a time when some want to abandon labels and become generic Christians, I'm not ashamed of my roots. I'm even glad for our diversity. I'm pleased to be seen as a denominational worker.

I struggle when individuals want to use my role as a minister to get what <u>they</u> want. I don't see myself as a "Marrying Sam" or as a dispenser of relief. But I <u>want</u> to be a servant of the Lord and of his churches. I'm glad to support pastors and churches whom I see on the front lines of ministry.

March 1987

George H. Davis

Too Southern?

Something happened recently that made me wonder if I'm getting too Southern. I wrote about being glad to be a <u>Southern</u> Baptist denominational worker. I'm a graduate of <u>Southern</u> Illinois University and of <u>Southern</u> Baptist Theological Seminary.

Here's the story. I was to pick up some of the missionaries for our World Missions Conferences. I would meet them at the airport and take them to Normal for a briefing meeting to begin the week. I asked my wife if she'd like to go along to Normal. She wondered if I'd have room for the missionaries and her. I responded, "I could ask Ken (Willoughby) to carry one."

As soon as the words were out of my mouth, I was aware that, for the first time in my life, I had used the word "carry" meaning 'take." I also realized that's a time-honored Southernism. That's why I'm wondering if I'm becoming too Southern.

I've been around Southerners for several years. I've thought that many of them talked funny and used strange expressions. Now, I find that it's contagious and I'm afraid it may be too late for a vaccine.

I'm a Yankee and proud of it. I used to talk like a Yankee. But not all Yankees talk alike. My kids get amused at the quick, clipped dialect in Chicago. They also remember how Aunt Jean greeted me at a rest stop in New Hampshire, "You must be Jäj." Later, as her grandchildren were trying to understand our children, they asked, "Do you have a cold?" We've had lots of fun talking about their dialect, but we loved and understood them.

We may come from various parts of the country and have differing speech patterns. We may even use different words or attach new meanings to them. But we can learn from one another and enrich each other's lives.

I remember an incident recorded in Judges 12 when accents were used to identify outsiders and they were promptly killed. Ephraimites crossed the Jordan River to quarrel with Jephthah for not waiting for them before he went to battle the Amorites. He replied that he had asked for help, but when none came he went on to defeat the enemy. Then Jephthah refused to let his critics return home. When any of them tried to sneak across the Jordan, his guards would ask, "Are you an Ephraimite?" If they answered, "No," they would ask them to say, "Shibboleth." But the men of Ephraim could not make the "sh" sound. They would say, "Sibboleth," and give themselves away. They were promptly put to death.

I hope we can have a little more tolerance for those whose speech sounds strange. But the real problem I see in the Judges story is that everyone who spoke with a certain dialect was presumed to be an enemy.

It's easy to be critical of anyone whose views are different. It's hard to listen openly to new ideas. We've already made up our minds about so many things. We've pre-judged what is acceptable; we might be referred to as prejudiced. When all we listen for is the "Shibboleth," we're in danger of killing some friends and letting some enemies pass.

April 1987

by George

The Class Of '57

The Statler Brothers recorded "The Class of '57" remembering a high school graduating class. They faithfully reported on the current status of each member except Mavis, "Where Mavis finally wound up is anybody's bet."

I started wondering about my class of '57--the Bachelor of Divinity graduates of Southern Seminary in Louisville, Kentucky. To begin with, I need to make it clear that actually I did not graduate in 1957. I was supposed to, but failed History of Doctrine my last semester. That left me three hours short of graduation. Fortunately, it was an elective, so I went back during July, 1958 and earned four hours credit. I then graduated during the centennial of the Seminary in 1959 during the Southern Baptist Convention in Louisville.

Anyway, I consider myself part of the class of '57. I can look back through old directories and find many people I remember. The Seminary recently published an Alumni Directory listing all the graduates they could find. I went through the list of those who earned their basic theological degree in '57 and was amazed at what I found:

- 2 Home Mission Board staff--Leon Boyd, Associate Director of the Metropolitan Missions Department and Kenneth Day, Director of the Communication Division.
- 1 Foreign Mission Board staff--Harlan Spurgeon, Vice-president and Director of Human Resources.
- 2 current foreign missionaries--Robert Holifield of Rome, Italy and James Yarbrough of Niger.
- 1 past foreign missionary--Ted Cox, who served in Japan.
- 1 former congressman--Honorable J. H. Buchanan, Jr.
- 4 seminary personnel--Harold Songer, Vice-president for Academic Services and Professor of New Testament Interpretation at Southern; Paul Debusman, Reference and Serials Librarian at Southern; Glenn Hinson, Professor of Church History at Southern; and Pierce Matheney, Professor of Old Testament and Hebrew at Midwestern Seminary in Kansas City, Missouri.
- 1 Baptist Sunday School Board staff--Joe Stacker, Director of the Church Administration Division.
- 3 state convention executives--Dan Stringer of Florida, Otha Winningham of Minnesota/Wisconsin, and Harper Shannon, an associate in Alabama.
- 2 state convention staff--Gene Puckett, editor of the Biblical Recorder in North Carolina and Charles Rabon, Director of Church/Minister Relations in South Carolina.
- 1 Baptist college dean--Charles Chaney of Southwest Baptist University in Bolivar, Missouri.
- 3 well-known pastors--James Carter of University, Fort Worth (by the way, I noticed he listed Cutler, Illinois as his home town), Doug Watterson of First, Knoxville, and Dale Clemens of Meadow Heights, Collinsville and our State President (also a former pastor at Farmer City).

George H. Davis

I found eight members of the class of '57 living in Illinois. Dale Clemens and Bruce Coltharp of Mascoutah are the only ones I remember. I think Bruce is a chaplain at Scott Air Force Base. I have a book he wrote in 1974 entitled <u>When They Crucified Our Lord</u>. It's a series of imaginary interviews with six men involved with Christ and His cross.

I'm sure there are scores of other important people I've overlooked. There also may be some like Randy and Mary in the Statler Brothers' song, "Randy's on an insane ward, Mary's on welfare."

They report that the class of '57 had its dreams. "But livin' life day to day is never like it seems. Things get complicated when you get past 18." Well, most of us were a little past 18 when we finished seminary. We'd put in four years at college plus three at Southern, so we were nearer 25. We still may have been naive and I'm not sure our dream was that well focused. We had yet to face the 60's with its criticism of the church and the 70's with its apathy.

I guess my hope for the class of '57 is that we haven't lost our dream or, as Bob Dale has challenged, that we can redream the dream.

May 1987

Good And Evil

I have struggled with the meaning of Diana Lyvers' life and death. I know she is more alive now than she has been for several months.

In the midst of my struggle, I read Genesis 50:20 "You meant evil against me; but God meant it for good." As I wrestled with the question of good and evil, God helped me understand some things.

1. What seems to be tragic and evil can serve good purposes.

Diana, like Joseph, was able to find meaning and a positive outlook in her situation. To me, her illness and death were such a tragic waste. She was so strong and courageous. Why couldn't she live on to touch many others? But then, she really left an impact on those who knew her. Would that have been as strong without her illness? I don't know. I do know that she found some peace in the midst of her suffering.

2. It is God who makes the difference.

So far as Joseph was concerned, the things that happened were not just coincidence. "God meant it for good," he said. He didn't claim that God sold him into slavery in Egypt; he said God worked in the evil circumstances in which he found himself.

I don't think God gave Diana cancer; I do believe that he strengthened her through the turmoil she and her family faced. What is it Paul says in Romans 8:28? "In all things God works for the good of those who love him" (NIV).

3. Sometimes it takes a while to get God's perspective.

It had been at least 28 years since Joseph's brothers had betrayed and sold him. His fear and anger had mellowed; God's grace had intervened. I doubt that he felt this way when he was in the pit waiting to he killed. Only after decades of experiencing God's providential care could he say, "God meant it for good."

If you read the context of Romans 8:28, you'll discover that Paul is writing out of bitter experience. He refers to sufferings, vanity, the bondage of corruption, groaning and travail, patience, infirmities, condemnation, separations, tribulation, distress, persecution, famine, nakedness, peril, sword, and death.

I recently watched "Shadowland"--the story of the marriage of C. S. Lewis and Joy Davidman. He was a bachelor of long standing but within a few years after their wedding, she became ill and died. I was touched by their story.

4. In the meantime, our attitude is important.

We are to trust, to seek to learn from what happens to us. This does not mean that we can never question or tell God how angry we are. There's probably more faith in honest doubt than in unexamined belief. I don't think God is shocked by our questioning, as long as we bring it to Him. I suspect He's hurt when we try to hide it from Him.

It has been hard for me to accept the standard interpretation of Jesus' words from the cross, "'My God, my God, why hast thou forsaken me?'" (Mark 15:34b). I know we say in that moment Jesus took upon himself the sin of the world and God had no choice but to turn His back on Him; He could not look upon sin.

I agree that Jesus suffered for our sin, but it's been hard for me to accept the idea that God actually forsook Jesus. I can believe that Jesus felt forsaken and I guess that's bad enough; but, it's hard for me to believe that God ever leaves us.

When I look at Psalm 22, from which Jesus was quoting, I wonder if he didn't have the whole psalm in mind and not just the first verse. I think the Psalm reflects God's continuing care for us in the midst of what seems to be unbearable evil. Verse 24 says:

For he has not despised or abhorred the affliction of the afflicted; and he has not hid his face from him, but has heard, when he cried to him.

Again, in verse 26:

The afflicted shall eat and be satisfied; those who seek him shall praise the Lord!

Psalm 23 is a favorite of many of us. But, before you get to trusting the Lord as a caring, resourceful shepherd, you may have to go through the valley of affliction in Psalm 22.

June 1987

"Upon This Rock"?

I recently heard a singer imply that the church was built upon the Bible as she held hers up while singing, "Upon This Rock." Did the Bible produce the church, or did the church produce the Bible? Well, here's my bias as a historian. Historically, the church existed for at least one or two generations without a written Bible, It was not until about 325 that there was agreement on what makes up the Bible. The last book of the Bible probably was not written until shortly before the end of the first century, even by conservative estimates.

George H. Davis

The church was called into being by the Living Word. They responded to His call. As eyewitnesses began to die off, others started writing down their memories of Jesus' teachings. Letters and gospels were put together and gradually the church produced the Bible.

Now, before you mount a high horse and accuse me of leaving God out of the Bible, let me remind you that the church can do no lasting work without God's guidance and power. This is no less true for the writers of the Bible. The written Word is the product of the Spirit of God working in the hearts of men.

I recognize that the Bible is instrumental in producing churches--more accurately that God uses the Bible to call out and grow his people. But, let's worship God, not the Bible.

I recognize the power of music to move us, but I'm also concerned that we avoid false teaching. Because music is memorable, it tends to stick with us. We find ourselves humming or singing what we've heard. The words sometimes become gospel for us. Thus we may incorporate a twisted or limited meaning into our theology.

It's not enough for a song to have punch; it also must be true. And it should be sung in such a way that the message is not distorted. There may be nothing wrong with the lyrics of the song I heard, but a false message was being telegraphed. The singer needs to think through what she is presenting, not just repeat what she's heard.

By the way, do you know why florescent lights hum?
Answer: They don't know the words.
With that, I'd better close.

July 1987

Education or Indoctrination?

I'm tired of seminary professors being maligned as liberals by those who've never heard them teach or read their writings. I guess it boils down to your concept of education. Should our seminaries be indoctrinating students or training them? If their only function is to teach students what they should believe and practice, then we don't need seminaries. We can provide that kind of indoctrination in our churches. If there's a standard Baptist mark we all must toe, then we can whip prospective ministers into line without expensive education. And, should someone step out of line, we simply can defrock him or her and get on with the business of producing stamped out stereotypes.

But, if we're interested in ministers who are willing to wrestle with tough problems and to seek biblical and Christian solutions, that's another matter. Personally, I'm not satisfied to be told what the Bible says about issues; I want to do some investigating for myself. I don't want a pastor who parrots what others are saying. I want to see some evidence that he or she has thought through the issues instead of just using catch words heard somewhere.

I believe we need seminary professors who will challenge and stimulate the thinking of young ministers. There are many church problems that can't be solved by seminary education, but if a pastor knows how to think independently and has reasonably good human relations skills, he or she is well on the way. By the way, some of us mature ministers still can use a challenge to our thinking. If a living being does not respond to a stimulus, we suppose it's dead. If all we want from our ministers is pat answers, we don't need them--computers can give us that.

I was in a seminar at Southern Seminary in Louisville, Kentucky this summer with Professors Wayne Ward and Paul Simmons. Dr. Ward refers to himself as "the resident fundamentalist" on the faculty. But he challenged some of my ideas and helped me to expand some of my beliefs.

Dr. Simmons is one of the most controversial members of the faculty. Part of that comes with his territory. As Professor of Christian Ethics, he is expected to bring the light of biblical studies and Christian teaching to bear on current issues. But, when he does, he gets shot at from both sides. If we just want someone to tell us what most Baptists believe, we don't need him; a poll can do that. But I heard Dr. Simmons say over and over again, as we discussed controversial issues, "Now, wait a minute. What does the Bible say about that?" And he wasn't willing to let you get by with quoting a few proof texts. He wanted you to examine them to see what they <u>really</u> said. He didn't demand that you agree with him but he wouldn't let you go until you had wrestled with the issues for a while. I came to appreciate him for that.

I won't get upset if you differ with him (or me), but I do take offense if you won't listen. When you prescribe the outcome of education, you have indoctrination. In some ways, indoctrination is simpler. If you want ministers stamped out of a mold in a preacher factory, you can get that. But somehow, that doesn't appeal to me. I guess I'm too much of a free thinker. I am willing to he accountable for what I believe but I want to be careful whose yardstick we use.

<u>Will you cut your pastor's salary?</u>

If your pastor gets less than a 5% raise next year, he or she may be taking an immediate cut. The new Church Annuity Plan provides that the member (minister) contributes before any other contribution is made. Then the church doubles his or her contribution, up to 10% of the salary. There's also a provision that a church may make the member's contribution.

If your pastor elects to put 5% of the salary in the new plan, he or she will only break even with a 5% raise. Granted, retirement credit is building, but that doesn't buy groceries or gasoline now.

August 1987

Should We Enforce Morality?

There's an old argument about whether morality should be legislated. It has taken some new twists in our day with the resurgence of the radical right religiously and politically.

There have been efforts to enforce some kind of prayer in public schools. It's not enough that students and teachers have the right of private prayer; activists would make sure that everyone prays, whether they want to or not. The rationale is,

George H. Davis

"it's good for them." Never mind whether it's meaningful: let's get prayer back into the public schools. To hear some tell it, our country's troubles started when prayer was "outlawed." This overlooks at least a couple of facts: (1) prayer never was an integral part of many schools and (2) prayer was not outlawed. What the Supreme Court ruled was that a mandatory prayer recited as a part of the school day was an unconstitutional establishment of religion.

More recently pressures have been felt in the area of sexual morality. Homosexuality evokes emotions so strong they're scary. The AIDS crisis has magnified our fears. Some would erect legal barriers against homosexuals, presumably to protect society from their "plague."

Homosexual practices have been around for a long time and have enjoyed widespread popularity. But, not everyone engaging in homosexual activities is a homosexual. One of our problems is that we have not bothered to define homosexuality. We say, "Everyone knows what that is" as we dodge the question. We may have driven some further away by treating them as untouchables.

Are irresponsible homosexual activities worse than irresponsible heterosexual activities? It may be that what the Bible describes is homosexual rape. Is God not offended by any act of a person imposing him or her self upon another? Does that not violate personhood when we treat another as some *thing* for our pleasure?

I sense a real danger when a majority (political or religious) wants to impose its standards upon all of society. I know we need moral standards but when I make mine absolute, I deify myself. That's idolatry!

I know we have inherited some of that Puritan tradition from New England and I know it's not all bad. But Baptists have fought for years to be free from imposed religion and I hope we'll continue even if we can join a conservative coalition to form a majority. I prefer a free church and a free state existing side by side. I fear church above state as much as state above church.

I'm not enamored with attempts to make ours a "Christian" nation. Such efforts got off on the wrong foot with Constantine. In the early centuries of the Christian era, armies were marched through a river, thus "baptizing" them. Of course, they were careful to hold their weapons above water so they could continue to battle their (and God's) enemies.

We are a pluralistic society. To attempt to force upon it "Christian" morality is to admit the failure of our evangelism. Isaiah and Micah have a concept of the mountain of the Lord's house being established as the highest of the mountains, and they say, "The nations shall flow to it" (Isaiah 2:2 and Micah 4:1). Normally, any flow is downhill, but there's a magnetic attraction that draws people. What's wrong that we must use force to bring people around? Is our religion too shallow?

I've been wondering

News reports a few weeks ago indicated that Pat Robertson resigned as a Southern Baptist minister when he announced his candidacy for the Republican Party's nomination for President of the United States. I've been wondering, "To whom did he resign?" I looked in the 1986 SBC Annual and didn't find his name; of course I realize that is not an official list. He may have been licensed and ordained by a Southern Baptist congregation. Did he return the license or ordination certificate to them? Did he turn them in to the church where he belongs? None of the reports I heard answered these nagging questions. I sense that news people did not take his action seriously; they still refer to him as "the Reverend..."

October 1987

Rambling Thoughts On Being Rooted Or Rootless

During the fall of 1986 I was back at my home church for a revival. I preached and one of my brothers, John, led the singing; it was like old home week for us. We saw people we were supposed to know but had difficulty giving them names. We also visited with people who had come into the church since we left in 1949 and 1953, when we went off to college.

I was struck by the number who had spent their entire lives (so far) in Patoka. It's a small town along Route 51, about halfway between Centralia and Vandalia. There seemed to be something good about living where you know everyone and they know you. At least, you know who you are: "You're Jake's oldest boy."

We haven't moved around very much, but sometimes I wonder where our children call home. They were born when we lived in Louisville and Altamont. They attended school in Altamont, Herrin, Grayville, Fairfield, and Champaign. Do they sometimes feel rootless?

Maybe there are two issues here--small towns versus cities and staying put vs. moving around. I suspect there's some correlation between small towns and staying put and between cities and moving around. I think studies have shown that people who live in cities tend to move more frequently. I don't mean to imply that those who live in small towns are sticks in the mud. There's a certain attractiveness in knowing who you are. However, there also may be a captivity in not being able to change who you are. People expect you to be the same person they've watched growing up. How much will they allow you to change? Isn't there such a thing as being root-bound, when the pot's too small for the plant?

When you move into a new community, it's relatively easy to adopt new patterns. That may be why some preachers move every few years--it's easier to move than to work through old problems. That points up one of the dangers of moving; sometimes it amounts to running. Another phase of the problem is that if one changes every time he moves, who is he? Is he only the latest style he has adopted, or is he a collage of all he's been?

There are some disturbing things about rootlessness. It's akin to restlessness; I think of a tumbleweed. But there is opportunity to grow. I suppose the real test of whether change is good, is whether there's purpose and direction to it.

I suppose before there can be growth, there must be a root system to provide nourishment. Is it possible that such a network can be developed away from ones ancestral home? Can a new "family" be found to offer such nutrients? Perhaps a Christian community can provide roots for uprooted people.

George H. Davis

I wonder why Joseph could find no shelter for his betrothed in his ancestral home. It must have been an empty feeling to go home and not find room. I wonder if he felt uprooted in the home town of his fathers.

I suppose family gatherings are the most significant part of my Christmas celebration. We don't have a lot of traditions, but the larger family getting together is a rather strong one. It's hard to get all the children, grandchildren, and great-grandchildren together, but a number of us will be there. I guess a part of what I'm wrestling with is that I see that tradition fading and it's painful.

I'm glad for the opportunities I've had. I see them more as God's plan than any design of mine. He's given experiences which have helped me become who I am. Some of them have been exciting and fun, others have been stressful and depressing; but I think I've learned from each. I'm not sure I'd change much if I could. But I miss not being known as "Jake's oldest boy."

December 1987

Renting Preachers

One of our churches is without a pastor and their interim had to be gone due to some previous commitments. They had used other supply preachers. A small girl in the congregation, noting the variety, asked her grandmother, "What are we doing, renting preachers?"

I guess it is important to have someone dependable in the pulpit week after week. We get used to a preacher and feel comfortable with him—but not too comfortable. Someone has said that a preacher's job is to comfort the disturbed and disturb the comfortable. We tend to get comfortable when we should feel uneasy about ourselves and situations around us.

I enjoy preaching. I enjoy it even more since I don't have the burden of coming up with three fresh messages every week; that's an almost impossible assignment. For me, nothing has improved my preaching as much as not having to do it every week. I have the luxury of preaching a sermon until I get it right!

But being a pastor is more than preaching. That may be the most public of his or her tasks, but there's also leading and counseling. Fifteen years ago, Ernest Mosley stated the work of a pastor, assisted by the deacons and staff, as follows:

1. Lead the church in the achievement of its mission
2. Proclaim the gospel to believers and unbelievers
3. Care for the church's members and other persons in the community

(Called to Joy, Nashville: Convention, 1973, page 24).

The tasks are best seen as interlocking and mutually supportive. There needs to be a balance between them rather than let one dominate the others.

I've spent half of my professional life as a pastor (1957-73); the other half has been as a director of missions (1973-88). I still consider myself a minister and try to live up to professional standards. All my training and experience is as a minister and I'm not afraid of being thought of as a professional. I'm aware that there are some unkind associations with professionalism. It sometimes evokes images of being cold and detached.

I'm sobered when I remember that it was professional religious leaders who gave Jesus the most trouble. He reserved His harshest criticism for those who had taken a detour on their way to the Temple; we call them Pharisees. In our language, that's almost synonymous with hypocrite. But I think there are other options open to religious professionals. We can strive to have an open mind, to be teachable. The best teachers are learners, too. We can seek to avoid the trap of thinking we own the truth rather than letting it own and direct us.

I've never met anyone who said he wanted to be a hypocrite when he grew up. I'm not sure I can remember anyone admitting to being one, but there's at least a little hypocrisy in most of us. That's why we hate it so; we're ashamed of that part of our lives.

Years ago, a good friend sometimes called me "Rev." Though I resented the nickname, I never got around to telling him so. (I think he was uncomfortable calling me George and was struggling for an alternative. He was a parishioner and a fishing buddy--he had a boat.) I liked him and could overlook his use of a nickname I disliked.

Like Amos, I would resent the suggestion that I could be bought. Economic issues are very real but there are others that matter more. Micah identified justice, mercy, and humility (6:8). I will come and preach at your church but I'm not for rent. If I'm true to my calling, God owns me.

January 1988

The fan's dilemma

What do you do when your team doesn't play up to its potential?

You cry, then you laugh and realize it's a game played for fun. But someone suggests it's more fun to win than to lose. Someone else notes that someone has to lose; that's the nature of the game. Then there's always someone who says that the answer is to fire the coach. It's his or her job to get their best out of a team.

Have you ever noticed how that carries over to church? When a church is not living up to its potential, someone suggests it's the pastor's fault. Had you ever noticed that Paul's athletic models for the church are individuals, not teams? He mentions the runner and the boxer, both individual performers. He also compares the church to a body and a building and they are corporate models, but we tend to focus on the solitary figures.

Why didn't Paul use team sports as models? Were they unknown in his day? Several years ago, the term "player coach" was suggested as a pastoral model by Elton Trueblood, I believe.

With our Baptist penchant for literalism, we are slow to grasp any image that's not spelled out in scripture. Our frontier mentality has compounded the tendency to glorify the rugged individual over the body. We tend to think of the priesthood of the believer wholly in individualistic terms, without realizing that a priest has intercessory responsibility for those he represents. We focus on individual responsibility and neglect corporate consciousness.

Why not think of the church as a team which must play together? What's needed is not individual "hot dogs" but a team that complements each other. Individuals recognize one another's strengths and perform unselfishly. Their goal is a team victory.

But they don't always win. What do you do then? Maybe you cry, like Jesus did over Jerusalem, "How often would I have gathered your children together as a hen gathers her brood under her wings, and you would not!" Then, maybe you laugh! Oh, I know it's more than a game, it's life and that's deadly serious. But it seems to me that laughter has something to do with forgiveness. When we take ourselves so seriously that we can't allow failure, we're setting ourselves up for defeat. Every human venture will have a note of failure about it and the church is a divine/human venture,

I think God must have a sense of humor. How else can we explain his creation and tolerance of man? Counselors tell us that being able to laugh at (and forgive) ourselves is a sign of mental health. Expecting perfection can become terribly demanding and unhealthy.

Another sobering question--do we get as upset over our failure to play well together in the church as we do when our team falls apart? You see, I am for forgiveness and laughing at our failure but I'm also for seriousness and responsibility. But let's recognize some corporate responsibility for one another and encourage fellow team members. Maybe a "high five" or a "low five" would be more appropriate than looking for a scapegoat.

February 1988

Surprise!

Yes, we were surprised when our children threw a thirty-fifth anniversary reception for us February 28th. We knew they were coming for the weekend, but didn't know all they had in mind. They managed to enlist co-conspirators for the Sunday afternoon celebration at Pennsylvania Avenue Church in Urbana. Even our pastor and our associational secretary were in on the secret and notified you. We're proud of and grateful to our children and enjoyed the day immensely.

I have many memories of our thirty-five years of marriage. We spent our first three months apart; I was in school in Carbondale and Leona was teaching in Coulterville. Though I still lived in a dorm, it was an easy drive fifty miles up Route 13 after I finished my dry cleaning route in the evening. I believe there were only six days we didn't see each other during that time. It may not have been an ideal way to start a marriage, but I suppose I'd do it again.

Then there was a year in Carbondale in Dr. Johnson's apartments. George Johnson taught Bible at Southern Illinois College of the Bible (better known as the Baptist Foundation). He also had some apartments behind his home on West Mill. One of the most memorable events during that year was the time we were expecting company for supper and I let the chicken burn up. The stove had a deep-well cooker which I was supposed to turn off before I left for class. I forgot and when we got home, the pot was black and so was the apartment--even the bones burned.

by George

We moved to Louisville, Kentucky so I could attend seminary. After a few months on a waiting list, we moved on campus into a one room apartment. There was a <u>small</u> kitchenette and a bath but the dining room, living room, and bedroom were one. A hide-a-bed couch, dinette set, dresser, desk, bookcase, and eventually a used television furnished that room.

For most of those three years, we made the trek to Louisville, Illinois every weekend. I had been called as pastor at Second Little Prairie Baptist Church, just north of town. Their pastor, Dale Clemens had invited me to preach a revival during spring break. Before it arrived, he resigned. They wanted me to come ahead and called me as pastor. So we had apartments in Louisville, Kentucky and Louisville, Illinois-- only the first Louisville was pronounced, "Lue-vil," the second sounded the "s."

My first full-time pastorate was in Altamont, Illinois. Our first child had been born in January before we left seminary in the spring. That fall, we moved our growing family into the parsonage at Altamont. The last three of our children were born while we lived there. For a long time afterward, they referred to it as "our house."

From Altamont, we moved to Herrin. One of the memorable things about that move was that we packed most of our belongings into banana boxes; they kidded us at Herrin about eating seventy cases of bananas. One of the features of the Herrin parsonage was a long, walk-through closet between the children's bedrooms. We had a few discussions about not running through it.

We moved to Grayville about Halloween and our kids didn't get to go "trick or treating" that year. Another thing they remember about that move was loading our dog and her new puppies in the dog house to move them.

Our next move brought the greatest changes. I became an associational worker and enjoyed it from the beginning but was unaware of my wife's feeling of loss of status. She went from being the pastor's wife with a built-in role to being just another church member. She had always said that I was her favorite preacher, but now I was no longer her pastor. She felt from before our marriage that she should be a pastor's wife and had been a good one. She enjoyed the role and did not feel forced into it. And she has adjusted well to her changing role as mine changed.

I remember how we celebrated our twenty-fifth anniversary. There was a reception we enjoyed but the family highlight was going to St. Louis and spending a weekend in a Holidome with three of our children--one was in college.

Our life together has been good; we're looking forward to several more anniversaries and we're learning how to celebrate. Thanks for you help!

March 1988

How Big is Your Church?

How do you measure the size of a church? You could find out how many members it has, or how many attend. You might look at the size of its budget, or a number of other values.

I have chosen, for the moment, to look at resident membership and average weekly Sunday School attendance. I'd like to look at worship attendance. Unfortunately, those figures are not available. For the moment, I'm ignoring financial strength. I recognize that churches are dynamic, not static; these figures represent only a slice of their history. They represent their size on or about July 31, 1987.

Church Size in ECIBA

Church	Resident Members	Ave. Wkly SS Att.	1986-87 Baptisms
Weldon	22	10	1
Bement	53	10	0
Lodge	35	20	0
Gibson City	44	23	0
Thomasboro	41	26	2
Fisher	50	28	1
Tuscola, Hillcrest	68	31	0
Tolono	90	41	3
Farmer City	90	47	3
LeRoy	110	52	1
Danville, Bethel	194	64	3
Rantoul, Immanuel	118	78	7
Monticello, Calvary	171	84	2
Champaign. Temple	174	89	3
Champaign, Garden Hills	206	95	1
Paxton	237	102	3
Normal, College Avenue	197	130	7
Bloomington, Vale	266	179	9
Urbana, Pennsylvania Avenue	452	337	8

Source: 1987 Annual, East Central Illinois Baptist Association

Half of the nineteen reporting churches in our association have fewer than 110 resident members; half have more. Half have fewer than 52 in Sunday School every week; half have more. LeRoy is right in the middle. In statistical terms, it's the median; half are below and half are above its numbers.

In an article in the April, 1988 Issue of *The Baptist Program*, Gary Farley says that "smaller churches baptize a better ratio of persons to membership than do larger ones" (p. 6). (By the way, that's an excellent article dealing with twelve characteristics of smaller churches. Ask your pastor for a copy.) I decided to check his statement out for our association.

I grouped our churches according to some natural breaks. We have seven churches who have 80 resident members or fewer and 40 or fewer in Sunday School weekly. Their 313 members baptized 4 persons last year for a ratio of 1 to 78. The three churches with 81 to 115 members and 41 to 60 in SS had a ratio of 1 to 41. The four churches in the next category--116 to 195 members and 61 to 90 In SS--had a ratio of 1 to 44. The five largest churches, with 196 or more members and 91 or more in SS, had a ratio of 1 to 48.

So, if you ignore the smallest group, the smaller churches tended to do slightly better. I recognize that you can't ignore any churches and that our association is too small a group to show any definitive findings, but it was interesting to check out, anyway.

What does all this prove? I'm not sure it proves anything. But, maybe it shows that bigger isn't always better. I hope you feel good about your church regardless of its size. How you feel about it may be more important than how big it is.

April 1988

Studies in Hypocrisy

Two news stories caught my attention over the weekend. The first was about the seizure of the yacht *Monkey Business* when some illegal drugs were found aboard. The federal government is implementing a "zero tolerance" program of confiscating vessels, vehicles, planes. etc. on which any amount of illegal drugs are found.

The second story was about a Champaign police SWAT team raid on a house where illegal gambling operations were thought to be in progress. The thing that tied these stories together for me was the seeming hypocrisy present in each.

You can hardly go to a ball game without being asked to pass beer to someone down the row. Beer and wine commercials are a major source of television revenue. We seem to have an unofficial public policy of promoting the sale and use of alcohol and, at the same time, of cracking down on the sale and use of other drugs. Yet, liquor continues to be our number one drug problem. I suppose there is a difference. We have declared alcohol legal and taxed it liberally. The lesson seems to be that if a drug is legalized and taxed, it's okay. As for gambling, you can purchase a lottery ticket at many grocery or drug stores and at a number of other outlets. There recently was a promotion encouraging clerks to ask *every* customer if he or she would like to buy a lottery ticket. Again, the lesson seems to be that it's all right for the government to conduct gambling operations, but it's forbidden to individuals. We can even license a business to operate horse race betting operations, as long as it is properly taxed. It makes you wonder if our primary concern is for the revenue which can be generated regardless of any moral questions.

I'm not at all sure it's the business of government to enforce morality but I'm pretty sure it shouldn't promote immorality. I recognize that not everyone will agree with my judgment on morality. Perhaps that's why I have second thoughts about

George H. Davis

asking the government to enforce my point of view. But we seem to be promoting things which clearly are detrimental to individuals and to society. At the same time, we're pouncing on persons who do the same kinds of things on their own. Is it any wonder people become cynical?

<u>Legal versus Moral</u>
It's time we realized that not everything that's legal is morally acceptable. Just because an action is permitted by law, is no reason for a person to assume it's harmless. The government does a poor job of protecting us from ourselves. Again, I'm not sure that's the proper role of government. Maybe it's time to realize that there's a better question than "What's legal?" Maybe we need to ask, "What's helpful?"

<u>Chances Are</u>
Your chances of dying this week are about 966 times greater than your chances of winning millions in the lottery. According to the National Center for Health Statistics, 100,536 persons died in Illinois In 1986, the last year for which figures are available. That's 1,933 per week. If you assume that two persons won the lottery each week (which is being generous), that means you have 966 more chances of dying this week than of winning the lottery. It would be interesting to see our media publish the *losing* lottery numbers, rather than the winning ones. That would be a real public service!

I recognize that nothing is easier than seeing the hypocrisy in someone else's actions, and few things are more difficult than being consistent in our own actions. I hope I can be as willing to see my hypocrisies as I am to point out other's.

May 1988

My Convention Highlight

One of my most memorable moments at the recent Southern Baptist Convention occurred on Wednesday night during the Foreign Mission Board report. I was <u>not</u> in a good mood. Auxiliary auditoriums had not been opened when we arrived; they wanted to fill the arena first. So we went up to the third tier, only to find it almost full. We finally found some vacant seats and made our way to them. Then we discovered why they were vacant; about all you could see was the light supports. Sometimes you could catch a glimpse of the speaker through the framework. But, we stayed put. At least we could hear. We could see the screen, but only from an extreme angle, so that wasn't very satisfactory.

Most of the votes during the day and the previous day had not gone my way. I've gotten used to being in a minority, so that didn't upset me greatly. I guess it left me more depressed than anything.

To top it all off, the program was running late. We frittered away time and the Foreign Mission Board report was twenty-five minutes late in getting started--8:30 p.m.--and they had an hour and a half scheduled. Our shuttle bus was to take us back to the motel at. 9:40. I wasn't in a very good mood!

by George

The report moved along well. At its focus was the appointment of seventeen couples and one individual as missionaries. Many of them gave testimonies. Keith Parks, FMB president, gave the charge to the missionaries and the congregation. The entire report was interesting and well done.

But what moved me most had not happened yet. During the invitation, persons were asked to come forward to tell a missionary about their commitment to missions. A decision card had been handed to everyone entering the session. It listed several types of commitment possible:

To explore a career in missions
To serve four months to two years
To serve up to four months
To pray for missions regularly
To nurture others
To increase my financial support through my church
To influence my church toward greater missions support
Other_____

Several persons responded. From the crow's nest, we had an excellent view of the floor of the arena. What moved me was seeing a lady in a wheel chair moving toward one of the missionaries to share her commitment.

I don't know what her decision was, but I was impressed. If she could commit her limited life to missions, why couldn't some of the rest of us do more? We give less than one percent of our income to all mission causes. And we give less time and energy than money. How can we be satisfied with what we're doing? I certainly can't believe God is. But, more than that, I was positively challenged to think about what I can do.

June 1988

FIREWORKS!

Factory Direct Outlet!

Seeing signs like this brought a lump to my throat as my wife and I traveled this summer. Our kids used to beg to stop at the sight. Now some of them are explaining the dangers to their kids. How things change!

I remember great fireworks displays when I was a kid. I had a couple of older cousins who ordered a generous supply every year, then they'd get the whole family together and shoot them off. I remember them using down spouts to guide skyrockets into their trajectory. Putting firecrackers in tin cans was also a favorite.

These were the same cousins who built a ferris wheel out of wood. It had two seats. Things slowed when one of the boys broke his arm in that endeavor.

They also built a small cannon and shot it into the side of the chicken house. That option usually was exercised only during the day when most of the chickens were outside.

George H. Davis

But, back to the fireworks. Why is it we're so uptight while we're raising our kids and can learn to relax and enjoy them only after they're grown? Is that why grand kids are so much more fun? You can have all the fun with limited responsibility.

I don't remember ever telling our kids they couldn't have something or couldn't do something because they were preacher's kids. Maybe they felt that and maybe others had those expectations, but I don't think we intentionally saddled them with that baggage.

July 1988

Will The Real Cardinals Please Stand Up

This has been a tough year for St. Louis Cardinal fans. We've watched as the team went from winning the pennant last year to struggling to stay out of the basement this year. It's been painful.

I know I'm not a very faithful fan. I don't follow the team closely. It was hard to build up interest early in the season when they were in such a tail spin. Then, about June, I got interested when they began to pull out of it and play well. Then came July and August and they fell into the doldrums again.

Will the real Cardinals please stand up?

I've wondered what's wrong. I know that baseball's a game of breaks. Is it just that the ball has bounced the wrong way? If so, isn't it time for a turn around?

Could they have given up? I was listening to a game the other night when a runner was attempting to steal third. The announcers said that the Cardinal third baseman didn't move to cover the bag. My family went over for a game August 20. The Reds beat us. I guess the crushing blow was when they pulled a double steal. For a team like the Cardinals, known for their speed, to get caught like that felt like a slap in the face.

Then I got to thinking like a preacher. Do ministers ever reach a point when they give up? When they no longer care what happens? I guess I'm confessing, but I think we do. You may call it burnout, disillusionment, or discouragement.

I think many professionals face times when it's hard for them to do their work. Staying "up" or feeling the challenge is not easy to maintain. There's always someone willing to prick your balloon or to tell you why your idea won't work. Pressures of more work than you can do get to you.

In a job where you're basically self-employed, you also have to be self-motivated. A minister is expected to be a motivator of others, too. (I realize there are those who say you cannot motivate anyone else. Each one of us can only motivate himself or herself.)

After a while, it's easy just to go through the motions without your heart being in it. Spiritually, we need revival. Socially, we need encouragement. Physically, we need rest. I suspect these are familiar feelings to many of us. Your pastor is not immune to them. I hope you'll pray for him, that you'll be his friend. He needs you at least as

by George

much as you need him. He may not lead you to win the pennant every year, but at least you'll stay in the game.

August 1988

I'm Encouraged

I'm encouraged by the attendance and participation at our annual meeting. We had more churches represented and more people present than in several years. And didn't Fisher and Bement do a fine job in entertaining us? Pastor Volie Pyles and Fishers pianist and organist were on the spot to provide for our needs. I had told the folks at Bement to plan on feeding about 40, but guess how many came to supper-- about 60. They were not caught short, though. They know Baptists. When we smell fried chicken, we flock around!

I'm encouraged by the number of pastors at our annual meeting. I counted sixteen; that's three more than last year. We have an excellent group (what do you call several pastors?) of pastors who enjoy warm fellowship. They're not all alike, but that's what makes them great. Each one is gifted in different ways and interested in various things. They are able to complement each other.

I'm encouraged by the workers we've been able to enlist this year. Our corps is almost complete, including some positions which have been vacant recently-- Christian life, stewardship, and youth. These program directors are the ones who do the work of the association. As part of our associational council, they help plan, coordinate, and evaluate our activities. And, by the way, if you wonder what the association has done for you lately, we've offered *thirty—five hours of training for Sunday School workers* over the past twelve months. That's in addition to the Vacation Bible School clinic.

I'm encouraged by the spirit of our people. Folks in our churches know they have a big task and that their resources aren't always adequate. But they're trusting God and believing that He'll provide everything needed for His work. I sense an enthusiasm which is contagious. I hope you've caught it.

I'm encouraged by the work being done across our association. We still don't have all the reports and the figures don't tell the whole story. Recently as I traveled to College Avenue in Normal, I saw a group of Japanese wives meeting to learn English. My wife is helping a Japanese family with conversational English. They had English lessons in Japan, but studying grammar and vocabulary doesn't mean you can speak the language. Lecia Carter is enlisting host families for international students. There's so much to be done, but we're tackling it!

I'm encouraged by our partnership with the state convention. Their supervision of the campus ministers serving in our association seems to be working well. We still have input into the process and the campus ministers are feeling more a part of the whole student ministry picture. And didn't Evelyn Tully represent the State well at our annual meeting? She's director of Woman's Missionary Union services for Illinois Baptist State Association. She'll be our liaison with the State for the year, so if you have a question about what's going on in Springfield, call her. I was especially glad to

George H. Davis

hear how associations have blessed her life. And didn't she represent the staff well? Of course, that's not too hard, considering the quality of our state staff.

I'm encouraged by the kind of help we can offer to one another. Part of what being an association means is that we're never alone--there are always others to help and encourage. We've received help from our state convention this year and we've given help. Some state staff have served as interim pastors in some of our churches. Some have spoken at our meetings and have helped us train workers. They've trained and supported our pastors and other leaders. I'm encouraged.

October 1988

In Praise of Independent Thinking

I am unwilling to give up my right to think and decide issues for myself. I know there's value in moral watchdogs, but I am unwilling to accept their judgment uncritically. Sometimes they bark at shadows. Sometimes they sleep while an intruder breaks in.

We have no shortage of groups and individuals who want to tell us how to think and vote. They presume to pass along the *Christian* position on any number of questions. Well, I happen to believe that Christians may differ on many of these questions and still be Christian. I doubt that any of us fully knows the mind of Christ. He may be equally shocked at and ashamed of all of us.

I've never received so much campaign literature claiming to be nonpartisan. All of it came from conservative groups intent on convincing me that their positions were the standard by which others should he judged. Some even came from my "Southern Baptist Friends." I think the reason I resented these mailings so much was that they claimed to represent *the* Christian viewpoint and expected me to use my influence to tell others how to vote. I believe that because they all addressed me as "Rev." or "Dr." One even supplied a comparison of candidates to be duplicated and distributed. With its use of emotionally charged descriptions, I saw it as blatantly partisan.

We may be dangerously close to idolatry when we allow someone else to do our thinking for us. We acknowledge our responsibility to give and serve and would not ask anyone to take our place in these areas. Why should the use of our minds be any different from other talents? If God has given us the ability to think and reason, and I believe He has, aren't we accountable for using that capacity? Will God allow us to shrug shoulders and say, "Well, Dr. Somebody said Christians should think this way." Who appointed them as your conscience?

I want to be very cautious about boycotting a company or a product just because someone doesn't like something they do. There may be just causes for using a boycott, but it had better be something I know about personally. I'm not willing to use that drastic tool just because someone else thinks I should.

I recognize that the mind can be twisted and depraved, but it also can be devoted to God's service and glory; I believe the choice is up to us. But we also need to remember that Jesus reserved some of his harshest rebukes for the lazy--the King James Version calls it "slothful." I wonder if this applies also to the use of our minds.

Have some of us buried our minds so that they do not become soiled? If we have, we come too late to the sad realization that they have rotted from lack of exercise. Who does your thinking for you?

November 1988

You Can Call Me George

A beer commercial a few years ago featured a guy proclaiming, "You can call me Ray; you can call me Jay; ... but you don't have to call me Mister." You may quarrel with my role model, but I want to say "You can call me George; you can call me Brother George; you can call me Brother Davis; but you don't have to call me Doctor."

The Lord willing, I'll receive the Doctor of Ministry degree from Southern Seminary in Louisville on December 16. I have finished all the requirements for the degree, including the oral defense of my project. For the past four years I've been a part-time student earning fourteen hours of credit in four seminars. Two were offered here in Urbana. I've also had three semesters of supervised field education and have completed a ministry research project--a total of thirty-two hours.

It had been twenty-seven years since I finished my basic seminary work. Going back to school brought back some painful memories. I remembered flunking Theron Price's "History of Doctrine' my last semester of seminary and being unable graduate with the class of 1957. I had to pick up three hours during summer school and graduated in '59.

These last few years have been good and challenging. I can count fifty-one books on my shelves that I've read during these studies. It hardly seems right to have an evening without homework. I won't quit reading, but I won't miss having four to twelve books to report on each semester. Case studies have been helpful in dealing with real ministry situations. But maybe the greatest benefit has been the fellowship of learning. I've made new friends and shared ideas with old ones. I can think of thirteen other Illinois ministers who've been in the program at the same time; there may have been others.

I've gained a renewed appreciation for seminary faculty. Bryant Hicks taught me valuable, practical ways of handling my feelings. Marvin Tate's biblical scholarship challenged me. Paul Simmons helped me wrestle with difficult, controversial issues and to see that there may be more than one "Christian" position. Christians may differ on tough problems. It really burns me to hear someone talk about "liberal professors" at our seminaries. I sometimes challenge them to name one and cite his of her heresy. That usually shuts them up.

The degree is in ministry, not just research. It isn't intended to be a diploma earned in the library, though I've certainly learned my way around there. I hope and believe I'm a better minister for the study and supervision. You have the right to judge that, too, because you're my flock. You have helped with the cost of this training and I'm grateful for that. You've allowed me time for study. I don't think I've neglected my work. I may have focused on different areas of ministry as a result of the program, but I think it's been healthy, overall.

Paul urges Timothy, "Do not neglect the gift you have…. Practice these duties, devote yourself to them, so that all may see your progress" (1 Timothy 4:14-15). I want my progress to be evident in my work.

I'm glad for the opportunity for study and am proud of the degree. But, I don't think I'll start referring to myself as Dr. Davis. Oh, I've received mail addressed to Dr. George Davis," but I'm usually suspicious of what they want. It has been a real turn-off for me. A colleague joked about teaching his young son to call him Doctor Daddy. I doubt that Doctor Grandpa sounds any better. I'll feel comfortable if you'll continue calling me whatever you've been calling me, as long as it's decent! You can call me George.

December 1988

Does God Wear a Watch?

I've been wrestling with a difficult question. Perhaps you can help me. Does God wear a watch? Did God make time, or is it man's invention? Bill Keane, Family Circus cartoonist, had Dolly say, "God invented time so everything wouldn't happen at the same time."

I'm a rather punctual person who would rather be twenty minutes early than five minutes late. It bothers me when other people waste time, especially mine. So, the thought that God may not wear a watch is almost blasphemous. How could God not be at least as concerned about time as I am (and don't tell me that he knows what time it is without looking at his watch)! Is it possible that God has a different relationship to time than I do?

The concept of time is very difficult for young children to understand. To tell them to wait until tomorrow is like putting it off indefinitely and the day after tomorrow *never* comes. Time seems to drag for children. Then in mid-life it whizzes by. This led Dale Clemens to suspect that:

> … a worldwide, subversive element has shortened the hours, weeks, months, and years. I also know that the distance of time between Thanksgiving and Christmas has been reduced.
>
> When I was a boy, Christmas drug and painfully arrived. That time just prior to Christmas was as slow as the hours one spends waiting with a toothache (Reminder, Meadow Heights Baptist Church, Collinsville, November 29, 1988).

But Austin Dobson wrote: "Time goes, you say? Ah no! Alas, Time stays, *we* go."

The Bible talks about two kinds of time: (1) "It was about the sixth hour" (John 4:6c). That's chronological time. (2) ". . . the hour is coming, and now is, when the true worshipers will worship the Father in spirit and truth…" (John 4:23). John Marsh calls that realistic time. It's "the right time." Jesus said, "My time is at hand . . ." (Matthew 26:18b).

The Bible also seems to indicate that the two kinds of time exist simultaneously. We live in chronological time but we also have the possibility of living in eternity. That's not something that begins when this time ends; it begins when I respond to God's grace. Then I, like God, am no longer bound by time. But, I'll still try to be on time.

January 1989

God Wants Every Church to Grow

I read the statement and had trouble digesting it. It said, "God wants every church to grow." Though it sounded good on the surface, there was an undercurrent that bothered me. Does God indeed want *every* church to grow? When did He say so? To whom? Is this a Biblical revelation, or is it post-Biblical?

To begin with, I have trouble with many statements which claim to portray the mind of God. Paul declares: "How unsearchable are his judgments and how inscrutable his ways! For who has known the mind of the Lord, or who has been his counselor?" (Romans 11:33b-34). I'm not sure everyone claiming to know Gods mind, does.

God's call to Isaiah was to preach to a people who would not listen. When he asked, "How long?" he was told to continue until no one was left to listen (see Isaiah 6). God's faithless people would be cut down like a tree, leaving only a stump. But, the promise of God was that "the holy seed is in its stump" (v. 13c).

The growth to which God calls us is sometimes quite different from our perceptions of growth. We're so immersed in our culture, we think "bigger is better." We expect a church to attract more members, adopt larger budgets, and build more beautiful buildings (just like any other human enterprise would). If they don't, we get nervous about the bottom line.

But, what is the bottom line? Is it the profit or loss we record, or is it faithfulness to God? He sent his Son into the world to suffer and die. The world calls that failure, not success.

It may be that we asked the wrong question in the beginning. Maybe we should ask, "What kind of growth does God expect?" It may be God's will for some churches to suffer and die, if that's what it takes to be faithful. Maybe some churches in racially changing communities should stay and minister rather than moving to the suburbs. It may mean that we should speak out on moral issues, even when it's unpopular and prominent members threaten to withhold their support.

I think it's hard for *me* to know what God wants *you* to do. Maybe that's why I have so much trouble swallowing the statement, "God wants every church to grow." Rather than heaping guilt on others who aren't growing, maybe I'd better concentrate on what God wants for me and for my church.

I need to be careful not to look for an excuse for my own laziness and self-centeredness. It may be that God *does* want my church to grow and that He wants me to give myself more freely so that His love is known and others are drawn into His Kingdom.

February 1989

George H. Davis

How long has it been since you harnessed a horse?

I remember hearing Evelyn Duvall ask, "How long has it been since you harnessed a horse, or baked biscuits from scratch?" She was speaking at a Family Life Conference at Pennsylvania Avenue Baptist Church in Urbana in 1968. I was pastor at Second Baptist Church in Herrin and had served on a committee to help Bluford Sloan plan and promote the Conference.

Recently I've been thinking about new skills I've learned. Dr. Duvall was pointing out that we all have skills we no longer use. I'm sure that's true. I haven't harnessed a horse in at least thirty-five years. I never *was* too thrilled with that job! Have you ever stood beside a work horse? They can be intimidating.

Meanwhile, leaving the ranch--I spent some time, early in my career as a pastor, learning to use a mimeograph machine. It's a dirty job, but somebody's got to do it. I learned that, if you keep the machine and the rollers reasonably clear, you can produce fairly acceptable copy. You can even do some color work, if you're willing to take the time.

All the time I was becoming a qualified mimeo operator, other people were talking about the superior work you could do with an offset press. But, that was intimidating. I understood mimeo; the offset was a strange machine. But, in time I became familiar and comfortable with them. In the meantime, copiers had made mimeos all but obsolete.

Then, people began talking about a new machine called a computer. It was supposed to be a wonder. I wondered. I'd found an addressing system that handled our newsletters very well. But, I kept wondering if we could save some time on our financial records. Eventually we plunged into the brave new world. Now I'm fascinated by the emerging horizons opened by computers.

This issue of the newsletter is the first for which we've used a laser printer to produce the camera-ready copy. I'm fascinated by the possibilities. No, we don't have a laser printer. But, I've found a firm that is willing to print out copy from our disk. The Lord willing, and the computer working, you'll see more of its design.

I suspect that the next decades will offer more skills for us to learn. We can either back off, intimidated, or press on fearfully. I hope we'll be willing to use the best tools available as we seek to serve the Lord.

March 1989

Pheeling Like a Pharisee

I've played several roles since my high school play days. As a pastor, I was the town drunk in a Christmas play. That role landed me on an Effingham radio station's version of the old TV show "What's My Line?" Nobody guessed what I was doing and I won a gift certificate from Stevens' Hardware. Last year I had a small part in "Meet and Eat: There *Is* Something More." This year I **played the part** of a Pharisee in "Joy Comes in the Morning." My only line was a wicked laugh as Jesus was condemned to be crucified. The problem was that I delivered it too convincingly. Some friends had the nerve to ask if I was acting.

I guess I'm enough of a Pharisee to know something about how the role should be played. I've always had sort of a love-hate feeling toward the Pharisees. I know that we've portrayed them as the bad guys, but that's not the way they started out. We equate Pharisee with hypocrite, but their original intention was to devote themselves to the Law of God. They were students and teachers of the Law. Their name comes from a Hebrew word meaning "separated." Were they the first Separatists? If so, they're very close to our heritage as Baptists. But somewhere along the way they became confused and thought that their understanding of God was God and that their interpretation of the Law was the Law.

I've never known anyone who planned to become a hypocrite. I've never heard a child say, "When I grow up, I want to be a hypocrite." I guess it's one of the ugliest words in the English language. One of the easiest ways to start a fight is to call someone a hypocrite. I think one of the reasons we hate this word so is that each of us has a little hypocrisy and we hate that part of ourselves.

It's so easy for religious leaders to become Pharisees. We're expected to know God and to be able to tell others about him. We're called upon to give moral direction. It's so easy to slip into feeling that we have the authoritative word. We tend to forget that it's **God's** word that's final, not ours. His word judges us--we are *not* the judge.

I used to think that only those who took the Bible literally could be hypocrites. But, I've come to realize that theological orientation has little to do with it. All that's necessary is a condescending attitude toward others. Trying to keep other people straight is one of their primary activities. Pharisees seem to enjoy blowing the whistle when someone breaks the rules. They seem to look down their long noses at others (I wonder if that's how I got the part—having the nose for it?)

April 1989

The Liberating Fellowship

What did God mean when He said that it was not good for the man to be alone? Surely He had more in mind than sexual companionship. I think He was as interested in humanity developing its full potential as He was in our procreation.

Is an isolated person fully human? Or, does our humanity have to do with our relationships with one another? I recognize that my background in sociology prejudices me, but I'm inclined to think that it's only in community that we become fully human. Stories of children being abandoned at birth and raised by wolves were used to show this. They were more animal than human when they were discovered. You may be prone to discount such stories as myth. I don't know. I've never seen such a creature, but I'm slow to say that they never existed.

I do know that language is a learned skill--it's developed in the human community. What distinguishes humans from other animals? The Bible talks about the image or likeness of God. What does that mean? Surely it doesn't mean that we look like God, or He like us. Maybe it means that we *are* like God. We can share in his creativity; we can have fellowship with him and with one another.

I believe that we reach our highest potential as we develop our freedom. One of the threats that religion poses is legalism--the notion that if we *do* the right things, we will win God's approval. The truth is all we can win is man's applause and that's often hollow. God loves us unconditionally; we don't have to earn his favor.

But, I'm not sure we ever develop our freedom to its highest potential without a caring community. Only there can we receive the support and confrontation we need to become our best. Left alone, we wallow in pride or despair. I tend to be a Lone Ranger--I feel very comfortable working alone. But, I recognize that I'm at my best in fellowship with others. My best ideas are born as they spark against conflicting or supporting ones. I'm anxious for others to see my work, hopefully to benefit from it.

I don't think churches are at their best when they try to exist independently. I feel our fellowship strengthens us; we learn from one another and learn to care for one another. It's only in this context that we are truly free. We need to be free to express our unique gifts. But, how do we know what these are unless we look at ourselves in comparison with and contrast to others. The attempt to exist in isolation is akin to the essence of suicide. The community doesn't give life--only God does that! But, the community can make life richer and fuller.

Associations have been described as "churches in fellowship, on mission in their setting." I guess I like the phrase "family of churches" better. It's not as descriptive, but it's warmer. The association is the first step most churches take toward mission beyond their communities. That first step is an important one. It is the beginning of the journey out of selfishness toward service. That's a constant crusade for the Christian and the church. Our sinfulness constantly pulls us back inside ourselves. It's our fellowship that helps to liberate us.

May 1989

Church Growth and Kingdom Growth

The growth that churches experience can be classified in four types: (1) *Regeneration growth* is the addition of new Christians to a congregation. Generally, these will be children, youth, or adults. Some may be the offspring of parents active in the church. (2) *Transfer growth* is the addition of members by transfer from another church or by statement. These folks are already Christians and church members; they simply are changing their church membership. (3) *Spiritual growth* is the development of individual Christians toward Christ-likeness. (4) *Organizational growth* is the development of a congregation to serve and witness to its community and/or the world in a better way.

Donald McGavran says that churches grow in three ways: biological, transfer, and conversion (*How to Grow a Church*, Donald A. McGavran and Win Arn, Regal Books, Glendale, CA, 1973). I question separating biological and conversion growth. By biological, he refers to children of Christian parents becoming Christian. I'm not sure how this is different from conversion, except that he restricts conversion to those coming to Christ for the first time. It may be a mistake to assume that children of church members almost automatically will become Christians. Too often they do not. A conversion is still required. It may not be as radical for a ten-year-old raised in church as for an adult who has no church background, but if sin is real, conversion is still needed.

Charles Chaney and Ron Lewis list four dimensions of church growth: numerical, maturational, organic, and incarnational (*Design for Church Growth*, Broadman Press, Nashville, TN, 1977). They omit transfer growth and separate spiritual growth into maturational and incarnational. They describe the latter as "seeing both the compassion and character of Jesus manifest in the various human cultures" (Preface).

But, my point is not whose list is the best, but that ***not all church growth is Kingdom growth***. Churches grow in all four ways (no matter whose list you prefer). But the Kingdom of God is enlarged only by types 1 and 3--regeneration and spiritual growth. The transfer of membership from another church may increase one's membership but it decreases the other's and the Kingdom likely is not affected. Transfer growth may have spiritual growth involved as an element, but it is the maturation of the Christian which expands the Kingdom, not his or her place of worship and service.

Churches may need to reorganize or expand their organization to be able to minister and to reach out more effectively. I would encourage this. But, I also would point out that though this may lead to Kingdom growth, it is not Kingdom growth, in and of itself.

All church growth is significant but the most significant is that which also is Kingdom growth. Churches that grow at other churches' expense are not building the Kingdom. They may be stealing sheep, or offering shelter to sheep that feel shepherd-less.

I believe our ultimate goal is to see the Kingdom of God increase. All that we do toward church growth must be measured against this standard. We may be doing some great things to help our churches grow, but they may not amount to much finally, in the Kingdom. Or, our church may not be growing much, but we may have the kind of growth that is measured in heaven.

July 1989

How to Make Ice Cream

The last time I tried to make ice cream, I failed. The paddle froze to the sides of the can and I was stuck. The electric motor shut off and would not restart (until I had given up on the project). I was trying to make a freezer to take to our Combined Worship Service but I wound up going empty-handed. My wife took the mixture and froze it in our food freezer.

Let me tell you about a fail-safe method of making homemade ice cream--one that doesn't depend on an electric motor. I don't know much about mixing up the fixings. You'll have to talk to my Dad or my wife for that recipe. I just handle the cranking (and eating).

You start with a fifty-pound block of ice, two gunny sacks, and a double bitted axe. Put one gunny sack inside the other and half of the ice inside them both. Lay that on a hard surface and proceed to crush the ice--*with the flat side of the axe*. Keep the rest of the ice wrapped in a tarpaulin, in case you need it later.

Begin pouring a little ice into the freezer while someone turns the crank. Put in a layer of ice and a handful of salt--I forgot to tell you to get the salt. Continue this until the tub is full. Then, put the gunny sacks on top of the freezer while it's being cranked. You'll need to check every once in a while to see if more ice and salt are needed (you'll also have to fight the kids to keep them from eating the salt).

When it gets hard to crank (and the sacks are almost empty of ice), you'll need to sit on the freezer (on the sacks, of course) to hold it down. This may sound like a chilling prospect, but it gives you something to do when the cranking gets tough. Sometimes the cranker will want to trade jobs.

When you've cranked as long as you can, drain the salt water from the tub (it's better to choose somewhere you don't want grass growing). Call for the "pan, cork, and spoon." That's the pan (dish) in which the ice cream was mixed, a cork to fit the hole in the lid of the can, and a spoon with which to get the ice cream off the paddle. Then open the can carefully, so you don't get any ice or salt or dirt into the ice cream. Lift the paddle out carefully, scraping most of the ice cream back into the can (you don't have to scrape it all off or you won't have any to taste). Put the paddle into the dish (pan). If there are too many kids around, you may have to get your taste from the can--they may claim rights to the paddle. Put the cork in the hole in the lid and put the lid back on the can.

It's best if the ice cream sits a while before being eaten. So, fill the tub back up with ice and salt (here's where you may need that extra ice). When the tub's full, cover it with the gunny sacks and put it in the shade. You may want to wrap it in a tarpaulin, too.

The last time I described this process, a friend invited us out for supper. When we got there, he handed me a double bitted axe, showed me a block of ice, and asked if I knew what to do with it. I did and we made ice cream.

However, for the last several years, I have depended on my trusty (until now) White Mountain electric freezer. I'll probably stay with it despite my recent disappointment--it's hard to find a source for block ice and gunny sacks are scarcer than hen's teeth, whatever that means. Besides, it's a little awkward trying to sit on the freezer to hold it down while you're cranking!

New ways aren't always as colorful or dependable as old ones, but they've won a place in our lazy hearts.

August 1989

Salesmen and Customers

There are two kinds of people in the world--salesmen and customers. Salesmen (I really should say salespersons, but the ones I have in mind are pushy men; though I know some pushy women, too) where was I? Salespersons tend to be well-dressed, confident, outgoing, and persistent. Customers come in many varieties but can be characterized as skeptical, reserved, unsure, and impatient.

Though I sometimes find myself cast in the role of a salesman, I think of myself as a customer. I enjoy that more than trying to sell.

I must confess to a love/hate relationship with salespersons. I sometimes give salespersons a hard time. Ask my wife. Sometimes I've embarrassed her by my treatment of them. I'm not proud of that. It's just that I don't want to be a pushover and it's hard for me to say, "No." It seems to be easier to belittle than to just say, "No."

There's one cookware salesman whom I admire. He's a good salesman. He took my abuse and came back. I think he called on us three times in different locations. His pots and pans seemed to be over priced and I told him so. He told me about the health hazards of eating food cooked in aluminum and I laughed at him. But he stayed with us and eventually sold us. It's one of the best investments we've ever made. We're still using it after fifteen years.

I respect a salesperson who's sold on his or her product or service and knows how to present it. I don't mind hearing his or her pitch, even if I'm not in the market. But I resent a pushy salesperson who tries to make the sale at whatever cost.

I also resent the idea that we're salespersons of the Gospel. Jesus didn't ask us to hawk the Gospel, but to announce or proclaim it. I think there is a difference.

However, we may be able to learn from salespersons when it comes to presenting the Gospel winsomely. I'm hesitant to try to force the Gospel on persons. I suspect that's due, in part, to not liking to be backed into a corner myself.

September 1989

I've Got Vanity

It's not something I would advertise, usually. But, I got it under unusual circumstances. Some of you have noticed it already. That's why I'm not ashamed to tell you I've got vanity--vanity license plates, that is.

My daughter bought them for me last Father's Day. They read

BY GEO 14

I'm not sure of the significance of 14. My wife said it could stand for my birthday--11/4. (She said 1 also can stand for 11 in puzzles and game shows.) I thought it could stand for my half of our wedding anniversary date—February 28. Anyway, it's 14.

The Secretary of State in Illinois will allow up to seven letters and numbers on vanity plates. That's a one-time fee of $11 extra. If you want letters only, that'll cost you $75 plus $10/year.

I've never used a clergy tag on my car. There may have been times when I didn't want to be identified. I know I don't expect special treatment as a minister.

Having plates that are easily identified has its hazards. If you speed, someone may recognize you. If you're parked illegally, you may be identified. However, I consider myself a better driver than most, so I'm willing to take the risks.

Perhaps greater risks are in store if I become vain or proud. Some might suggest that it's too late to worry about that.

I want to take a healthy pride in myself and my work. But when it's unhealthy, it's destructive. Proverbs is full of warnings:

When pride comes, then comes disgrace;
but with the humble is wisdom (11:2).

George H. Davis

*Pride goes before destruction,
and a haughty spirit before a fall* (16:18).
*A man's pride will bring him low,
but he who is lowly in spirit will obtain honor* (29:23).

In the Bible, vanity refers to emptiness or hollowness. "Thou shalt not take the name of the Lord thy God in vain" means not to claim to be God's child if it's an empty claim.

The two ideas--vanity and pride--are brought together in Isaiah:
*We have heard of the pride of Moab,
how proud he was,
of his arrogance, his pride, and his insolence—
    his boasts are false* (16:6).

When our claims are false, they may be based on unhealthy pride. I hope that's not the case with BY GEO 14.

October 1989

You May Be Penalizing Your Pastor

You may be throwing an "unintentional flag" on your pastor. The problem is that, unlike football, with the Internal Revenue Service an unintentional penalty still costs him. The penalty is not assessed in yards but in dollars of tax he has to pay because of the way your church pays him.

No, I'm not advocating that your pastor shouldn't pay taxes. What I am asking is that you be aware of tax laws so that he does not have to pay *unnecessary* taxes. Now, I'm neither a tax man nor the son of a tax man (but I do have a son who's an accountant—does that count?)

If your church pays her pastor a car allowance, he may be paying taxes on money that should be handled as reimbursement for business expenses. The car allowance often is not enough to cover expenses. Under the Tax Reform Act of 1986 (as I understand it), he can deduct unreimbursed business expenses only to the extent that they exceed 2 percent of his adjusted gross income. This means that he has to swallow a big chunk before he gets any tax relief.

Ministry related expenses such as car, convention, continuing education, books, and hospitality can be handled as reimbursement for actual expenses. That's the way such things are commonly done in the business world. Jesus encouraged his followers to "be wise as serpents and innocent as doves" (Matthew 10:16b). He also warns that "the sons of this world are more shrewd in dealing with their own generation than the sons of light" (Luke 16:8b). Maybe we need to smarten up!

Your church also should be providing adequate insurance and retirement protection for her pastor. Medical insurance is almost a necessity in our society. It's one of those things that you can't afford but you can't afford to be without, either. Many young ministers shortchange their retirement because of the press of current expenses. It's hard to think about 30 or 40 years down the road when there are bills to be paid. Churches should encourage their pastors to take a longer view. This may mean that the church needs to provide more for current living expenses.

Some people have the notion that ministers don't pay taxes. I don't know where that fairy tale originated, but it's false. It's true that they can claim some of their salary for a housing allowance (as military persons can). But, it's also true that they must pay Social Security as a self-employed person. That means that for 1989 they pay 13.02% of their salary and housing into Social Security as compared to 7.51% for employees. In the end, your pastor probably pays as much taxes as others in his income bracket.

I suppose the most common problem regarding pastors' salaries is that they feel excluded from the negotiation process. Often they have good reason for feeling shut out. Budget committees frequently ask ministers to leave when they're ready to discuss their salary. I'm not sure there's a good reason for this. There needs to be some setting where the minister and a representative group can talk about his work and his needs. Some may do this with a Personnel Committee. Other denominations have Pastoral Relations Committees. I think that's a step in the right direction.

Information is available for a church considering how to pay her pastor. Come by the office and borrow the Annuity Board video. Attend a tax seminar scheduled for February 8 at Pennsylvania Avenue, Urbana.

November 1989

Don't Be Bamboozled!

During the next few days, some well-meaning but misguided persons are going to tell you that we're about to enter the last decade of the twentieth century. Don't you believe them. We're still a year away.

The 1980's aren't over until the *end* of 1990. Some thoughtless people will try to tell you they end with the beginning of 1990.

But, let's think this through carefully. What's the first year? Is it 0 or 1? Of course, it's 1. What's the last year of a decade, 9 or 10? Yes, it's 10. What's the last year of the first century, 99 or 100? You're right again, 100.

So, 1990 is the last year of the 1980's. Now, don't be confused by all the hoopla over the end of the eighties. But, speaking of hoopla, you haven't seen anything yet. Wait until 1999 when shallow thinkers try to tell us we're about to enter the 21st century. Keep in mind, that won't happen until 2001.

* * * * * * * * *

Now that we have that thorny question settled, let me tell you about a situation where my thinking was not so unclouded. Last fall I received a new bird feeder for my birthday. The old one was mounted on a wooden pole and was frequently occupied by squirrels..

I decided to get a new metal pole, complete with squirrel baffle. It worked great.

Last spring I took it down and stored it in a back room. This fall I started looking for the section of the pole I had driven into the ground so I could put the feeder up again.

George H. Davis

I walked across the area where it was supposed to be, trying to get lined up just right with the patio window. No pole. I got down on my hands and knees to examine the area more closely. Still no pole.

I looked for my stud finder, thinking that the metal pole might trip the magnet that is attracted to nails in a wall. I didn't find the stud finder.

I did find an ice pick with which I probed the area thinking that it might be just below ground level. My wife joined me in looking. Still no pole. A few rocks, but no pole.

I even tried to bamboozle my family into helping me look for it while they were here for Thanksgiving. But no luck. They were more interested in other things.

Well, last week I found the bottom section of the pole--attached to the other two sections in the back room. I remembered that the whole thing had stuck together when I put it away last spring. No wonder I hadn't found it in the back yard!

Oh well, I guess even your mind has to rest once in a while. Now, if I could just find my stud finder.

December 1989

My New, Red Harley

I doubt you've seen it yet, but I have a *new, red Harley*. It's not that I'm ashamed of it; it's just that I usually don't wear my underwear on the outside where it will be seen; most of the time, I try to cover it up.

Yes, my daughter bought me a pair of long, red Harley Davidson underwear for Christmas. The Harley logo is emblazoned on the chest and each sleeve proclaims *Harley Davidson*. My real identity is inscribed across the back—*Grandpa George*. She couldn't wait for me to open them, so I got them early. I obliged by putting them on promptly and wearing them proudly.

All this brought back memories of skipping school because I had to wear long underwear one winter day. I was mortified at the thought of having to undress for a high school PE class and have everyone know what a sissy I was. In those days it was not fashionable to wear long underwear. I guess I was born a generation too soon.

I've since come to value comfort above pride and frequently wear long drawers during the winter. Further, fashion has changed and long drawers and tops are in. I still don't feel comfortable wearing them as outerwear. Maybe I should reconsider. Would you pick a fight with someone wearing red Harleys? Or, does it take more than a Harley to make a person tough?

January 1990

More on Salesmen

I did it again! I allowed a salesman to rob me of two hours of my time. No, I didn't buy his product but I felt cheated that he could fritter away my most precious possession. I was angry at myself for allowing him to intrude in my life.

by George

I'm usually pretty adept at avoiding salesmen I don't want to see. I can turn them away or tell them I'm not interested. But this time my wife had made the appointment. I asked her what he wanted to talk with us about and she wasn't sure. Our power was off when he was supposed to call. He called back for another appointment and this time I was home. I asked him whom he represented and he mentioned an air purifier. Then he mumbled something about a forty-five dollar gift.

"Well, whatever," I thought. "For forty-five dollars I'll listen to his spiel." The young man was very courteous and I tried to be, too (sometimes that's a struggle for me). But after he left I got angrier and angrier. I felt like I'd been lied to. He had tried to sell me a *vacuum cleaner*. Of course he called it something else, but it was a vacuum cleaner. And it was overpriced.

To satisfy myself, I looked in the telephone book the next day. Sure enough; his company is listed in the Yellow Pages under vacuum cleaners. I came close to calling the company and telling them what I thought of their tactics, but I didn't have that much of my mind to spare. Then I realized how some people calling our office feel. They look in the phone book and find us listed under Churches. They call to see if we can help them or they want to talk with the pastor. When I tell them we're not a church and don't have a pastor, they're confused.

Our alternative is to be listed under Religious Organizations and I'm not sure that's a good one. Who would think to look under Religious Organizations for us? But then, who looks for us in the Yellow Pages? I don't know what's best. But, I do know I felt cheated. The knives were worth maybe twenty-five dollars, but they did have a forty-five dollar tag in the box.

From now on I'm telling salesmen that it will cost them thirty-five dollars an hour to talk to me—"How long do you want?"

February 1990

The Christian (?) Connection

Recently I received some campaign material from a group calling itself "The Christian Connection." Of course, they denied that it was campaign literature—they called it an educational leaflet. But I've learned to sniff through smoke screens; it was campaign material for this month's primary election.

If they admitted it was campaign literature, they might be in danger of losing their tax exempt status. Further, their purpose in mailing samples to churches was to get them to order and distribute this campaign material—arguably a violation of our tax exempt status.

How did I know it wasn't educational material? To start with, they didn't list all of the candidates for governor; they left Robert Marshall off. Apparently they didn't want to educate me about his candidacy. Maybe it was just an oversight, but that's a rather serious shortcoming for educational material.

I also noticed that the issues listed were stated in prejudicial language: "tax increase," "abortionists," and "unborn children." The wording clearly was slanted toward the viewpoint of one candidate and against the other two listed.

George H. Davis

Four of the seven issues listed related to abortion. I have no problem with any Christian taking a stand on this issue but I do object when he or she claims it to be *the* Christian view. Christians differ on this emotional issue. I'm not willing to infer that those who differ from my view are not really Christians and I resent the implication when it's aimed at me.

There was no mention of any Christian commitment or connection on the part of any of the candidates. I was disappointed. I had hoped for something about their religious background. But, I guess they didn't want to educate me about that either.

The leaflet clearly supports "tax rebates for parents who choose non-public schools" but it also urges me to vote my convictions. Well, I surely will.

I'm all for Christians becoming informed and active in politics. But I'm also afraid when certain issues become Christian issues. "Christian" includes a wide variety of viewpoints, some of which may be closer to the mind of Christ than mine.

March 1990

Have You Noticed?

Have you noticed that weather forecasters enjoy predicting unusual weather? Bad weather seems to turn them on. When everything's normal they get kind of down in the mouth and dull. But let a storm blow in and they perk up—their juices really start flowing.

Then what happens? Likely as not they'll go overboard. They'll call for three inches of rain or eight inches of snow with blizzard conditions or temperatures in the high nineties with high humidity. They seem never to have heard the motto, "Moderation in all things." They go hog wild.

And when their forecast does not materialize, are we disappointed? No, we're usually relieved. Maybe that's why they do it.

Have you noticed that writers tend to go overboard, too? Often they overstate the case to prove their point.

I'm told that one of the prerequisites to being a good writer is that one must feel deeply about some things. Well, how can one feel deeply and write with moderation?

But who wants to read something which has all the excitement of pabulum? If I'm going to read, I want something that's entertaining or challenging. I don't want something predictable. If it is, I'll skim it.

Have you noticed that preachers tend to deal with extremes? They don't talk about middle of the road attitudes or behavior. They deal with raw prejudice or bizarre actions.

They don't spend a lot of time telling us how good we are; instead they drag out our hidden side. They berate us for our evil thoughts; they cajole us into acting more civilized.

Wouldn't it be nice to hear the weather person say, "Tomorrow's temperature will be normal for this time of year"? Or, would you sleep through a forecast like that?

by George

Wouldn't it be nice to hear a sermon about how well we are doing? Or, would you sleep through it? How can you sleep through lies like that?

Weather forecasts always seem more ominous than the weather that actually develops. It's as if the producer had pinned this poem in the studio:

>Wetter or drier
>Be sure it's dire.

April 1990

Looking Up; Seeing God

"I will lift up mine eyes unto the hills, from whence cometh my help." So reads Psalm 121:1 in the King James Version.

The Revised Standard Version more accurately renders the second half of the verse as a question (the answer is in the next verse, which, incidentally, doesn't change much from King James):

I will lift up my eyes to the hills.
>From whence does my help come?
My help comes from the Lord,
>who made heaven and earth.

It's God, not the hills, that provides our help. That message is there in both versions, if you read far enough. But there's something about being in the hills and the woods that rejuvenates my spirit.

Our family spent a recent weekend in Pope County. Even though it rained most of the day Saturday, I enjoyed it. On Friday evening I spotted a new bird (to me). I noticed its bright red bib and got out my Peterson's Field Guide to find it. As I fingered through the pictures, I saw some possible matches but then, there it was--a rose-breasted grosbeak. While that may be a rather common migrant through our area, I don't remember having seen one before. At least, I hadn't identified it. I guess that's one thing I enjoy about the hills and woods--their endless variety. The Psalmist acknowledges that God made heaven and earth. I know so little about heaven and am only beginning to learn some things about the earth.

Our oldest son, Mark, pointed out various species of birds in our backyard a few years ago. From then on, I began watching. The richness of God's creation challenges my imagination. If he made such great variety, why do we get so intent on looking and sounding alike?

May 1990

Remembering And Being Remembered

I answered the phone last Wednesday night and heard the caller identify himself and say he was a salesman from Florissant, Missouri. Up to that point, I was not too thrilled.

But he went on to ask if I knew Billy and Claudia Mitchell. Well, I don't know if my tone changed but my attitude surely did. Billy Mitchell had been pastor of my home church while I was in college. It was he who directed my thinking toward Southern Seminary in Louisville, Kentucky when most of my peers were looking toward Southwestern in Fort Worth. Billy has been special in my family's life. Claudia is his gracious wife--his source of strength and stability. He became an Interfaith Witness consultant for the Home Mission Board and retired in Atlanta about fifteen years ago. We saw them from time to time at Home Missions week at Ridgecrest, but it had been a few years. I had heard that they had gone to St. Louis to live with her niece. Well, this salesman was the niece's husband. The last thing Claudia had told him when she knew he was headed for Champaign was to get in touch with me. And he had.

We visited on the phone and he came by the next evening and we visited some more. I enjoyed reliving memories of the Mitchells and sharing them. On Sunday I called my dad and told him of my experience. He said he felt like he'd had a visit with them just from the second-hand conversation.

Meanwhile, back home I picked up the mail on Thursday. I noticed a letter from Hazel Walker of Marlow, Oklahoma. Because we are appointed by the Home Mission Board, we sometimes get cards and letters from people we don't even know. At first glance, I put this one in that category. But I didn't have to read long to recognize we had known her as Hazel Prater. She had been treasurer of First Baptist Church in Altamont, my first full-time pastorate.

She and Mike had retired and moved to Bowie, Texas. We had visited them there and Mike had shown our kids a horned toad. Mike had died and Hazel has remarried. She saw our names in **Open Windows** and had written to Altamont to get our address.

Remembering and being remembered. Those two experiences added years to my life and, more importantly, life to my years.

June 1990

Who Really Believes The Bible?

What about the seminary professor who has devoted his professional life to studying the Bible? He has become proficient in Greek and/or Hebrew so he can read the Bible in the language in which it was written, not just from a translation. He also is able to read German or French or Spanish so that he can read commentaries and studies not available in English.

This is his full-time job. He spends several hours each day in study. He also has the opportunity to discuss the Bible with colleagues--those who have similar interests and abilities. He may challenge traditional viewpoints and open new possibilities in Biblical interpretation. That's part of his job.

We owe a great deal to such persons. They have enriched our understanding of the Bible and, more importantly, the God of the Bible. No one would claim that they are inerrant, but few would deny their love for the Bible.

Or, consider the pastor who proclaims his loyalty to the Bible. He has studied, sometimes under the tutelage of a seminary professor and sometimes on his own. He preaches messages from the Bible to his congregation.

It becomes evident that he prefers a particular approach to Biblical interpretation. It also becomes apparent that his interpretation of the Bible is the standard by which he judges others' faithfulness.

When someone proposes another view, he accuses that person of not believing the Bible. It probably would be more accurate to say that they have different interpretations of the Bible, but that wouldn't stir people to action and that's part of a preacher's job.

Which one believes the Bible? Well, I suggest that both do, imperfectly (I'm skeptical about anyone claiming perfection--even in faith). The fact that they interpret the Bible differently does not denigrate either of them. But when one starts attacking the other, that's cause for concern.

Our innate distrust of education makes us susceptible to attacks on teachers. We do well to recognize our own feelings of inadequacy and jealousy which fuel the fires of distrust of those with more training. I'm not suggesting that we worship seminary professors. Only that we treat them with the same respect due every other human being. I believe the Bible says something about doing unto others as we would have them do to us.

July 1990

How Much Help Do We Need with Reports?

Recently I received eighteen and one-half pages of instructions on how to fill out the 1990 Uniform Church Letter. They were mailed to every pastor of a Southern Baptist Church in Illinois. That's in addition to the twelve-page *Guidebook/Worksheet* and one page of instructions on "The Reporting of Missions" included In the 1990 Church Clerk's Packet.

It set me to wondering how much help we need in completing our annual reports. Have they become so complicated that we need someone to lead us through them, item by item? Are we so bored with filling out reports that we get careless and don't read simple instructions? Have statistics become so important that denominational workers' job performance is judged by what is reported?

In his new book *Effective Church Leadership*, Kennon Callahan says:

> In a number of mainline denominations there is a nervous, strident preoccupation with membership decline. Bureaucratic leaders of boards and agencies hark to the statistics each year within their particular denomination.
>
> It is most important, at this point, to note that the focus on membership is a characteristic mark of a churched culture. . . . membership becomes a mark of a "successful church." Statistics reporting membership numbers are pleasingly noted.
>
> ....

George H. Davis

By contrast, on a mission field the characteristic mark that is of predominant concern for the Christian church is salvation, not membership. On a mission field, the focus is on sharing the good news of the Kingdom and on winning persons to Christ. The central concern is helping persons to claim "Jesus is Lord" in their lives, whether they become members of a specific denominational entity or not (Harper & Row: San Francisco, 1990, pp. 23—24).

He goes on to argue that we should see ourselves as working on a mission field rather than in the churched culture of the late 1940s and the 1950s.

One of the weaknesses of our goal-oriented system is that we tie success to enlisting people. We have not developed comparable means of measuring what happens in their lives as a result of their enlistment.

I suppose I'll go on using our statistics. They are a means of measuring. But Callahan makes me wonder whether we're measuring the right thing. He kind of shakes me up. Maybe God is trying to get through to me.

August 1990

The American Redstarts

You may have thought they were sparrows, but they're a little smaller. The young and females are brownish with an almost grey head. They have a pale yellow wing bar and a yellow or orangish dab on their shoulders. Their tail is tinged with yellow on the sides and is often fanned.

Binoculars are of little help in identifying these restless insect feeders--they're always on the move. They hop and flit about from branch to branch scaring up and devouring their prey. Some have described them as butterfly-like. They belong to the wood warbler family with thin needle-pointed bills.

They are on their way south to winter in tropical America. They have provided me several minutes of relaxation and enjoyment this month. Their activity and color have brightened and cheered our back yard. At times I've spotted as many as three or four at once, but have seen few mature males. They are darker (almost black) and orange replaces the yellow.

I continue to be amazed at what's going on around me once I take time to observe. I sometimes wonder what else I'm missing.

God, help me to see people as clearly as I see birds!

September 1990

My Latest Goof Up

The phone rang.

Jo said, "We're ready to trim your books but found a spelling error. Do you want us to go ahead?"

"Is it on the cover?" I asked fearfully.

"Yes," she replied.

by George

I picked up a copy on my desk and there it was—bold as life!

"Yes," I said sheepishly, "go ahead."

Immediately I was reminded of Murphy's Law. Actually it's Jones' Law of Publishing: "Some errors will always go unnoticed until the book is in print" (Arthur Bloch, *Murphy's Law, Book Two*, Los Angeles Price/Stern/Sloan, 1980, p. 23).

We had assembled 628 copies of the annuals (including those for Central Association and ours) without noticing the streamlined spelling. I had designed almost identical covers for both books so I couldn't blame Eulonda.

One of the beauties of computers is that you can multiply your errors endlessly. You just copy one page to create another, misteaks and all! I had used the spell checker earlier on the main text but failed to do so for the covers. After all, who would misspell what he writes dozens of times a day! Oh, well; live and learn--hopefully.

One thing I've learned is that I'm prone to error. Another is that I'm intolerant of error. Now that makes a strange combination. Handling error (my own and others') is sometimes difficult. It's not easy to forgive myself or others. How could I be so careless?

One test of a sense of humor is being able to laugh at yourself. It takes no special grace to laugh at others; in fact, it may be cruel to do so. But I believe it's a sign of health when a person can laugh at his or her own stupidity. You may think it's irresponsible, but I suggest that we should not take ourselves too seriously. If we expect perfection, we're doomed for disappointment.

I remember when I tried to overhaul my VW bug and couldn't get it running right. Finally I took it to Nile Deputy in Mt. Carmel. He opened the back, took a quick look and asked. "Do you have your spark plug wires crossed?"

I shrugged my shoulders and watched while he switched the wires and started it up. It purred like a kitten.

"What do I owe you?" I asked sheepishly (I seem to be in that mode rather frequently, don't I?).

"A cup of coffee," he replied, "and I promise not to tell anybody, until I see them."

He was as good as his word. When we got to the coffee shop, he asked a friend. "What do you think of a preacher, who thinks he's a mechanic, who drives from Fairfield to Mt. Carmel to get his spark plug wires uncrossed?"

Well, in both cases the amateur was separated from the professionals. Try as I may, there are many fields in which I am still very much an amateur. The sooner I make peace with that, the better—for all of us.

November 1990

The Lonely Lamb

My name is Rachel; it means "ewe." I am six months old; I was born just before Passover, last spring.

Though I'm really quite grown up, I've noticed some strange things happening tonight. There seemed to be some commotion followed by singing. It was not the kind of song I'm used to hearing from the shepherd. I know his songs and this one was different; it almost had a heavenly tone about it. Then most of the shepherds left, as if they were on a mission.

Oh, they left young Joshua here and I'm not afraid! I *am* nearly half grown and mother *is* nearby should I need her. We're bedded down with other flocks in a sheepfold just outside David's town—Bethlehem. I'm not afraid because I know I'm well cared for. It's just that I'm—I guess the word is—lonely.

Usually, when I can't sleep, I make my way over to the shepherd and he comforts me, but tonight he's gone. They said something about going to look for the Messiah. They sounded excited!

I know about Messiah. The shepherd says Isaiah described him as a *lamb*. I've heard some of the male lambs talking about being the Passover lamb. It must be a great honor in be chosen—a year-old male, without blemish. They all try to be especially careful not to fall into a crevice and break a leg or get caught by a wild dog and be disqualified by the scars. They try to imagine what it would be like to be offered as a sacrifice and to have their blood smeared on the doorway, symbolizing God's protection. Then they'd nourish the family as they gathered to rehearse the blessings of God through the years. Oh sure, some of the young lambs don't think that's such a great honor; they'd rather live!

One of the shepherd's favorite stories is about some poor folks who bought one little ewe lamb and raised it as one of the family. One day their rich neighbor had company and, instead of killing a lamb from his flock, he stole their pet lamb and fed it to his guest. When my shepherd tells the story, he really gets riled; I can almost see the hair on the back of his neck bristle. He says that's the way King David reacted when he heard that story for the first time.

The shepherd says that the prophet said that Messiah would die, like a lamb, and that his death would be for others. I'm not sure I understand all that. I do remember the shepherd telling about Abraham going to sacrifice with Isaac. The boy thought they had forgotten the lamb but his father said, "God himself will provide the lamb for a burnt offering, my son." Then he found a ram and offered him in place of his son. I'm not sure I understand that, either, but I know Isaac was glad for the ram.

I wonder how Messiah will feel about being God's lamb. Will he ever feel sad and lonely?

December 1990

Mixed Messages and Oxymora

Have I been watching too much television this winter, or is it really getting worse? It seems like almost every show finds a way to say that casual sexual intimacy is natural. It's become a social or recreational pastime for TV couples.

I'm not talking about the soaps; I seldom see any of them. I'm talking about prime time shows. Oh, I know that we have "graduated" to soaps during prime time, but I don't watch them either. I tend to prefer action shows but I'd rather most of that took place somewhere other than the bedroom.

by George

With our growing concern over sexually transmitted diseases it seems to me that we're getting mixed messages. Commercials and public service announcements warn us about these dangers while, during the program, couples engage in activities we're warned against.

It's almost like telling a person who's drinking to "know when to say when." The first casualty of alcohol is the ability to think clearly. How can one be expected to exercise sound judgment when that is impaired?

And, speaking of oxymora (that's the plural of oxymoron)—Webster defines them as "a combination of contradictory or incongruous words." I won't stoop to "government intelligence" or "city worker." Rather, let me propose "Baptist doctrine." It used to be that Baptists generally agreed on some basic principles. Oh, we've always had our disagreements. Some wag said, "Show me two Baptists and I'll show you three opinions."

I cherish the right to disagree over non-essentials without breaking fellowship. But then, who's going to decide what's not essential?

Until the last few years Baptists were known for their staunch support for the doctrine of the priesthood of the believer. One of its tenets is that every believer has the right to read and interpret the Bible for him or herself, without someone telling him or her what it means.

In 1988 leaders of the Southern Baptist Convention felt the need to affirm pastoral authority at the expense of the priesthood of the believer. It makes me wonder whether we should quit acting as if there were such a thing as Baptist doctrine. Do we have any commonly held, essential teachings? Or, are most of our understandings subject to the whim of the moment? Are we willing to sacrifice doctrine on the altar of pragmatism? Is growing churches more important than being the church?

January 1991

"On the Other Hand"

Caught in the currents of cultural and political change, Tevye (in "Fiddler on the Roof") frequently found himself saying, "On the other hand," as he struggled to understand the whole situation. When his middle daughter married a gentile, he pondered, "Can I deny everything I believe in? On the other hand, how can I deny my own daughter?"

Some people have trouble living with ambiguity. For them everything is either black or white; there are no shades of gray. I'm not sure why this is so. Maybe it's a personality trait or a predisposition. Some can argue either side of an issue; others see only one side.

T. W. Hunt, writing about the need for faith, says, "Uncertainty is the enemy of faith" (*The Doctrine of Prayer*, Nashville: Convention Press, 1986, p. 68). Well, for me, it's one of the **reasons for** faith. If you are certain of something, you don't need faith. I know that he may mean that faith leads to certainty but I'm haunted by the fact that some of the Jewish leaders of Jesus' day were certain they were Abraham's children; He called them sons of the devil.

George H. Davis

You may not know how to take this column. I may seem to express conflicting opinions at times. Well, I guess that's who I am. I don't intend for this to be a final word—only God has that and He hasn't spoken it yet. I intend for these to be thoughts in passing. If you don't agree, that's ok. I guess what I want is for us to think. We don't have to agree but to refuse to think would be unthinkable!

I know some people are uncomfortable with ambiguity. They want everything nailed down. They'll even quote 1 Corinthians 14:8: "If the trumpet gives an uncertain sound, who will get ready for battle?"

But I see ambiguity in the Bible. There are two accounts of David numbering the Israelites. In 2 Samuel 24 we read that the LORD moved David to count the people. It's Satan who moves him in I Chronicles 21. I can live with both accounts without trying to explain them away. God seems to be telling us that when we take too much delight in our strength, we're in trouble.

I recognize that my personality may make ambiguity palatable while to others it is disgusting. That doesn't mean that either of us is wrong. It means we're different. We're both members of His body, created by His hand. Both are equally valued by Him.

Lord, help me to remember that

February 1991

The Search for an Ideal Family

I'm struck by the fact that I know very few ideal families. I've spent much of my life in and around churches but I'd be hard pressed to name a family that approaches perfection.

I know a lot of ministers and most come from families that fall considerably short of the ideal. How can families, which contain such obvious flaws, nurture children who become ministers? Well, I suppose the short answer is that there are no other kinds of families.

But there's also a longer answer—we are what we are not just because of our past but also because of our vision of the future. Anthony Campolo points out that some oppose the claims of behaviorism:

These social scientists believe that human beings are "deciding" creatures. They believe that we *will* our behavior and are responsible for what we do. They view the task of sociology and psychology as the defining of the social conditions that provide the setting for social action. Social action theorists do not deny that the psychological makeup of the actors and the social circumstances in which they are compelled to act limit the options available to human beings. However, these realities only provide the limits to human behavior. According to the social action theorists, they do not *determine* which of the options actually will be chosen by the actors. Given the makeup of a person in alternatives presented by the social setting, there may be a very limited number of choices available. Nevertheless, there are alternatives, and each person is required to decide from among the options that exist (*A Reasonable Faith: Responding to Secularism*, Waco: Word, 1983, p. 74).

Furthermore, Campolo asserts, "what we envision and hope for impinges on what we are in the present so as to modify our behavior in seemingly unexpected ways" (*ibid.*, p. 76). He notes Victor Frankl's studies of persons in Nazi concentration camps during World War II. "The major difference between those who survived and those who did not was in their respective views of the future.... The hope for the future conditioned their ability to deal with the present." Campolo concludes, "humans have the ability to imagine what the future might be" (*ibid.*, p. 77).

So, instead of just searching our past for what makes us tick, maybe we need to work on our vision of the future.

March 1991

Driving Like a Pharisee

Lord, I'm thankful that I don't drive like other people do! I don't speed; I wear my seat belt; I almost always signal to turn.

But, Lord, have you noticed some of these ~~idiots~~ drivers? They act like the speed limit hasn't been invented. They can't wait for a green light. They stop astraddle the cross walk. Lord, you wouldn't believe some of the things they do!

Why, Lord, the other day some idiot didn't think I was passing a truck fast enough so he tried to cut in ahead of me. But I showed him. I cut him off.

What, Lord? What's that you say?... Why do I let other drivers get my goat? Is that what you asked?

I don't know, Lord. What should I do?

Oh! "Just drive safely regardless of how others drive," is that it?

But, Lord, sometimes they make me so mad. Somebody should teach them a lesson!

Oh, that's not my job, huh?

Well, Lord, the police aren't always around when you need them. Somebody should report these idiots.

Oh! You've seen me drive in an idiotic manner, too? Well, maybe once or twice. "What about when…?"

OK. OK. I get the point. You don't have to tell everybody.

So you want me, in my driving as in living, to be true to you and to myself and not to worry that someone else may not be following the rules as carefully as I am? Is that it?

Lord, help me to keep my eyes on you and on the road and not to worry about whether others are competing fairly.

What? "Who said this was a race?"

Well, Lord, I just thought…

April 1991

George H. Davis

A Statement about the Layoff of Campus Ministers

I was shocked by the decision to lay off two campus ministers—one being David Russell at Illinois State University in Normal and at Illinois Wesleyan University in Normal. I have heard the rationale for it but I'm still struggling with my response.

Lyle Schaller writes about several factors that have changed since the late 1950s to make this a different world in which to minister. He identifies one of these factors:

> In the 1950-68 era churches were serving in a society marked by rapidly expanding resources. The pie was growing every year and thus it was relatively easy not only to give everyone a larger slice every year, but also to share a piece of that economic pie with newcomers. From 1969 to 1987 the national economic pie has remained about the same size, after allowing for the impact of inflation, and that has made it more difficult to allocate resources among competing and expanding demands (*It's a Different World*, Nashville: Abingdon Press, 1987, p. 30).

Churches and denominations added staff and programs rather dramatically during the 1950s and 60s. Now cuts are being made.

I can understand the short-term financial benefit of the decision. I recognize that the cost of salaries and benefits is increasing rather rapidly. I know that it is the churches who provide the money for Illinois Baptist State Association. So it makes sense to keep all those staff persons working with the churches.

However, I question whether we should make such decisions on the basis of where we get the money or on where there'll be the least protest over layoffs. It seems to me that we must be involved in some ministries whether or not they pay off in the short term. I see campus ministry as one of these areas. It was through the work of a Baptist Student Union that I became serious about following Christ and felt a subsequent call to ministry.

There's another problem I have with the layoffs. They increase the percentage of our total IBSA staff in the state office and reduce the percentage working out on the field. That is contrary to the overwhelming needs in our society and the direction that planners are pointing. For the most part, our state staff trains those persons working with the people of Illinois—they are at least one step removed from the deepest needs of our society. Campus ministers and some others are working directly with these people. We need more work directly with students and other groups, not less.

May 1991

"You Don't have to Follow the Leader When He Goes Wrong!"

On our way to the Southern Baptist Convention, Leona and I spent the night in Huntsville, Alabama with my brother, John, and his wife, Agnes. We had talked of driving only one car to Atlanta but couldn't get all our luggage into one, so we took both. John and I enjoyed visiting and so, I suppose, did Agnes and Leona.

by George

As we neared Atlanta, the ladies decided that the men should drive. We stopped at a rest area and got directions to our hotel. John took them and led the way--each of us picked up a map. As we proceeded, Leona thought John missed a turn. I followed him but she said to me, "You don't have to follow the leader when he goes wrong!" "You do if he's your brother," I declared.

I told that story at Curt Bier's installation as pastor at Calvary Baptist Church in Monticello. Then I pledged that I'd think of him and treat him as a brother.

One of the tragedies in the current crisis in our Convention is that we too often think of each other as either "one of us" or "one of them." We begin to try to size each other up by the way we look, the way we talk, or where we went to school. Sometimes we go by how the person votes.

We're apt to try to cram each other into pigeonholes rather than to allow each one to be a person. I don't mind telling you how I feel, but I do resent being pushed into a cramped space full of pigeon droppings. Most of our classifications amount to about that. We reserve them for people with whom we disagree and don't understand.

It's harder to pigeonhole someone you know on a face to face basis. They tend to defy classification. They may fit your definition at one point but not another. I guess that's one reason why we have better fellowship among the pastors and churches in an association. We may differ on theology but still respect one another. That's not to say that theology doesn't matter but perhaps the real faith is that by which we live, not what we spout!

If I think of you as my brother, I'll give you the benefit of the doubt, even if I think you've missed a turn!

June 1991

Churches in Association

"Independent, Bible Believing"—that's what the church ad said. The more I thought about it, the more I was convinced I had just read a contradiction, an oxymoron, if you please.

As I understand the Bible, a church is absolutely **dependent** on God. Its members also are ***inter*dependent** on one another. Churches also are interdependent.

Churches live in relationship to other churches. There's no way out of that situation. We can ignore others and pretend to live in isolation, but churches are in association with one another. We do have some say about the *quality* of that association.

We can compete with each other. I remember a community in southern Illinois where the competition for members seemed severe. The pastor from one church would meet a competing pastor on his way to visit a prospective family. There was intense pressure to get there first with the best offer!

Competition may not be all bad. At least it's a recognition that we're in the same business.

We can complement each other. In our area, there's so much room for growth that competition hardly enters the picture—at least if we keep our focus on unchurched persons rather than only on Baptists moving into town. We can focus on our strengths and minister out of them, giving our blessing to those who choose to affiliate with another congregation.

Churches can no more exist independently of one another than can Christians. We recognize the need each individual has for fellowship, encouragement, and guidance. Of course there are unparalleled values in private devotion, but that does not take the place of public worship. Christians need other Christians.

It's the same with churches. We cannot afford to ignore one another. If we do so, we penalize ourselves. We go our way, blissfully ignorant of the wealth that fellowship with Christians from other churches can offer. We, too, may have something for them.

If our only concern is what we will get out of a relationship, we need to recognize that attitude as antithetical to Christianity. It's also a spirit that's willing to use others for selfish ends.

July 1991

Will the Circle Be Unbroken?

Denise Gardner grew up in Alabama with Barbara Joiner as her Acteen leader. As a teenager she was involved in ministry to migrant families, persons Joiner has since identified as "invisible" people. Denise has carried that memory with her into adulthood—though some would argue that Denise has never grown up!

She's married now, has four children and a busy life. She teaches a Sunday School class for high schoolers, is an Acteen leader, and will become youth director in her church this fall.

Denise moved to the Joliet area in 1980 (after serving as a summer missionary and a church youth worker there) and began ministering to migrants in that area. A few years ago, she and her family moved to LeRoy. She learned that migrants worked in our area and began pushing for a ministry here.

Through her efforts more than fifty people from at least thirteen churches have been enlisted and an effective ministry conducted this summer.

As I observed some of our teenagers that were involved in the ministry, I wondered if one of them would catch and carry the burden of ministry to "invisible" people into adulthood. Migrant workers may not be around forever; they may be replaced by machines. But "invisible" people are likely to be here as long as we are preoccupied with ourselves and our programs.

The old country gospel song asked whether the circle would be complete in heaven. I wonder if the cycle of inspiration for ministry will be complete. I'd hate to see it fizzle.

Such motivation usually is caught from a charismatic leader. Denise has that kind of inspiration and has become that kind of person. I wonder who's catching her dis-ease (with the status quo). Who'll keep goading us to reach out to people who will not ask for help but need our love?

There's a crude proverb in the apocryphal book of Sirach:

by George

If you blow in a spark, it will glow;
If you spit on it, it will be put out;
    and both come out of your mouth (28:12).
What's coming out of your mouth?

August 1991

How Important Are Church Letters?

The Uniform Church Letter is a form each Southern Baptist church is expected to fill out every year. It's our primary source of information about church size and gifts. It's the best statistical source we have but its accuracy depends on a common understanding of how reports are to be made.

I've become increasingly concerned that on the associational and state convention levels we've made UCLs essential to participation. Our associational constitution says that failure "*to send a Uniform Church Letter*, messengers, or financial contribution for three (3) consecutive years (italics mine)" is one ground for dismissal from the Association. The state convention's constitution calls for submission of a church letter at least every other year.

Each of these requirements raises submission of a UCL to a level above what's intended. Is our purpose to get an annual report or to work together on mission? It's great to receive a report of work done but doing the work is more important than filing a report. We seem to have elevated reporting to a required activity.

I like reports. They tell us where we've been and where we're headed. But I dislike confusing our priorities. Our purpose is not to generate reports but to serve God together. When reports become essential to our fellowship, we've confused our purposes.

I suspect that one reason we're so anxious to get complete reports is that we've discovered how to grow by reporting. Incomplete reports will not show numerical growth—complete reports may! There are some dangers in worshipping at the altar of numerical growth. One is that we forget there are other measures of faithfulness.

September 1991

A Letter from the Past (with Pictures)

I thought I had lost touch with Marguerite. It seemed like it had been a few years since we heard from her, until I received a letter earlier this month. It stirred up a lot of memories.

Marguerite Wooldridge has been an important person in my life. My mother died when I was eight and she came to help Dad care for me and my three younger brothers. Dad remarried after about a year and a half, but Marguerite has remained a family friend.

George H. Davis

She later went to work at the Baptist Children's Home in Carmi. When their director, Wade East, moved to Texas, he asked Marguerite to come to work there. Now she's in a retirement home in El Paso.

She had sent the letter to my folks, asking them to forward it to me. I guess she had lost my address in the move.

She sent some pictures of us boys, taken when we were about 10, 8, 6, and 4—sometime after Mom's death and before Dad's remarriage. We were splendidly attired in our knickers and hats. Oh, Don's long underwear is showing above his stockings and John is struggling with a shirt collar that's too tight, but we're family! Don now lives in Tennessee, John in Alabama, and Dick in Arizona but we're probably closer now than we've ever been.

The four of us and our wives plan to get together again next summer. We're going to New Hampshire, near where Mom grew up. She came to Urbana to attend the University of Illinois, staying with an uncle who taught engineering here. She married and began raising her family here. I think I remember a couple of trips to New Hampshire as a child. I also took my children out there several years ago. Then, Mom's sister and one of her daughters came to visit us a few years ago.

Maybe it's getting in touch with our roots. There have been many influences for good in my life and I want to understand and appreciate each one. Marguerite certainly is high on that list. She visited us when our children were at home. They were amused to meet "Dad's baby sitter."

If Robert Fulghum is right and the really important things are learned early in life, then Marguerite was one of my builders. Long before I heard of kindergarten, she was teaching me.

October 1991

A Conversation with God

God; this is George Davis.

What's that? Oh. Yes, the one who's director of missions in east central Illinois.

Oh? You've been hearing a lot about me lately? How's that?

Oh. Yes, I've gotten the message that Girls in Action, Acteens, and Baptist Women's groups have been praying for me. I've received 264 birthday cards from them, but who's counting?

Oh. Yeah? You say that's only a fraction of those who've prayed for me, my family, and my work? Kind of like an iceberg, huh?

Well, it's been a special experience to hear from so many. Some have written special messages. Some have told me about themselves. I've heard from a few I knew but I now feel like I have hundreds of new friends. One fifteen-year-old girl wrote that it sounded like I already had enough wisdom but that she'd pray for me anyway.

What? She told you that, too? Oh.

And you said what? Oh. Well, I'm glad she went ahead and prayed, too. One never gets too much wisdom.

What? "Not a chance"? Is that what you said?

by George

Let's talk about something else. One little girl sent me a quarter wrapped in cellophane. A ninety-year-old lady sent me a check, suggesting I buy myself a birthday present.

Lord, it's been exciting and moving to open the cards and read the messages. It's staggering to think of the hundreds of girls and women across the country who are praying for me.

You say, "The women pray for missions and the men plan the budget"? Yes, I've heard that, too. I did hear from a few RAs. I guess they're just not that big on writing.

Oh? They did pray, huh?

Well, there's no telling what kind of a mess I might have gotten into without the prayers of all these folks.

Oh? You say that's what you thought, too?

November 1991

Birthday Letter

Here is one of the 365 birthday cards and letters I have received. Will you join in praying for this girl and for me as I seek appropriate responses?

by George

Dear george

My name is _____ . I am eleven years old. My birthday is August 12. I like helping people too. I am praying for you. will you write me back and will you be my pen pal. I want to know will you pray for me, daddy, mom, and my two brothers because we are split up. My daddy is in prison. well my mom is at home but I don't get to see her much. one of my brother's is with Grandma and the other brother is with a freind. and I am with Grandmother. let's be freinds....

December 1991

Coming Home—Going Home

Everyone wants to be at home for Christmas but sometimes we have difficulty deciding where home is. Is it where we are living now or where we were raised? And if we're looking toward our ancestral home, which ancestors?

We enjoyed the best of both worlds over the holidays. All our children and grandchildren were at our home Christmas Eve. Two of the grandchildren stayed until Sunday.

We went to Patoka for dinner with the larger Davis family on the Sunday following Christmas. That afternoon, the five boys and their families honored their parents with a reception celebrating their fiftieth wedding anniversary.

It was a memorable afternoon seeing old friends and meeting new ones. Dale Wyatt from Newton and his family were there. Our families used to raise Hereford

George H. Davis

cattle; he still does. I learned that he had been honored as an exhibitor at the Illinois State Fair for fifty consecutive years.

Someone told me that a history of Marion County was being published and they thought it would be incomplete without an article on the Davis family. Well, you can bet that I paid attention to him. Wheels started churning in my head and before the afternoon was over I was checking out ideas.

When I returned to Champaign, I dug into some material I had gathered. I discovered that when my father retired in 1982, it was the first time in at least 110 years that a Davis had not been farming southwest of Patoka. My great-grandfather, grandfather, and father all farmed the same land! But my father and stepmother are the last of the Davis clan living in Patoka.

Though I've experienced some sadness about that, I'm also buoyed by the knowledge that we're carrying on family traditions in new locations. I guess anniversaries are times for remembering and celebrating—turning loose and taking hold.

The poet wrote, "Change and decay in all around I see." But change and decay are not necessarily synonymous. Not all change leads to deterioration. Sometimes change may bring blessing. We still need to finish the rhyme, "O Thou who changest not, abide with me!"

January 1992

Things Don't Stay the Way I Remember Them

"I used to have a pair of heavy—maybe wool—socks. They were gray with maybe red or orange trim around the top. Do you know where they are?" I asked my wife.

She couldn't remember them. But the next day one of them showed up on our bed.

"Where did you find it and where's the other one?" I asked.

"It was in the rag bag," she replied. She didn't know about the other one but surmised that I had worn holes in the toes and thrown them away.

I had supposed that one of the boys borrowed them. I wasn't upset about that for they left a few shirts, trousers, and sweaters they had outgrown.

Then I got to figuring how long it had been since I had seen those socks. It could have been as much as twenty-five years. I think I bought them for hunting and I haven't hunted since 1969.

Then I got to wondering what else had slipped away while I wasn't looking. I remembered a recent Sunday afternoon. I had been staying with the folks for a few days to help them get stabilized. While they were napping I walked down the road toward "the other place." That's a home place located one-half mile west of the folks' home. I lived there as a youngster. When Grandpa and Grandma Davis moved to town, we moved into their house and from time to time "hired hands" lived at "the other place."

by George

As I walked and remembered, I cried. Things had changed radically. Most of the neighbors were gone and so was "the other place." Nothing remained to show a family had lived there. Added to that was the loneliness and heaviness I was feeling.

I wondered too, if we're not looking for long-discarded socks at church. Do we recognize when we've worn something out and go on to new ways or do we fret over the way it used to be?

Then I remembered these lines from James Russell Lowell:
New occasions teach new duties; Time makes ancient good uncouth;
They must upward still, and onward, who would keep abreast of Truth;
Lo, before us gleam her camp-fires! We ourselves must Pilgrims be,
Launch our Mayflower, and steer boldly through the desperate winter sea,
Nor attempt the Future's portal with the Past's blood-rusted key.

Then I remembered that this kind of poetry no longer appeals to moderns and I wept again.

February 1992

EDUCATION CUTS DON'T HEAL!

I saw this bumper sticker a few weeks ago and my immediate reaction was, "That's clever." However, as I mulled over the message, I was troubled.

I know that school districts and universities across the state and country are facing mounting financial problems with faltering government support. But the sticker seemed to be saying that education should be immune to budget cuts.

That's what bothered me. I asked myself, "Is education an ultimate value, or does its worth derive from its service to something more basic? Do we want education for its own sake, or does it serve more basic societal goals?"

As these questions rumbled through my mind, I decided that when you have anything for its own sake, you're making it an ultimate value—a god, if you please. At its best, education glorifies God; it does not seek to replace him. I recognize that publicly-funded education cannot be sectarian. It must not favor one religion over another or over none. But it can serve broadly-based societal goals.

Another question, related to education, is the nature of the subject. What is education? There seems to be a rather deep division. Some think it is giving people right answers. Others see it as teaching them how to solve problems. Those who favor indoctrination want correct responses. Those who lean toward skills development trust people to come up with workable solutions, which may differ from current wisdom.

Robin Williams, as John Keating in "Dead Poets Society," says, "I always thought the idea of education was to learn to think for yourself."

"At these boys age? Not on your life! Tradition, John. Discipline. Prepare them for college and the rest will take care of itself," replies Dr. Nolan, principal of Welton Academy, a preparatory school for boys.

Another way to see the problem is to ask whether solutions are to be found in the past or in the future. Admittedly, we cannot ignore our history, but some of the

George H. Davis

answers we've come up with are no longer working. We need some new approaches and I doubt we'll come up with them in an indoctrination approach to education. I'd rather teach a person to think and question and trust him or her to come up with a solution.

"I stand on my desk," Mr. Keating said, "to remind myself that we must constantly look at things in a different way. You see, the world looks very different from up here.... Just when you think you know something, you have to look at it in another way" (Touchstone Pictures, a Peter Weir film, written by Tom Schulman).

March 1992

The Word of God—Bigger Than You Imagine?

When we use the phrase "the Word of God", we're usually thinking of the Bible. However, the Word of God is much more. I know that neo-orthodox theologians have been widely maligned by evangelicals, but one of the best, Karl Barth has the strongest doctrine of the Word of God I've read.

Barth begins by pointing out that first and foremost, there is the revealed Word. John's Gospel opens with "In the beginning was the Word, and the Word was with God, and the Word was God" (1:1 NRSV). He certainly was not referring to the Bible but to Jesus, the Christ. He continues:

> He was in the beginning with God. All things came into being through Him, and without Him not one thing came into being....
>
> He was in the world, and the world came into being through him; yet the world did not know Him....
>
> And the Word became flesh and lived among us, and we have seen His glory, the glory as of a father's only son, full of grace and truth (1:2-3, 10, 14).

According to Barth, God is known only in his revelation—"Through God alone can God be known." He goes on to say that revelation is mediated to us through Holy Scripture—the Written Word. As Scripture bears witness to God's grace in Jesus, it is the Word of God. Then there's the third step—the Spoken Word. As we witness to God's grace in Christ and as the Holy Spirit brings our witness to life, it becomes God's Word.

I remember how I struggled with Barth. I found him hard to read but exciting. His theology rang true. I also remember the circumstances in which I discovered Barth. I was ready to graduate from seminary but failed one class my last semester, leaving me three hours short. To say that I was disappointed would be an understatement. But I commuted to the campus during the summer, a year later. Fortunately, I had completed my required courses and could pick up any combination which would add up to three hours. I took a course on the theology of Barth and another one. I found his *Church Dogmatics* to be challenging expositions of Scripture.

What had been a depressing experience and a chance encounter became a source of excitement. Now, when I hear shallow references to "the Word of God," I think of how much more there is. When I hear disparaging remarks about so-called liberal or neo-orthodox theologians, I recoil. I remember that Barth felt he was correcting the liberal theology of his day.

Another outcome of that frustrating, failing experience was that I graduated during the Southern Baptist Convention. The 1959 Convention was meeting in Louisville, Kentucky in honor of the Seminary's 100th anniversary. Though I could have graduated in the Winter of 1958, I chose to wait until Spring. Then, in Freedom Hall on the Kentucky State Fairgrounds, during the meeting of the Convention, I received my diploma.

April 1992

Law and Order?

It seems strange that law and order would be such a popular campaign issue when so many of us deliberately ignore laws and some even buy devices to avoid being caught. Why is it that traffic laws are made to be broken but laws protecting property must be strictly enforced?

I deplore lawlessness and disregard for persons. But I'd like to include all laws and all persons. I cannot pretend that I've never disobeyed any law. I've already been too confessional for that. And it's hard to claim absolute honesty—hypocrisy is so sneaky.

But I'm bothered by our double standards. You can't drive long without being aware that a large number of drivers have chosen to break speed limits. I suspect that there's little difference between Christians and non-Christians here. Both speed.

I'm not sure what our rationale is—we're careful drivers; we're in a hurry; the limits are for those out of control. None of these reasons work. It's always risky to place ourselves above or beyond the law.

Laws (even traffic laws) were made for our benefit. We can hardly claim it's of no consequence if we exceed speed limits. Look at the outrageous cost in human lives because of careless driving. Speed is often the culprit.

Have you heard this definition? "What you do and I don't do is sin." I guess that applies to crime, too. We've made some law breaking acceptable. Maybe we need a keener conscience.

May 1992

The Motherhood of God

One of Jesus' favorite ways to refer to God was as Father, but it certainly wasn't the only way He thought of Him. Do you remember how He expressed His grief over Jerusalem?

> Jerusalem, Jerusalem, the city that kills the prophets and stones those who are sent to it! How often have I desired to gather your children together as a hen gathers her brood under her wings, and you were not willing! (Matthew 23:37 and Luke 13:34 NRSV).

As he describes his and God's love for Israel, he likens it to that of a mother hen.

Isaiah has passages which focus on the feminine characteristics of God:

But Zion said. "The LORD has forsaken me,
    my Lord has forgotten me."
Can a woman forget her nursing child,
    or show no compassion for the child of her womb?
Even these may forget,
    yet I will not forget you (49:14-15).

and

You shall nurse and be carried on her arm,
    and dandled on her knees.
As a mother comforts her child,
    so I will comfort you;
    you shall be comforted in Jerusalem (66:12b-13).

A passage in Hosea has sometimes been interpreted from a father's perspective, but it may make more sense from a mother's:

When Israel was a child, I loved him,
    and out of Egypt I called my son.
The more I called them,
    the more they went from me;
they kept sacrificing to Baals,
    and offering incense to idols.
Yet it was I who taught Ephraim to walk,
    I took them up in my arms;
    but they did not know that I healed them.
I led them with cords of human kindness,
    with bands of love.
I was to them like those
    who lift infants to their cheeks.
I bent down to them and fed them (11:1-4).

Wherever you look in the Bible, you'll find a God with the tenderness of a mother as well as the strength of a father.

June 1992

The Biggest Room

Where's the biggest room in your church?

As you ponder your response, let me suggest that it's the room for improvement.

I don't mean to say that you're not doing anything right but that there's always room for improvement (I almost said Jello). When we think we're about as good as we can be, we're in trouble. The inner circle of disciples (Peter, James, and John) wanted to pitch three tents on the mount of Transfiguration. "It just doesn't get any better than this," they seemed to be saying as they eavesdropped on the conversation between Moses, Elijah, and Jesus. However, Jesus led them back into the valley of human need. He seemed to be saying that worship without ministry is short-circuited.

We recognize the need for development and improvement in almost every other area of our life but sometimes resist change at church. How do I know this? By observing...myself. I sometimes find change painful.

No, I don't believe all change is good. But it is inevitable. Maybe the most we can hope for is to plan for and try to manage change.

"Build a better mouse trap and the world will beat a path to your door." Some churches are adopting this attitude. They're different. They stand out from the crowd.

No, I don't believe that drawing members from other congregations constitutes real kingdom growth (though it may result in individual growth). I think we must focus on the unchurched population.

Some are bold enough to ask unchurched people, "If you ever went to church, what kind of church would it be?" and then they start a church to meet these needs. This may be difficult to do in an already established congregation.

Some object that the Bible is our pattern for church. We shouldn't try to make the church fit people's expectations but God's. Well, if people aren't involved in church, there's little chance of them getting acquainted with the Bible or God.

One of our weakest senses is the imagination. One reason for that is lack of use. We don't encourage creative thinking; we reward party line thinking. Teachers of children have recognized that the use of coloring books may inhibit creative development. It may be better to give them a blank page.

Yes, some will argue that children need to learn to "color between the lines." I respond that there's always plenty of pressure to conform.

July 1992

On Golden Pond

Three of my brothers and their wives and my wife and I spent a week in New Hampshire last month. We stayed near Ashland-near Squam Lake, where the movie "On Golden Pond" was filmed. Of course, we took the tour of the lake and saw the cabin, Purgatory Bay, and the loons.

The film is about an elderly couple going back to their summer home. It deals with the aging process and its problems. Their daughter and grandson also figure into the story. It features Henry Fonda, Kathryn Hepburn, and Jane Fonda.

One of the first things we learned on the tour was that there is no Golden Pond; it was simply named that in the movie. However, because of the movie's popularity, a few tourist attractions were renamed. We ate at "The Common Man," a restaurant in Ashland where, according to local legend, the Fondas were told they'd have to wait an hour.

George H. Davis

We were in New Hampshire because that's where our mother had grown up. She came to Urbana to attend the University of Illinois because her uncle taught engineering here. She and Dad met and married as students here. They moved back to Dad's home in south central Illinois and began farming and raising a crop of boys. We were 8, 6, 4, and 1 year old when Mom died.

We went back to her home area to recapture some of the feeling of the people and places where she was raised. One of our cousins hosted a family reunion while we were there and we got to meet relatives we knew only by name. I visited with Jim Dinsmore. He's a retired professor of psychology at Indiana University. His father had married a sister of our Grandmother Moore and worked for Monsanto in St. Louis. He has a cabin on nearby Lake Winnipesaukee where he spends a few weeks every summer. I remembered visiting their family in Webster Groves as a child.

We saw the normal tourist attractions-the Old Man in the Mountain and the Flume at Franconia Notch. In visiting my father at home last week, I found old, framed photographs of those places. Evidently, my mother had brought them to remind her of the beloved mountains. Several years ago, her sister told me that Mom got homesick for the mountains here on the prairies of Illinois. Maybe that's part of the reason that mountains hold such a fascination for me. We saw Mt. Washington but didn't attempt to climb it.

It was a really good week. We all got along reasonably well and even had some experiences which we'll be reliving for a long time. Maybe one of the best things that happened was that we had the chance to visit with each other and exchange memories.

Maybe there really is a Golden Pond. It was a happy, reminiscing time for us and we even brought home some New Hampshire maple syrup to remind us how sweet it was.

August 1992

Baptisms and Evangelism

I frequently hear or read about the number of "churches in the Convention (or State, or Association) that have not won anyone to Christ or baptized anyone over the past year." It usually distresses me when I hear that, partly because it's not based on accurate data.

The annual Uniform Church Letter (the nearest thing we have to an official report) asks for the number of persons baptized but there's no question about the number won to faith in Christ. There's a real difference in winning a person to Christ and baptizing him or her. Not all the people we baptize have been saved through our ministry; some are already Christians. Not all the people we win choose to follow up with baptism. So, to infer that because a church reports no baptisms during a year, they have won no one is a faulty assumption. And to assume that all persons a church reports baptizing were saved through their ministry, is also faulty. Is that a double fault?

Another thing that bothers me about statements about no baptisms is that, I believe they're based on a misunderstanding of evangelism. I spent over twenty years in the pastorate and found that you win people in spurts. One year you may win very few and the next year you may he flooded. We all long for the floods, until we come face to face with the task of developing those new Christians. That, alongside evangelism, is one of the tasks the Lord assigned us.

We also have different gifts. Paul said, "I planted, Apollos watered, but God gave the growth" (1 Corinthians 3:6). I think it's an insult and a put down for churches and pastors to make statements about "going a whole year without winning anyone to Christ." What makes our division of time into years sacred? The speaker or writer often knows very little about the fields or the workers.

I don't want to sound like evangelism is unimportant, but I do regret that we feel compelled to criticize each other's performance. It's all right to look at our own records and to find areas needing improvement, but it seems a little presumptuous for us to stand in judgment of one another.

September 1992

It Only Takes a Spark

It only takes a spark
   to get a fire going.
      Pass It On, Kurt Kaiser, 1969

The truth of these words has been demonstrated again in our association:

Denise Bean grew up Alabama with Barbara Joiner as her Acteen leader. Migrant ministry was one of her involvements as a youth. She married (becoming Denise Gardner), moved to this area and has been instrumental in getting scores of people involved in ministry to families of migrant workers. She has taught us to see migrants instead of looking past them to "someone of significance."

What if Barbara Joiner had not agreed to work with girls in her church? What if she had wanted to spend her time with someone who would contribute to her church instead of someone who would require ministry? What if she had not so impressed Denise that she continues to minister out of that inspiration?

It only takes a spark.

A few years ago, Starla Yeager moved to Rantoul. Her husband had been transferred to Chanute Air Force Base there. She had training and experience in literacy missions and began to interest others in the opportunities around them. Among those she touched was Ella Moore.

Now Ella carries the torch for literacy missions. She put together training classes for leaders this fall and the fire is spreading. Internationals and their spouses are learning conversational English. Adults are sharpening their skills at reading and writing.

What if Starla had not come to this area? What if Ella had not been able to see the potential for this ministry?

George H. Davis

Well, we're thankful that God had brought the people together and has provided the spark it took to ignite the fire. Because He has, we're richer and hundreds of lives are being touched. This year, we've ministered to at least 230 families of migrant workers. Scores of Internationals can understand us better and can make themselves understood. We've had opportunities to tell some of them about a God who loves them. Some have decided to follow Jesus.

It only takes a spark.
Kaiser's verse concludes:
And soon all those around
    can warm up to its glowing.

October 1992

"Lord, turpentine his imagination"

One of our greatest needs in the church is for leaders with imagination. It's laziness that makes us boring. We often don't do much to cultivate our natural curiosity. We teach children to color inside the lines rather than to express themselves more creatively. Sometimes we're so straight-laced that we can't even think outside the lines. We're afraid to ask. "What if ...?" There may be a fine line between using our imagination creatively and destructively. I believe fantasy can be healthy as well as harmful. Imagination can be turned toward evil as well as good, but isn't that also true of other things? Power can be used to benefit others as well as to harm them.

It's unthinkable not to think. God gave us minds to use and we dishonor him by not stretching them. I remember a phrase from a prayer for the preacher, "Lord, turpentine his imagination . . ." (James Weldon Johnson, *God's Trombones. Seven Negro Sermons in Verse*, New York: Viking, 1927, p. 14).

We need to understand our traditions but we should not be afraid to break with them when there's good reason. I'm convinced that the best ideas haven't been thought. There's nothing wrong with the tried and true but there are better ways for much of what we're doing today.

In 1973 the Foreign Mission Board published a booklet that stated:

> Edutainment is what you get when you imagineer. In fact, education can be entertaining... and entertainment can be educational.
>
> Only in modern history have entertainment and education been separated....
>
> Edutainment is exciting. Edutainment is creativity, discovery, and imagination purposefully used for learning new things, relearning old things, and understanding familiar things in new ways—ways that put education and entertainment back together again:
> - seeing what you think,
> - thinking what you see,
> - seeing what you never thought of,
> - doing what previously you could only think about,
> - hearing what you think, and

by George

- thinking about something you've never seen!

("Imagineering: A Handbook," Broadman. p. 2).

November 1992

Joy and Sorrow

Tears and laughter must be best friends; I often see them together. Sometimes I cry when I'm happy. When I'm sad, you may hear me laughing.

I'm not sure about the source of emotions but I have a hunch that remembering triggers them. I don't think I live in the past but I do have a lot of memories, mostly good.

My family is fairly close. We're scattered geographically, but emotionally we're close. My brother Don is near Nashville, Tennessee. Jim is near St. Louis. John is in Huntsville, Alabama. Dick is in Arizona. Linda is in Missouri. Four of us and our spouses took a vacation together this summer. You've got to be close or crazy (or both) to attempt that!

I was on vacation in eastern Tennessee when I got word that Dad had died. When I got the call, my first thought was one of relief that he didn't have to go back into a nursing home. Dad just didn't fit into their system; he wasn't an institutional person. He'd lived all his life with a fierce sort of independence and didn't want to give it up now.

His wish was to die in the house in which he was born and he almost made it. You may feel that you know my father's house better than you know him. Well, he was a big part of what made it my *father's* house. He wasn't the consummate father but he was *my* father, and I am grateful for him.

When my brothers and I get together for his funeral, we not only shed some tears, we also shared some joys. Four of our children shared remembrances of Grandpa at the funeral.

Some of us were able to stay and clean out the house and get it ready to rent. Those were busy, touching times. We worked hard, had some fun, and shed a few tears. There are a lot of memories tied to that place and those people.

We decided to go ahead with our traditional Christmas reunion at the Patoka Community Center. With kids, grandkids, and great-grandkids, we long ago outgrew the house. Our traditions may take on a different bent or go in new directions but I suspect that Dad's spirit will be present.

December 1992

It Was a Good Year

I'm having a hard time turning loose of 1992. It's not that I'm still writing "1992." I've made that adjustment but I'm still holding on to some of the things that made 1992 a good year.

One of the highlights was receiving hundreds of cards and letters from GAs and RAs across the country. Information about me appeared in their magazines a year ago last fall and I began hearing from them. A number of women wrote to let me know that they were praying for me, too.

Just when I thought the letters were about to play out, I would get another one. I don't know whether some groups are using the old magazines or whether they're relying on other sources.

Then, this fall my name appeared in "Missionary Moments," a packet used by Southern Baptist churches during their Sunday services to remind them to pray for missionaries.

After Dad's death, I heard from several friends across the country. They assured me that they cared and that I was not alone.

Last year saw the fiftieth wedding anniversary of my parents. But it also witnessed the killing of my step-brother's youngest daughter and the death of our folks. Yet I can think of it as a good year because I was reminded that I'm not alone—I have family and friends.

I'm not holding my breath

I've been looking for bumper stickers or buttons that encourage the support of our troops in Somalia, but I haven't seen any. We seemed to be quick to show our support of troops sent to Saudi Arabia but slow to express that same attitude toward those in Africa.

Could it be that we're more interested in being in a situation where military superiority can be demonstrated than we are in giving humanitarian aid? Is winning more important than helping?

Can we get excited about assisting people with basic human needs or are we only interested in assuring our position in the world? Can we become world leaders who have a genuine interest in helping others whether we profit from it or not?

While I'm looking for the bumper stickers and ribbons, I'm not holding my breath. Somehow, these causes are not so glamorous and their heroes are soon forgotten. They probably won't write books or go on the banquet circuit.

January 1993

It Stands to Reason

If "the husband of one wife" (1 Timothy 3:3, 12 and Titus 1:6) is interpreted to mean that a pastor or a deacon must necessarily be male, why don't we interpret "men and brethren" (Acts 15:7, 13) to mean that only men should participate in the church's decision making processes?

Indeed, Paul wrote:

Let your women keep silence in the churches: for it is not permitted unto them to speak; but they are commanded to be under obedience, as also saith the law. And if they will learn any thing, let them ask their husbands at home: for it is a shame for women to speak in the church (1 Corinthians 14:34-35).

by George

Few would attempt to practice this literally. Most would say that what Paul wrote was socially conditioned; he was writing for his time and situation but not for all time.

This is not to take lightly what was written but to take it seriously. What were the reasons behind this kind of instruction? What else does the Bible say about the relationships between men and women?

If we're going to take the Bible seriously and not merely use it as a club to enforce our prejudices, we need to look at it as a whole. Paul also wrote:

> For ye are all the children of God by faith in Christ Jesus. For as many of you as have been baptized into Christ have put on Christ. There is neither Jew or Greek, there is neither bond or free, there is neither male nor female: for ye are all one in Christ Jesus (Galatians 3:26-28).

Before he wrote, "Wives, submit yourselves unto you own husbands, as unto the Lord." he wrote, "Submitting yourselves one to another in the fear of God" (see Ephesians 5:21-22).

When we arbitrarily decide that women are not eligible for the offices of pastor or deacon, we are ignoring a rich tradition of Scripture. *Harper's Bible Dictionary* notes:

> Women were not excluded from the functions of prophecy in the O. T. period. The following are represented as speaking by divine inspiration: Miriam, sister of Moses (Ex. 15:20, cf. Num. 12:2); Deborah, wife of Lapidoth (Judg. 4, 5); Huldah, wife of Shallum (II Kings 22:14); . . . Anna, of the tribe of Asher (Luke 2:36ff.).
> ....
> In N. T. times women were recognized prophetesses, like the four daughters of Philip (Acts 21:9). They seem to have been numerous, for rules concerning the veiling of their heads during prophecy are included in Paul's First Corinthian Letter (11:5). A false prophetess, Jezebel, is mentioned in Rev. 2:20 (Harper: New York, 1952, p. 585).

Then there's Phoebe, described as "a servant [deacon] of the church which is at Cenchrea." The Roman church is urged to "receive her in the Lord, as becometh saints, and that ye assist her in whatsoever business she hath need of you" (Romans 16:1-2).

February 1993

It Makes a Difference Which Way You're Facing

Have you noticed how much more welcome a 30° day is in February or March than it is in November or December?

I think the difference is hope. Our experience tells us that when we see a 30° day in December, it is only a preview of colder days ahead. But a 30° day in February is a harbinger of spring. We look forward to warmer days.

Not in my back yard!

George H. Davis

This has become a common phrase as we search high and low for places to locate landfills for our growing crop of trash. Though everyone may agree that we need new ones, no one wants them close by.

This same phrase may he heard as we look for sites needing new churches. We tend to get protective of our turf and to suggest their location somewhere else.

The truth is that boundaries of church fields are almost nonexistent. There's hardly such a thing as a neighborhood church any more. Most churches draw members from a wide area. Many persons drive by other churches to get to the one they attend.

Where we go to church is becoming increasingly a matter of taste; denominational loyalty is on the wane. Churches minister to some groups better than they do others. I doubt any church can minister uniformly well to all groups.

We've long recognized that new Sunday School classes grow faster and reach more people than do old ones. Isn't this same principle true of churches? If we want to reach new people, one strategy is to start new churches targeting them.

And who says churches must live forever. It may be that a church will reach people for a while then die when the community changes. Is that wrong? Oh, maybe it would be better if they could change to meet the needs of the changed community, but that seldom happens.

When Jesus said that the gates of Hades would not prevail against his church, was he talking about **the Church** or **the churches**?

March 1993

Who Is Our Enemy?

Isaac Watts asked:
Are there no foes for me to face?
    Must I not stem the flood?
Is this vile world a friend to grace,
    To help me on to God?

I think one of the questions we face is, "Who is the enemy?" Is it the world, the flesh, and the devil? Some tend to see these as synonymous. They don't see much difference.

Granted that "the world" is sometimes used by Paul as meaning "the world without God," he also sees "this world" and "the world to come" as intersecting. He refers to "the ends of the ages" as having come upon us (1 Corinthians 10:11). He speaks of Christians as having received "the earnest" of God's inheritance (Ephesians 1:14).

Some see us living "between the ages." I guess I would prefer to think of our time as an intersection or an overlapping of kingdoms.

Some seem to think that whatever is happening to us now is designed to destroy true Christians. They see government and society as out to eliminate us. I think it starts with the idea that the world will become worse and worse until Christ comes to redeem it. I don't see that concept as entirely biblical.

by George

Jesus warned about misleading signs and misleading leaders. The oft-quoted "wars and rumors of wars" is actually a false sign. Jesus said. "...see that you are not alarmed; for this must take place, but the end is not yet" (Matthew 24:6). The one true sign Jesus gave for the end of the world was that the gospel would be preached throughout the world, as a testimony to all nations (v. 14).

Christ has come and the redemption has begun! After two thousand years, his Spirit and his followers have made an impact. It's not as great as it should have been, but we can see evidences of Christ's work in our society and world. The work is not done, but it has begun!

Jesus taught us to pray:
Thy kingdom come,
Thy will be done,
    on earth as it is in heaven (Matthew 6:10).

School boards and other governmental bodies are not our enemies. If we can get over our paranoia, we may even find friends there. Television is not the enemy. It may seem like a wasteland, but there are tremendously creative forces at work there, too.

Let's not ignore the good in our search for enemies. There's a great deal of good going on around us, even in the midst of all that's wrong.

One of the risks in really looking for enemies is that we may find them in surprising places. Remember the words of Pogo, "We have met the enemy and he is us."

April 1993

The Guilt of the Lambs

In the wake of Waco, much has been written and spoken about the guilt of David Koresh. He was the leader of a Branch Davidian compound where scores died when federal authorities stormed their stronghold.

While questions remain about the grounds for and the strategy of the raid, I would not dispute Koresh's guilt. Leaders bear heavy responsibility for the kind of leadership they offer. But, have the followers no responsibility?

Several years ago I heard about an article in a German magazine. The title could be translated "The Guilt of the Lambs." Its thesis was that Hitler kindled a fire that swept Europe but that it would have died out if it had not been fanned by the complicity of hundreds of ordinary, minor officials. The guilt belonged not only to the leaders, but also to those who followed.

I recently heard about a movie called "The Silence of the Lambs." I decided to check it out to see if there could be any connection. Trust me; there's none!

Meanwhile, back to the ranch. I don't believe anyone has the right to turn his or her mind over to someone else. That is the essence of idolatry. It sets aside God's word for someone's twisted interpretation of it.

People are not sheep. They are human beings, created in God's image. Part of that image involves responsibility for our actions. We cannot get around that responsibility by saying that someone told us to do something. That is as irresponsible as saying,

George H. Davis

"The devil made me do it." Flip Wilson made that line funny a generation ago, but it's really a tragic excuse.

People are not robots to be programmed. It makes no difference whether the orders come from a so-called religious leader. Esther Burroughs, at the state Woman's Missionary Union convention, said, "Don't turn your priesthood over to your pastor." I agree. God holds me responsible for my actions. My pastor is responsible for his.

I remember reading an article by Buckner Fanning. In it he said, "It takes two fools to put a preacher on a pedestal—one to put him there and the other to stay there."

I agree that we should respect our leaders. But, I also believe that respect must be earned—it is not automatic! Sometimes leaders are not worthy of respect.

I'm not talking about disagreement. I believe we can disagree with one another and maintain respect. In fact, that may be the essence of respect. There's little self-respect if we knuckle under to pressure.

May 1993

Prayer in School?

I do not remember a teacher leading in prayer during my public school years. That included eight years at Patoka Grade School and two at Patoka High; by that time the kids were so ornery that the school was closed (I doubt that prayer would have saved it). We went to Sandoval for the last two years of high school. Then I went to Southern Illinois University in Carbondale where I crammed four years into five.

I remember some good teachers. Rettie Simcox was my first and second grade teacher (kindergarten hadn't been invented yet). Homer Potts taught me in grades seven and eight. He was a strict disciplinarian. His specialties were orthography and geography. His "what and where" tests were legendary. He also was a gifted artist. In high school I remember Mr. Robertson for physics and Miss Kostanzer for Latin. In college none surpassed Dr. Caldwell in history. He taught us how to do research and write a paper. He had a surface irreverence and a deep respect for truth.

In the twenty-one years I don't remember any of them leading a class in prayer; Dr. Caldwell did invite us to attend church with him one time, I don't feel I was deprived. I don't remember any of them making fun of Christianity either. Oh, there were some who challenged common ideas but their intent was our growth. I never thought it was their job to teach me faith. My family, Sunday School teachers, and pastors were busy there.

Some are saying that this country was founded as a Christian nation and should include prayer as a part of school program. I remember learning that when settlers came to this country some started here the only kind of churches they knew in Europe—state supported ones. Others were not allowed to practice their faith; dissident clergy were arrested. It was not until we were well into the nineteenth century that the last vestiges of state churches were abolished. I don't want to go back (some would argue that we have gone back already).

by George

Someone has observed that, as long as there are exams, no one can keep students from praying—it's easier, if less effective, than studying. But when prayer becomes part at classroom procedure, it slips easily into coercion. To my thinking, coerced religion is worse than none; it deceives us into trusting it. To be meaningful, religion must be free.

I didn't learn that in public school; that came in seminary and I'm still living by it. When I got to seminary, all my teachers began class with prayer. It was appropriate and often meaningful there because it was a Christian school.

June 1993

What Makes a Person Homosexual?

You may be uncomfortable hearing or thinking about homosexuality. I'm uncomfortable when I'm asked to make decisions without any agreement on definitions.

Webster defines homosexuality as "erotic activity with another of the same sex" (*Ninth New Collegiate Dictionary*). One thing making us so uncomfortable is that many of us engaged in a variety of "erotic activity" as we were growing up. Does that make us homosexual?

No; I don't think so. I think that was a stage in our development. Does that mean that the homosexual is in a state of arrested development? I don't know. There's a lot I don't know about homosexuality. Some claim genetics is involved. I cannot say it's not.

I guess part of the question is whether it's the preference or only the action that brands one homosexual. Is a person heterosexual only when he or she participates in sexual activity with a person of the opposite sex? Is a person homosexual who, despite his or her attraction to another of the same sex, abstains from sexual activity?

Why are we so much more tolerant of a heterosexual person who is always on the prowl for sexual conquests than of such a homosexual? Isn't all use of another person simply for one's pleasure wrong?

According to L. H. Marshall, Paul:

insists on continence before marriage and fidelity in marriage as the obvious duty of Christian people. His viewpoint on the matter is exactly the same as that of his Master (*The Challenge of New Testament Ethics*, London: Macmillan, 1950, p. 280).

In 1 Corinthians, Paul lists several groups that are moving away from God:

Do you not know that wrongdoers will not inherit the kingdom of God? Do not be deceived! Fornicators, idolaters, adulterers, male prostitutes, sodomites, thieves, the greedy, drunkards, revilers, robbers—none of these will inherit the kingdom of God. And this is what some of you used to be. But you were washed, you were sanctified, you were justified in the name of the Lord Jesus Christ and in the Spirit of our God (6:9-11).

Before we start branding people, maybe we'd better check our own pedigree!

George H. Davis

Well, that's probably more than I know on the subject and maybe more than you want to hear.

July 1993

Cholesterol Revisited

I'm not sure how to spell it; I'm not sure I'm pronouncing it right. I've made fun of cholesterol, saying I didn't believe in it!

It's hard to believe in things you didn't know about while you were growing up. It's not impossible. Some of us manage to adapt to space explorations and computers although they've been developed within our lifetime.

I knew a man who refused to believe in space flights; he thought the whole thing was being done in a television studio. At least he was right about one thing—television can make anything look real.

A few days ago I went to my doctor for a physical. I hadn't had one in ten years and felt I probably was due. He gave me generally good reports and wanted to do some blood tests. A few days later I received a note saying that the laboratory tests "were all negative or normal." Then a note that my cholesterol was 213, "just over normal for your age—normal 159-210."

The doctor had been kind enough to enclose a fat controlled diet and suggest that I follow it. Now that's what I call picky! Three points over normal and he suggests I limit my fat intake!

I remembered that I had made all kinds of fun of an article in our newspaper a few days earlier. It was entitled "Keep the fat out of homemade ice cream." I didn't even dignify that piece of trash by reading it. I made some smart aleck remark about nothing being sacred anymore.

After a day or two I looked over the diet. It suggested that I limit red meat to no more than three meals a week! Limited sausage and cheese. Limited donuts. That's all right; I'm not that crazy about donuts. But, skim milk?

It's enough to shake your faith in doctors. Don't they have something better to do than question our pleasures? I think that's why I've been skeptical about cholesterol all along. But then, they could be right. Am I willing to risk being wrong? Maybe I'll follow it every other day.

Then I began wondering—how would I feel if someone sought my advice, then refused to follow it? Oh, well. It's only food!

August 1993

The Ties That Bind

I tried to call two of my brothers and talked to each of their answering machines. Then I called my youngest brother in Arizona. He told me he thought John was in Alaska. A couple of nights later John called; they had been to Anchorage visiting their son. The next morning Don called; they had just returned from Siberia.

by George

I told them both that I was going on vacation, too—to Osage Beach, Missouri!

Well, it may not sound as glamorous as Alaska or Siberia, but it was an enjoyable week at Lake of the Ozarks. We didn't fish; we didn't swim; we didn't boat. The nearest we got to the water was the spa. We enjoyed the area and the company—some friends from southern Illinois joined us.

I was reminded how hard it is for me to get away from computers. We went to Wal-Mart Monday morning. (Isn't that what you're supposed to do on vacation?) I browsed through the magazine rack and noticed the cover of a well-known computer magazine.

No pin up could have been more enticing to a computer junkie. (Does that say something about my age?) I argued myself out of buying it, reminding myself that I was on vacation. That argument didn't work the next day; I'd heard it before.

Though I had a book of Robert Frost's poetry back at the cabin, I bought the magazine with it's tempting software reviews. I told myself that I'd only glance at it when there was nothing else to do.

Frost's poetry will likely outlast anything I read there but I was reminded how hooked I'd become. I guess the apron strings have been replaced by computer cables. But at least I went a whole week without Solitaire!

Some day I may go to Anchorage or even to Siberia, but for now Missouri is fine. After all, those trips might take two or three weeks and I'm not sure I can be away that long. Maybe that explains the popularity of laptop and notebook computers—their owners can't be weaned from Solitaire!

September 1993

Isn't Imagination Wonderful?

She smiled warmly and spoke as my wife and I took our places, two tables away at a small restaurant. I had noticed the attractive, younger lady as we crossed the room. She looked familiar but I couldn't come up with a name. Her husband seemed preoccupied with the newspaper.

I sat facing her but was frustratingly unable to identify her. She was obviously too young to have been a classmate, though this was the community where I finished high school. She had smiled like she knew me. How? Where?

We finished our meal and went on to the funeral home in my hometown. After a while, she and her husband came in. She mentioned seeing us again and it dawned on me; she was the librarian from whom my Dad had borrowed books. I had accompanied him on at least one occasion and had returned some after his death.

Imagination suddenly evaporated and reality was realized. She was not a former girl friend nor the daughter of an old class mate. My acquaintance with her was much more recent and much less romantic. Isn't imagination wonderful?

Wonderful is one of those two-edged words; it cuts both ways. Webster says that a wonder is "a cause of astonishment or admiration" (*Ninth New Collegiate Dictionary*). Wonder reminds me of another two-edged word—awe. If something is awesome, it may be awe inspiring or awful. You may be awe struck by something terrible.

George H. Davis

There's a passage in Judges where an angel of the LORD asks Manoah, "Why do you ask my name, seeing it is Wonderful?" (13:18). Clyde Francisco, late professor of Old Testament at Southern Seminary in Louisville, Kentucky, used to argue that "Wonderful" should be capitalized in that passage. He tied it to Isaiah 9:6 where Messiah is described as:
>	Wonderful, Counselor, Mighty God,
>	Everlasting Father, Prince of Peace.

He felt there should be a comma after Wonderful here, since it was a name for God.

The next time your imagination shifts into overdrive, be aware of what's going on. It's a wonderful gift that enables us to discover new truth. Without it, we'd still be reading by candle light. Edison dreamed of another way to produce light and imagineered the electric light bulb. But, Hitler dreamed of a Germany run by a superior race.

We can imagine evil as well as good. Which way is yours running?

October 1993

"Now, which one are you?"

If you grew up with more than one brother or sister, you surely heard this question more than once. I still hear it when I return to my hometown, but I'm reconciled to it now. My brothers and sister and I get along well. We used to fight frequently but it's been years since we heard Mom call out. "Don't bend John's glasses."

A second cousin helped revive my interest in family history. I told her that I had been unable to trace my Davis roots past my great-grandfather. I had visited his grave at a small cemetery in the woods near the place where I was raised. He had moved into that area about 1870 and began farming. For about 115 years a Davis was farming that land.

My genealogically literate cousin traced the family tree back to David Davis, born in 1756 in Wales. He immigrated to North Carolina and the family made its way to Jefferson County then to Marion County, both in Illinois.

I had squirreled back some material on my mother's family. Getting it out, I traced the Moore's back to the 1600's in New England.

My wife had some information on her dad's family that went back into the 1700's. It has been fun putting all this information together. Here are some observations growing out of this project.

Many families seemed to have a child about every two years. I guess that shouldn't be too surprising. Children became part of the work force and there was always a need for more workers on the farm. Large families were common. Some had eleven or more children.

Many children died before reaching school age. Early cemeteries are filled with graves of infants. In my Grandpa Davis' family, he was the only one of seven to live into his thirties. The flu and pneumonia took many children and youth.

One of the favorite names in the Davis family was Squire. How does that sound? You can call me Squire Davis. It has a sort of distinguished sound, doesn't it?

I remembered too, the warning of John the Baptizer, "Do not presume to say to yourselves. 'We have Abraham as our ancestor'; for I tell you. God is able from these stones to raise up children to Abraham" (Matthew 3:9 NRSV). I guess that sort of puts everything in perspective, doesn't it?

November 1993

Christmas Music

You'll soon discover (if you don't already know) that I'm neither a musician nor the son of a musician. My dad had a pretty fair tenor voice but had no formal training. I remember my grandfather leading the singing in our home church on at least one occasion. The thing I remember is that he had us sing the third stanza only—he said they'd been neglected too long. That was before the current rage for singing every stanza.

Christmas brings out some of the best and some of the worst music possible. Some of the songs we sing have poor theology, some have terrible tunes (I told you I was no musician).

But music is one area where almost everyone has an opinion. More people seem to feel good or bad about music than any other element in a worship service. There is so much potential in the emotional baggage we bring to the music.

I tend to like simple, straightforward music. Music that has a lot of repetition or uses vague expressions doesn't do much for me. I think lyrics ought to be understandable and don't care for words or phrases that aren't generally understood, especially if they're Hebrew, Latin, or Greek. I have studied these languages and (given enough time and the appropriate lexicon) I can figure out the meaning of most words. But communication depends on clear usage. Our purpose is not to impress but to express.

Phillips Brooks speaks to me when he says, "The hopes and fears of all the years are met in thee tonight." It's hard to improve on his description of what happened in the Little Town of Bethlehem:

How silently, how silently
    The wondrous gift is giv'n!
So God imparts to human hearts
    The blessings of His heav'n.
No ear may hear his coming,
    But in this world of sin,
Where meek souls will receive Him, still
    The dear Christ enters in.

To me that's more powerful than:
And heav'n and nature sing,
And heav'n and nature sing,
And heav'n, and heav'n and nature sing.

George H. Davis

Maybe the fault here is in attempting to adapt Isaac Watts' text to Handel's music. The words had to be repeated and repeated to come out, to come out right. I guess that just shows that each of us has different tastes in music, or that some of us have no taste!

December 1993

Not a Drop?

Some candidates for Secretary of State in next month's primary election have proposed that a young driver with any alcohol in his or her system lose his or her driver's license. At first glance, this seems to be the kind of idea that deserves support. ***Not.***

I support efforts to fight driving while intoxicated, but there's much about the current proposal that concerns me:

- Would this mean that a teenager could no longer drive the family home from church if their congregation insisted on using wine for the Lord's Supper?
- Why single out young drivers? If any alcohol interferes with safe driving, why not enforce "Not a Drop" across the board? Why single out drivers under twenty-one? You say, "Young drivers are impressionable and are forming life habits." I suggest that by the time a person is sixteen, he or she should have enough maturity to make responsible decisions. If not, they should not be driving—with or without alcohol.
- I'm bothered by attempts to impose our standards on others. Just because I don't drink, doesn't mean that I should try to keep everyone from drinking. To try to force my standards on others goes beyond responsible citizenship. I believe it's possible for some to handle moderate amounts of alcohol. I'm aware of the dangers of alcoholism, but that's a separate issue. If we're really concerned about that we shouldn't tackle just the driving privilege.
- The proposal smacks of hypocrisy. It says. "If you're under twenty-one, you cannot drink any alcohol and drive, but if you're old enough to have good judgment, you may drink in moderation." Good judgment does not depend on age. I've seen some people who were well into adulthood make some remarkably poor decisions. I-low can we expect youth to make good decisions if we take responsibility away from them saying, "We know what's good for you"?
- Hypocrisy sneaks out in another way, too. As Baptists, we're notorious as "those who don't drink (in front of each other)." We pay lip service to abstinence but recognize that for many in our ranks, the pledge is hollow. We're likely to support this proposal because it sounds good; we're suckers for grandstanders. If something sounds good, we'll support it, without thinking it through.

I'd rather our grandkids didn't drink, but I'd like for that to be their decision, not mine. I think they're smart enough to make that decision and whatever it is, they're still our grandkids (I know; it's easier for me to say that now than when our kids were home).

February 1994

Is Yours a Corrugated Fellowship?

We're familiar with corrugated boxes. They're boxes made of paper formed into alternating ridges and grooves. The material is not very strong by itself, but put together as they are, these boxes can withstand a lot of wear and tear.

According to *Merriam Webster's Collegiate Dictionary, Tenth Edition*, corrugate is from a word meaning wrinkle. Do you sometimes feel that the fellowship of your church is kind of wrinkled? No, I'm not talking about the age of your members; I'm referring to the unevenness of the fellowship. We're not always smooth and wrinkle-free. In our culture, wrinkles are seen as a sign of age and are to be avoided at all costs. I'm not so sure that's right.

Corrugated boxes aren't very pretty. They're made out of rough, cheap materials and are glued or stapled together. There's not a lot of craftsmanship that goes into their assembly. As in a family where you don't chose your brothers and sisters, fellow members are given to us. They share our parents but may not be much like us.

The size and shape of the boxes do not always tell us much about their contents. Things may be packed inside in any number of ways. Sometimes there's more packing than merchandise. The box may get dirty or torn or punctured and still protect what's inside. We've learned to look inside before deciding whether we want the contents.

Churches are a little like that. They are often made up of layers of materials glued or stapled together. The materials are not finely polished nor highly finished. Sometimes there's a hole or a scrape. The box may be beautifully gift-wrapped only to be ripped apart.

There certainly are finer, more handsome materials available, but it's hard to beat the durability and protection of a sturdy corrugated cardboard box. Some think churches should be prettier or should be more gaily decorated. But the way we ship boxes, pretty paper doesn't last long; ribbons are soon shredded.

Some have suggested that if the Church were not from God it would have died many centuries ago. All the trouble it's been through and all the ugliness done in its name would have killed it.

March 1994

Is Bigger Better?

We've got a problem! The unforgivable sin in Southern Baptist groups is failure to submit an annual Uniform Church Letter. Our state convention constitution says:

> A church will be considered a cooperating church when it has submitted an annual church letter for one of the two preceding church years and has contributed financially during the preceding year to fulfill the nature and purpose of the

George H. Davis

Illinois Baptist State Association.

Our constitution says:

Should any church maintain doctrine, polity, or practices contrary to the purposes of the Association, or fail to send a Uniform Church Letter, messengers, or financial contributions for three (3) consecutive years, the Credentials Committee may, upon failing to reconcile such church, recommend dismissal. A three-forth (¾) majority vote in annual session shall be required to withdraw fellowship from a church.

But, the Old Testament takes a dim view of counting people. The Lord warned Moses that a tax should be levied during the census "then no plague will come on them when you number them" (Exodus 30:12b NIV).

The most interesting census in the Old Testament is that ordered by David. There are two accounts—one in 2 Samuel 24, the other in 1 Chronicles 21. In 2 Samuel "the anger of the Lord burned against Israel, and he incited David against them, saying 'Go and count Israel and Judah'" (24:1). In 1 Chronicles "Satan rose up against Israel and incited David to take a census of Israel" (21:1).

In each account, Joab opposes David's intent:

My lord the king, are they not all my lord's subjects? Why does my lord want to do this? Why should he bring guilt on Israel? (1 Chronicles 21:3; compare 2 Samuel 24:3).

However, King David wanted to know how many soldiers he had. Eventually he recognized and confessed his sin; seventy thousand died in Israel in the ensuing pestilence.

So, what are we to do? The sin is not so much in counting as in pride at our size or strength. A related sin is idolatry—we turn from trust in God to rely on our power and ingenuity.

Will we continue to ask for annual reports? I doubt we'll stop. But we can learn to use those figures more honestly. We need to be careful how we interpret the data we collect. But, most of all, we need to recognize that salvation is from the Lord, not from the church!

What will be our pestilence? God may just leave us to our own devices—to accomplish what we can, in our own strength.

April 1994

Another Area of Concern

I've read concerned stories about the decline in the number of baptisms our churches are reporting. I share that concern; since about 1972 that figure has been declining.

There's another figure that is even more alarming; that's the number of other additions reported. These are people who join our churches by transfer of letter from another church or by statement (when no letter is available). Since 1975 that number has dropped dramatically (see the graph on page one).

by George

After the first two years of our Association's life, our churches reported between 300 and 500 other additions each year until 1976. Since then, we've never received 300 and in all but three years, we've been under 200.

You may agree that's quite a drop but ask, "What does it mean?" The obvious meaning is that we can no longer rely on receiving a steady stream or members transferring into our churches; it's been slowed to a trickle.

You may not see this as a matter at concern. You may think we should focus on the number of new members we receive by baptism--after all, that's Kingdom growth! Well, it *may* be. Let me remind you, however, that some of those we baptize have been Christians for some time.

Back to other additions—why has the number dropped? While I can think of a few reasons, I don't know the full answer. I'd like to see a study over a wider area.

- Denominational loyalty is not as strong as it was a generation ago. It's part of a general shift away from brand name consciousness. The question has changed from "what brand is it?" to "what does it offer me (us)?" Lines between denominations have become blurred as factions grasp for control. Several nonaligned congregations have emerged.
- Church membership is no longer valued as highly as it was. Most of our churches have persons who are involved in our life but do not become members. Their commitment may be limited.
- People from the South are not moving into our area like they were during and after World War II when many came looking for work. They were from areas where Southern Baptist churches predominated and they joined churches or started new ones here. That migration pattern has changed. Now, some of those people are retiring and moving back south.
- While I'd like to cite our denominational controversy as a factor in the decline, I'm not sure that can be documented. It may be part of the reason for the lack of enthusiasm for church membership, but I'm not sure how much the denominational struggle has reached into our churches.

May 1994

How did they do that?

My wife was in Springfield, grandmaing our newest grandson. I was to pick her up and we would travel to Mt. Vernon, Illinois to help our daughter and her family get acquainted with their new computer. She had consulted with me several times before the purchase and now wanted help getting it set up. On Sunday we would come back to Patoka for a family reunion.

Before I left Champaign, I checked with Leona to be sure that I didn't forget anything we might need for the weekend. She instructed me to bring her yellow dress and Sunday shoes. I also was to pick up a package of handkerchiefs. No problem—I set the things out the night before and packed what I thought I needed.

I set out confident that everything was all right. I got to visit again with newborn Tyler Matthew Davis and his almost three-year-old brother Clayton in Springfield then we traveled on to Mt. Vernon. When we arrived, Cody and Kelsey (more grandchildren) ran out to meet the car before we got in.

We had a good visit. I got a database set up for Jane's day care. We enjoyed a trip to Rend Lake where Steve's folks had set up a camp site. Returning to Mt. Vernon, we planned to get on the road in time to worship at First Baptist Church in Patoka, my home church.

As we were getting ready Sunday morning, I thought things were going rather well. One small problem, I could not find Leona's shoes. I couldn't imagine what could have happened to them. Well, she was gracious, as always, and wore her everyday ones.

As we started toward Patoka, I was still troubled about the missing shoes. I went back over things in my memory and decided that Cody or Kelsey must have gotten them out of the trunk and taken them into the house. We just hadn't found them.

Well, the day at Patoka was very enjoyable. It was good to visit with my brothers and to see their families. The day wore on and everyone began to leave. We headed back to Champaign, refreshed and tired.

Well, when we arrived home. I found that my suspicions had been confirmed. Cody or Kelsey **had** carried the shoes in but had put them in *our* house in Champaign instead of theirs in Mt. Vernon. There they were, on the bed. It was strange; that was about where I had put them Thursday night, so I wouldn't forget them.

Now the mystery deepened. How had *they* traveled that distance, gotten into *our* locked house, and left the shoes precisely where *I* had placed them? There wasn't an easy solution to this mystery, but the answer had to be along those lines. I couldn't have forgotten them, could I? Somehow, my wife figured things out differently.

June 1994

Another translation of the New Testament?

That's just what we need!

You may have detected a note of sarcasm in my voice. We've already got more versions than a computer software company. There's the New King James, the New American Standard, the New International, the New Revised Standard, and that's just the better known ones.

But when I read that Eugene H. Peterson had done a translation of the New Testament, I could hardly wait to find it. I'd read and been challenged by his *Five Smooth Stones for Pastoral Work* and *Working the Angles: The Shape of Pastoral Integrity*. I had been excited by his ideas and the way he expressed them.

I was not disappointed when I began reading *The Message* (NavPress: Colorado Springs. 1994). It's a free translation using current language and idioms. He argues that the New Testament was written in everyday language and that it should be read that way.

As I began to read, I found myself chuckling then wincing as expressions amused me and struck home. It's really a translation I have trouble putting down; I just want to read on.

by George

Someone has suggested that Peterson is a nineties counterpart to J. B. Phillips, who began publishing his New Testament translations in the late forties. He became immensely popular during the fifties.

There may be parts of Peterson's work I won't like, but that hasn't happened yet. When I got back to the office with it, I read Mark, later 1 and 2 Peter. Now I'm reading Matthew.

Let me give you a sample of how he renders the Sermon on the Mount:

"Don't pick on people, jump on their failures, criticize their faults—unless, of course, you want the same treatment. That critical spirit has a way of boomeranging. It's easy to see the smudge on your neighbor's face and be oblivious to the ugly sneer on your own. Do you have the nerve to say, 'Let me wash your face for you.' when your own face is distorted by contempt? It's this whole traveling road-show mentality all over again, playing a holier-than-thou part instead of just living your part. Wipe that ugly sneer off your own face, and you might be fit to offer a washcloth to your neighbor" (Matthew 7:1-5).

One problem you may have is that it's hard to keep track of verses since they're not numbered. References are printed at the top of each page, listing the contents of that page. Chapter numbers are placed throughout the text.

Peterson was for many years pastor at Christ Our King Presbyterian Church in Bel Air, Maryland. Now he teaches at Regent College. I'd encourage you to read whatever you can find that he's written but don't miss *The Message*.

July 1994

I Remember Ruts

During my early years, we lived a mile from the gravel road that led to town. Town was Patoka, a village of about 600, located along Route 51, sixteen miles north of Centralia. Illinois.

Later that dirt road was oiled, then graveled, but I remember walking that mile to catch the school bus. Later, the bus came to our house. Sometimes we would leave the car out at the gravel road and take a team and a wagon to it; the horses would await our return.

Sometimes we would get brave and try to drive that mile of mud—I remember ruts. The path you normally took soon was cut deeper making ruts. There were advantages and disadvantages to ruts. The ruts could keep you from sliding into the ditch and that was always appreciated, but if the ruts became too deep you could get hung up. The frame of the car would get stuck and the wheels hardly touched the ground. When the ground was frozen solid, you might venture out of the ruts, but you realized that if the sun was shining, the surface might be thawed enough so that you'd slip into a rut.

Another risk of ruts was that you might meet someone in the same set of ruts, going the opposite direction. That was seldom a worry for us; traffic wasn't that heavy.

We use "rut" for a pattern of doing things. The same benefits and dangers apply to our familiar patterns. If we don't have some way of reacting in a given situation, we have to come up with a new solution every time. But if we always respond in the same way, we're going to take a wrong path sometimes.

I don't know who coined the seven last words of the church—We've never done it that way before. There's another saying that's worth remembering—Don't throw out the baby with the bath water. Some things are worth saving. Not every old way is bad, or good. Not every new way is good, or bad. We need the wisdom to know which is which, or as Kenny Rogers said. "You've got to know when to hold and know when to fold."

There's no virtue in change for its own sake nor in stubborn refusal to change. An old story tells about a motion made in a church business meeting—"I move that we buy a chandelier." A contrary member rose to his feet and said, "I'm against this motion for three reasons: first, we don't have anyone who can play it; second, we don't have anyone who can spell it to order it; and third, what we really need is more light."

I told that story thirty years ago and a lady told me she was at that business meeting; I guess we've all been at one like it.

August 1994

"Drag your feet and hurry back!"

I had taken a pair of dress shoes for new half soles and heels. I had noticed a small hole in the sole the last time I wore them (Doesn't that have a nice rhyme to it? Hole in the Sole—there's got to be a song there. Oh well, where was I?).

The shop called to tell me the shoes were ready and I went to pick them up. As I paid the bill and walked out with my new-looking shoes, the cobbler sang out, "Drag your feet and hurry back!" Somehow he caught me by surprise.

As I reflect on his wish for me, I see it as more sincere than the generic "Have a nice day." You may criticize him for being so bent on business (There we go again—bent on building his business. More music!). But I applaud him for being direct.

I remember talking to a carpet salesman about using different qualities of carpet in a church sanctuary. I thought the aisles and altar area should be of good quality and that under the pews we could save a little. He said that the carpet under the pews wore out faster than that in the aisles—more evidence of foot dragging and scuffing.

I'd heard a lot of people suggest, "Pick up your feet. Don't shuffle." Maybe I've even said it a few times. This was the first time I'd been told to drag my feet.

I guess the advice you give or get depends a lot on perspective. I can see that he was giving me good advice, from his perspective. The generic advice we hand out isn't always good—"Keep your chin up!" You're liable to get it popped if you stick it too far out.

I won't forget his advice soon; it was unusual enough to stay with me. Sometimes it takes an unexpected word to stick to our word-weary ears. We hear so much and so much of it is so predictable. One of the qualities of Jesus' teaching was that it was unpredictable. He didn't just repeat what he'd heard.

September 1994

Dwelling in Beulah Land

I was still feeling good about our annual meeting. Everything had seemed to be on a high plane, from the music, to the Bible studies, to the sharing time, to the reports, and the sermons. I was feeling satisfied and when I heard a senior adult choir sing Dwelling in Beulah Land, I said to myself, "That's how I feel."

The choir was from Edwards Road Baptist Church in Greenville, South Carolina and they were singing at Pennsylvania Avenue Wednesday night after our Associational annual meeting. I hadn't heard the song for several years but had been thinking of it recently. Actually, there are at least two Beulah Land songs, Beulah Land by John R. Sweney and Dwelling in Beulah Land by C. Austin Miles. During our recent senior adult reunion, I got to thinking about songs I hadn't heard in thirty years.

I remembered singing both of them, I believe out of the old, soft back *Songs of Faith* hymnals. Sometimes my grandpa would lead the singing, but more often it would be Artie Rogier.

The words and a feeling of affirmation came back as the choir sang the last stanza:

Viewing here the works of God,
    I sink in contemplation,
Hearing now His blessed voice,
    I see the way He planned:
Dwelling in the Spirit, here
    I learn of full salvation,
Gladly will I tarry
    in Beulah Land.
I'm living on the mountain,
    underneath a cloudless sky, (Praise God!)
I'm drinking at the fountain
    that never shall run dry;
O yes! I'm feasting on the manna
    from a bountiful supply,
For I am dwelling
    in Beulah Land.

©1911, Renewal 1939 The Rodehaver Co., Owner.

When I got home, I started wondering about the source of the Beulah Land reference and found it in Isaiah. Even though his land had fallen into enemy hands, he saw brighter days ahead when the land would be restored to God's people:

You shall no more be termed Azubah (Forsaken) and your land shall no more be termed Shemamah (Desolate); but you shall be called Hephzibah (My Delight Is in

George H. Davis

Her), and your land Beulah (Married); for the LORD delights in you, and your land shall be married (62:4).

I felt like I had visited Beulah land.

October 1994

What Color Are Your Glasses?

We have a saying about looking at the world through rose-colored glasses. The inference is that it causes a rosy tint to all our perceptions.

A month or two ago, I caught brief parts of the Whitewater hearings then being conducted by the United States Congress and Senate. It was rather obvious that the interpretation of information was influenced by the presumptions of the participants; there were no disinterested parties.

Similar partisanship seems to show up in the civil war among Southern Baptists; our interpretation of events is colored by our predisposition. We see people as friendly or as opposing our ideas. We become the judge of who are "good guys" and "bad guys." I know that some of us have been more deeply involved in the fight than others but almost all of us have been affected.

I'm suggesting that no one is unbiased. Our best hope is to recognize our bias. As a history major in college, I was taught that every historian writes from some bias; there's no such thing as a completely objective historian. Our bias determines what we include in our history. Lots of things are omitted because we decide they're unimportant. Someone else might object that we've overlooked major events and skewed our history; the truth is that all history is skewed. We tend to agree with some skews and be repulsed by others.

All of us see the world through the lens of our experience and education. The way we were raised has a profound effect on our view. We may rebel against our heritage only to find *that* influences how we see things.

One principle I've tried to live by is that people are more important than ideas. I believe that it's wrong to run over people to get your way.

I vividly remember being in a meeting more than thirty years ago when a leader was absent. A speaker said, "I don't know where he is," implying that the leader was negligent in his duties. I was aware that the speaker *did* know where the leader was and I said so—I felt such a public attack should not go unchallenged.

Not everything is worth fighting over; some things don't make that much difference. But there are a few things worth going to the wall for. One of life's struggles is deciding what's worth fighting for and what's not. I'm not sure any of us can decide that question for anyone else; I think each of us has to make his or her own decision there.

It may be that my presumption of the importance of each person comes as much from our culture as from the Bible. There certainly are Biblical examples of people being bulldozed by others, but I'm not sure that makes it right. Almost every behavior has been justified by Biblical references.

November 1994

by George

Remember Pearl Harbor?

That motto was meant to be punctuated with an exclamation mark, not a question mark. However, after fifty-three years, it may be going the way of the Alamo. At one time, "Remember the Alamo" was a battle cry. It was a call to focus on the bravery of those defenders of Texas soil. Now, at least outside Texas, the interest seems to be more historical—we're no longer stirred to action by 19th century heroes.

How long does an event have the power to galvanize us into action? Is it only during the lifetime of those alive when it occurred? How strong is second hand memory? Is there a difference between experiencing an event and being told about it? Did you really have to be there?

It's hard for me to remember that more than 80 percent of our population was not yet born on that 1941 "date which will live in infamy." I believe it makes a difference if you can remember where you were and what you were doing when you heard about the attack on Pearl Harbor. Of course, the survivors of the attack might argue that you can't *really* remember Pearl Harbor unless you were there! I'm not going to argue with them.

We recognize this principle theologically—you have to know God first hand; a second hand, hearsay experience will not work. We say, "God has no grandchildren."

How do we translate this principle into church life? Most congregations began with a dream. Someone had a vision of what needed to be done; others caught it and a ministry was launched. Often the vision had a specific focus, a certain group or area. Others were not excluded; they just were not the primary focus.

What happens when the focus group changes or disappears? What happens when the original dreamers disappear? Can their successors carry out the quest? Isn't there a saying, "No one is lazy except in the pursuit of someone else's dream"?

Some of our churches were begun to give new comers to the area a church like they had back home. Home was southern Illinois, Kentucky, or somewhere else *South*. When the migration during and after World War II stopped, the available field of transferring Southern Baptists began drying up. Those transferring in now may not come from an area where Baptists predominate. We never told those native to the area that they weren't welcome; we just planned for those like ourselves.

Can we reinvent churches for our changing communities, or must we be tied to a dream that's two generations old?

December 1994

Be Careful What You Ask For

Somewhere around Thanksgiving our daughter asked me what I wanted for Christmas. "I don't know," was my unhelpful reply. A few days later, I was talking with her again. In the meantime I'd seen a dazzling commercial on television for a gnarly radio-controlled car called Ricochet™. It could bump into walls, turn over, and go on running—it could run on either side.

George H. Davis

So when we talked again I told her I wanted a Ricochet™ for Christmas. "What's a Ricochet™?" she puzzled. Well, apparently between my explanations and her kids' interpretation, she got the idea. So, guess what I got for Christmas. That's right, a Ricochet™. How did you guess?

What does a sixty-two-year-old grandfather do with a radio-controlled car? Well, he walks it, of course. That is, when the grand kids aren't around to monopolize it.

I recognize the problem. What do you buy for a grandfather of eight who has everything? At least, it feels like I have all I really need and many things to enjoy. Eight of the things we enjoy are our grandchildren. I suspect they'll claim part ownership to the Ricochet™, but I'll maintain custody!

My problem now is, do I put my age on the warranty registration card? Maybe I could put 62, and they'd think I was six. Maybe I should fill it out with a pencil, or better still a crayon—left-handed!

I guess the real challenge I face is learning to play. It's not hard for me to goof off because it just looks like I'm resting then. But I sometimes have a hard time seeming to enjoy myself too much. Maybe there's more of the old Puritan work ethic left in me than I've recognized.

Is it a sin to enjoy oneself? I certainly hope not. Is it sinful to pursue enjoyment for its own sake? Well, I may have to wrestle with that. In the meantime, I've got a sneaking feeling God is watching me and laughing. I think he'd like to take my Ricochet™ for a spin.

In the meantime, if you'd like to challenge me to a race, come on down. Just be sure that your vehicle operates on 27 MHz because mine is 49 MHz. I wouldn't want us to become confused over who has the meanest machine!

January 1995

Slipped a Cog?

I value my wife's feedback. After reading my last column, she asked, "Do you remember how old you are?" I guess, in my enthusiasm to tell you about my new racing car, I did forget a birthday.

What bothers me is that I am noticing this kind of behavior with increasing frequency. I recently made a trip to a hardware store to purchase three O-rings to repair the faucet at our kitchen sink. While there, I bought a package of garden hose washers. When I got home, I laid the washers on the dining room table and promptly attended to the faucet.

Once that task was complete I decided to run the dishwasher. By then I was beginning to notice hunger pangs, so I got out the peanut butter, bread, milk, cookies, and pumpkin pie. After finishing my balanced meal, I proceeded to put everything away. I finished with the food and started looking for the washers.

They belonged in the plumbing parts box in the garage but they had disappeared. I remembered seeing them on the table but now they were gone. I tried to imagine what could have happened to them. My wife was gone so I couldn't ask (blame) her. I tried retracing my steps. I distinctly remembered seeing them on the table but they were no longer there. I was the only one home and I had spent most of my time in the kitchen or at the table.

I tried walking into the kitchen then back to the table, thinking the washers might reappear! No luck.

Then I began thinking about the dumbest place to look. They surely couldn't be in the refrigerator, but there they were, under the bread I had just put back in its place. Apparently I had set the bread on top of the washers on the table. When I picked up the bread to put it away, I had picked up the washers too. So, it's possible that I could slip a cog now and then.

I guess, if there's an encouraging note, it's that I often notice this before anyone else does. Sometimes I'm even able to correct it. The other day I saw a license plate holder that read:

OF ALL THE THINGS I'VE LOST
I MISS MY MIND THE MOST.

The driver wasn't that old so I know it's not age playing tricks on me. I guess that it's just that I have a lot on my mind, wherever it is!

It's a good thing I found the washers. If they had stayed in the refrigerator, they might have wound up as topping on a pizza. They were bright yellow so they would have added color but I'm not sure about the taste of vinyl. And what about their cholesterol content? Or, the calories, or fat? I guess, if you're eating pizza, you don't worry about such things.

February 1995

Save Me from Myself

One view of the current Major League Baseball strike is that the owners have said "Save us from ourselves. We want to limit the amount we can pay players because when we get to bidding for all-star players, we don't know when to stop. We can't help ourselves; we just go crazy and we need to be protected from our own excesses."

Some hear Congress saying, "Save us from ourselves" on the proposed balanced budget amendment to our Constitution. "When we start saying where federal money will be spent and there's the possibility of some of it going to our constituents, we can't help ourselves; we go a little crazy. We want to be forced to limit spending to the amount of money available. We don't have enough backbone to stand up to special interest groups on our own."

For the last several years I had tried to save enough from each paycheck to make quarterly payments for state and federal income taxes and Social Security. I'd heard that I could instruct the treasurer to withhold a set amount from my salary and deposit it for me but I thought that I just as well do it myself and have the use of my money a little longer.

Well, it wasn't working; every few years I would have to borrow money to finish paying my taxes. That was painful. Not only did I have to pay interest on the borrowed money, I had to admit my self-discipline was not as strong as I thought it should be. It seemed like there was always something we needed the money for—some emergency.

It happened again this year so I decided to have some withheld. That was a painful decision. I like to think of myself as a well-disciplined person. It hurt to admit that I needed more control.

Money is such a powerful thing that we have difficulty controlling ourselves when spending it. It gives us such a sense of superiority and fulfillment to buy what we want. We're frustrated when we see others with things we'd like to have.

While I've finally admitted to needing help with my money, I wonder about other areas of my life. What about my time? It seems to me that time has become even more precious than money. We may be more stingy with our time than our money. Maybe it's because we have some discretionary money—some that's not absolutely necessary for survival.

We think of time as the essence of life—we say, "He lived 81 years." Yet, that's not a complete measure of his life. What kind of life did he live? Was he productive? Was he helpful? These questions have to do with how he spent his time.

I suspect I'm a poorer steward of my time than of my money and that's a little scary. If I need more control in managing my money, what about my time? How do I go about having some withheld for vital uses?

March 1995

Finding the Will of God

Is finding the will of God a matter of discovering what God has predetermined? Or, is it an interactive search where each of us plays off the other?

In pastorless churches I sometimes hear persons pray, "Lord, guide us to the one you have already chosen to be our pastor." If this is the way God works, I think we're taking the wrong approach. It doesn't take a five-person committee to find a needle in a haystack; it takes divine guidance and one person may be better at understanding what God has already decided than a committee.

Instead, we've chosen to use committees to look at the church and discover its needs. God has given us intelligence and judgment and I believe he intends for us to use them. What kind of pastor do we need? How does this person fit those needs?

I suspect there may be several persons whom God could use as our pastor in a particular set of circumstances. I believe God is more interested in who a pastor is than where he or she serves. I don't believe God deals with us as robots to be manipulated for his predetermined purposes.

I don't mean to suggest that we're left to our own resources in finding God's ways. We need to pray for wisdom and guidance throughout the process. God can help us to be sensitive and aware of what's going on around us. He can help us gain insight to how someone would respond in our church.

Our judgments are fallible. We sometimes make wrong decisions. God usually doesn't overrule us; he leads us to learn from life's experiences. God does not give up on us when we make a wrong turn. He still works with us.

by George

The Bible says that we walk by faith, not by sight. For me, following God's ways is not a certain path but a tentative, step-by-step journey. Bunyan's pilgrim kept the destination in view but struggled through many detours and difficulties along the way.

April 1995

Remembering My Mother(s)

I've had two mothers. My biological mother died when I was eight and I barely remember her.

She was raised in New Hampshire and came to Urbana to attend the University of Illinois. Her dad's brother taught engineering here and she stayed with him and his family.

Mom was a student of the Classics—she studied Latin and Greek and graduated with honors in 1931. Attending University Baptist Church in Champaign, she met and eventually married Jake Davis, a farmer's son from Marion County in south central Illinois. After a year or so near Elmwood, west of Peoria, they moved to the family farm, near Patoka.

It's been painful for me to recognize that most of what I know about Mom is second hand—someone else had to tell me about her. I have pitifully few direct memories of her. I've found a few pictures and some written information. I remember Grandma Davis praising Mom and Dad helping fill some gaps, but there's so much more I'd like to know.

A few years ago, Mom's sister came to visit us here and helped give me a feel for her. Then, my three full brothers and I and our wives went to New Hampshire a few years ago and spent a week roaming over the area she loved. I still treasure that trip.

But the only Mom I knew for more than fifty years was my step mother. She signed on to help Dad raise four boys less than eleven years old. She brought a nine-year-old son to the marriage and she and Dad had a daughter a few years later.

Mom had her hands full with us. Just keeping the household going was more than a full time job. Dad and Grandpa owned and operated a 435-acre farm with cattle and hogs. All but about 100 acres was devoted to crops—soybeans, corn, and wheat.

We all worked hard and long. There wasn't much time for mischief but we did manage an occasional fight—that's what brothers do, isn't it? Mom was always worried that we would bend John's glasses. I know we gave her a hard time.

Our home was not ideal. Mom and Dad had at least their share of disagreements. Dad dealt with them by getting out of the house—working outside or going somewhere. Mom frequently threatened to leave.

Fortunately, in their later years, they found some accommodation and lived more peaceably. It has taken me a while to realize how much I owe her. We often challenged each other and sometimes I hated her but that passed, too.

My father gave me his family name and much more but I've come to realize that I've been shaped by my mothers, too. They both were real mothers and both were

George H. Davis

involved in raising me and giving me the kind of groundwork I've needed for a good life.

May 1995

Will Any of These Work?

I was speeding...

because everybody else was doing it. I set my cruise control for 65 mph and everybody was passing me, so I bumped it up a little.

because I was in a hurry; I got started a little late and needed to make up some time.

because it's a shame to have a car like this and not be able to open it up; it's made to run faster.

because the police expect you to speed; they won't stop you unless you're ten miles over the limit.

because I didn't really notice how fast I was going; I was just keeping up with the traffic. Isn't there a law against obstructing traffic?

because I wasn't thinking about how fast I was going; I've had a lot of things on my mind lately.

because my speedometer doesn't work right. I really don't know how fast I was going.

but I can afford it; what's the fine, $50?

and you people should get busy catching real criminals and leave us law-abiding citizens alone.

because that seems too slow for this area; don't you think it should be faster?

but my cousin is a policeman; do you know him?

but if I get one more ticket, I'll lose my license. You wouldn't want to do that to me, would you?

but I give to the policemen's benefit drive; didn't you notice my sticker?

but it must be this high octane fuel I'm burning. I was using the cheap stuff but the last time I filled up I got the good stuff. Maybe that's it!

because that guy up there cut in front of me and I was just trying to catch him; I don't think he even saw me.

Will these excuses work any better for other transgressions than they do for speeding?

June 1995

Who Owns "by George"? Let's Fight it Out!

I heard recently that George Foreman has an autobiography out called (you guessed it) *By George*. I'm hurt that he didn't ask my permission to use this title. After all, I've been using it as a byline for twenty-three years.

by George

I've known all along that I didn't have exclusive rights. A friend told me of a television weatherman in Florida who used it. I met a man in Kentucky who used it as a byword. His wife had died and he was interested in a certain widow in the church but his interest wasn't being reciprocated. He complained, "The Bible says, 'Love the brethren,' and by George she's not loving the brethren."

I stumbled onto this byline and it may be the best thing I've ever done. I've tried to use this column to show the human side of ministry; I've never been much for ceremony. I remember reading that it takes two fools to put a pastor on a pedestal—one to put him there, another to stay there.

It's my view that the minister was a human being before he or she became a minister and that possibly a little of that humanity remains. He (or she) is fallible and subject to dozens of other human ailments.

Sometimes we try to hide our humanity by our language. We seldom say anything (publicly) stronger than "by George." We use a ministerial vocabulary like—"bless you, brother." How many real people do you know who talk like that? We may even assume a ministerial tone when preaching.

In this column I've told about some of the stupid things I've done and some of my off-the-wall opinions. I've intended for most of them to be taken seriously. I want you to laugh with me at my stupidity. I want you to argue with me about my ideas; I'm not looking just for agreement. Most of all, I want you to think.

I guess gullibility ranks pretty high on my list of worst sins. Not everybody claiming to speak for Christians or even Baptists is worth following. I'm not sure I was born skeptical, but I've become cautious of people who want to do my thinking for me.

It's flattering when people agree with my ideas but it certainly is not essential; it may not even be healthy. I think my opinions are important but they're not infallible. Sometimes I'm wrong; just ask my wife! I hope I'm still growing, mentally if not physically. Some of the best ideas haven't been thought yet and I'd like to claim a few.

For now, George Foreman, how about a fight for the right to use "by George"? C'mon, let's duke it out—one grandpa to another.

No! No! Wait. I was just kidding.

July 1995

Roll Call of Church/Ass'n Leaders Lost

Over the last several years we've lost members who have been leaders in their churches and in the Association. I remember a time in the mid-80's when five deacons from Pennsylvania Avenue, Urbana died within a few months: **Jim Bryan** (whose widow, Helen Watson died a few years later), **Clyde Thomason**, **Mason Younker** (who had spent most of his church life in Paxton), and **Stanley Dill**, a former pastor at Fisher. **Paul Jacobs** also died about this time, though I'm not sure he was a deacon. **Ray Bartels** was a deacon; he and Margaret had worked among Indians in the southwest.

George H. Davis

Then ***Diane Lyvers***, the pastor's wife at LeRoy died. ***John Ivers***, a deacon at Temple, Champaign was an encourager to me. ***Alice Gillespie*** was the wife of the first full-time pastor at First Southern, Bloomington (now Vale). She also was a college class mate of my wife and me. Her husband, Rodney spent a lot of time in Urbana when she was *hospitalized at Carle.*

Jack Sanford was a pastor at Pennsylvania Avenue who went on to the Memphis area, then to be an associate editor of *Western Recorder*, the Baptist paper in Kentucky. ***Ralph Neathery*** was faithful at Bement. Bo***b Stout*** had been pastor at Immanuel, Rantoul then became an area missionary for the state convention.

Then we lost ***Neva Smith*** and ***Truman*** who had been pastor at Tolono for twenty years. Garden Hills, Champaign lost ***Georgia DeJarnett***, then ***Dan***. College Avenue, Normal lost ***Beth Loving***.

Gene Goble of Weldon had been pastor at Lodge. Then ***Alma Dubson*** whose husband, John is a deacon at Fisher, died. ***J. P. Cragar*** died in Arkansas; he had been pastor at Fisher. ***Henry Johnston*** of Fisher had been pastor at Carroll (later Pleasant View), Urbana.

Jim Torry died in retirement in Arkansas; he had been a deacon at Pennsylvania Avenue and trustee chair for the Association. ***Richard Bryant*** had been a pioneer missionary in central Illinois and had helped start fifty churches, including Vale; he died in Louisiana. ***J. S. Bell***, former pastor at Temple, died in Kentucky.

Pennsylvania Avenue lost ***Nellie Martin*** and ***Audine Smith***. Garden Hills lost ***Mary Askew***. We also miss ***Harry Hubbart***, a deacon at Tolono and longtime Finance Committee chair for the Association. ***Herman Baker*** was faithful at Bement.

That's a lot of leadership to lose over the last twelve years or so; I wonder if we're developing others to take their places. You may not recognize every name but I've known almost every one and I'm sure there are others I've missed.

August 1995

"Why did you heat this [Jell-O]?"

My wife, Leona recently was hospitalized for surgery. When she returned home, a couple of days later, Betsy Lewis brought in our supper. She had included several dishes—chicken and noodles, green peas, homemade bread, apple sauce, and a cherry gelatin dessert. What was supposed to be warm still was and we enjoyed it. There was enough that we put some away for another day.

She had brought it over in plastic containers, saying we could dispose of them when we were done. So, the next day I got them out of the refrigerator and we had another meal, compliments of Betsy's thoughtfulness. I popped the chicken and noodles and then the peas into the microwave and took them to the table. Leona said the chicken and noodles weren't warm enough, so I gave them another minute or two. Even after this second meal, we had food left.

We had company over the weekend and, with Leona's direction, I cooked a roast with potatoes, carrots, and celery. (I'm not much of a cook when you get past breakfast, unless it's on a grill.) We ate off that for a couple of meals.

by George

On Monday Leona was to return to the doctor's office, so we had lunch a little early. I brought out the chicken and noodles, peas, apple sauce, and dessert and began the microwaving process and setting dishes on the table. Leona sat down and asked why I had heated the gelatin dessert. I realized I had put the wrong container in the microwave; the chicken and noodles were still cold!

Well, I heated them up and we enjoyed the remnants of Betsy's generous provision. I asked Leona if the dessert might not still be good and she gave me permission to check it out. I did and it wasn't bad; I guess I preferred it jelled, though.

There must be a lesson here, I thought to myself. The containers looked enough alike that even after opening them and leaving the lids sitting on top, I had heated the wrong one. How often had I done something like that?

I guess it happens when I grab sermon notes out of the file and preach without giving serious thought and prayer to the setting; not all sermons fit every occasion. It may happen when I hear about a situation and suggest my last successful solution; each situation has its own unique ingredients and deserves its own attention. It may happen when I know of a pastor wanting to move, if I send a copy of his résumé to every pastorless church I hear about; not every preacher fits every church, anytime.

I remember the old saying, "If your only tool is a hammer, everything looks like a nail." I resolved to try and pay more attention to each task I approach and not to microwave gelatin again.

September 1995

Do you have the courage to read Burden of a Secret?

I met Jimmy Allen when he became President of the Radio-Television Commission of the Southern Baptist Convention. I was serving as a trustee of that agency.

In recent months I had read news accounts about his family going through an agonizing ordeal with AIDS. So, the first book I picked up (using the gift certificate the pastors gave me at the annual meeting) was *Burden of a Secret: A Story of Truth and Mercy in the Face of AIDS* (Moorings: Nashville, 1995).

He describes how four members of his family contracted AIDS. His daughter-in-law received tainted blood during the difficult birth of her first child, but it was not until after the birth of a second child that they learned of the danger to which they had been exposed. The son tested negative for HIV but the daughter-in-law and both children were positive. Then another son informed his parents that he, too, had tested positive.

Jimmy writes frankly about the difficulties his family faced and the loneliness they felt. After the youngest grandchild died in the mid '80s, they tried to find a place where the surviving child could attend Sunday School. He tells of their disappointment:

Despite our publicly announced intentions to follow Jesus—to live as he did—most churches were following the dictates of fear. Jesus voluntarily touched lepers,

George H. Davis

but he did not die of leprosy. He died at the hands of religious leaders who were so anxious to hold onto their power they wouldn't touch a leper to save their lives.

It hit me hard when I realized that the church as an institution had so failed that it could not summon the cleansing touch of Jesus for a four-year-old child. I vividly saw a reality I did not want to see. I saw that in many churches the strategy of gathering new members has become a science. We have learned well the techniques of church growth. To thrive in the user-friendly, what's-good-for-me era of modern Christianity, churches are supposed to be homogeneous, well-cared-for, comfortable, and entertaining.

The competition for new members is severe. The debt on buildings required for modern-day mega-churches is high. We don't minister to those in need because we cannot afford to offend and lose paying members or prospects for membership. The fear of deadly disease is enough to cause widespread panic in our church, not because the hurting people would fail to find us or refuse to come in, but because the comfortable and complacent people would be in such a hurry to get out (pp. 98-99). *Permission to quote has been requested.*

This book ought to be required reading for all pastors and church staff. Lay persons could also profit, but I warn you—it's not enjoyable reading. Read it where you're not ashamed to cry!

November 1995

I Never Put It in My Coat Pocket

Sometimes I've written about dumb things I've done, but, until now, I haven't revealed anyone else's flaws. I believe that having a healthy sense of humor begins with the ability to laugh at one's own folly; to laugh at others can be cruel.

However, at some risk, I'm going to tell on my wife. I'm doing so only because I think the situation is a snapshot of our society and I have her permission.

Recently she lost her driver's license. They were in a plastic pouch she usually carries in her purse. There were a few credit cards and other identification in the packet, too.

For several days she retraced her steps, turning the house upside down and revisiting stores where she might have had the packet out. All of this searching and inquiry proved fruitless.

Reluctantly she canceled the credit cards and waited for an opportunity to get a replacement license. Meanwhile she asked for a ride to Church and I drove her around. Two days after getting her new license, she found the old one. It was in the pocket of a coat she seldom wears—she still doesn't remember putting it there. "I *never* put it in my coat pocket," she protests.

One problem is that she has two winter coats; she gave another away. Of course, when I stop to count, I can think of six coats in my closet. One is an all-weather with a zip-out lining; it should be thrown out. Another is a down-filled jacket I inherited from a son. I rescued it from some clothes my wife had assembled to give away.

Tony Campolo writes about shopping for people who have everything:

by George

Just think about last Christmas season. Your biggest problem was probably not figuring out where you would get enough money to buy presents for family members and friends. Instead, it was trying to figure out what to buy for people who had everything. The answer to that problem should have been self-evident. What you should buy for those who have everything, is nothing. But you didn't have the guts to pull it off, did you?

No!

Instead you went up and down the aisles of department stores having anxiety attacks. Panic-stricken, you searched, yea, even prayed, that somebody somewhere had invented some new things that nobody needs so you could buy them for people who have everything. This is not an absurd description of a reasonable world. It is a rational description of an absurd world (*Carpe Diem*, Dallas: Word, 1994, p. 36).

December 1995

Doing Laundry

Laundry is not something I do regularly. In fact, I guess it had been thirty years since I had done much. I'm quite sure I did some while our kids were small and I clearly remember doing laundry during college. I also remember taking or mailing laundry home to be done when I was in college.

But when my wife was in the hospital for an unplanned visit over New Year's, I found myself doing laundry again. It had been a long time but I still knew to sort it into three piles. If you had asked me to describe the piles, I might have been in trouble. One was whites, one was colors, the other was whatever didn't seem to fit in the previous categories.

I'm getting bogged down in details, so back to why I was doing laundry. Leona had mentioned feeling numbness in her left arm and hand one evening. The next morning her whole left side was feeling numb. She called her doctor's office and was advised to go to the emergency room. We spent most of the day there and, after several tests and conferences with doctors, she was admitted. She spent the next four days undergoing tests and being medicated.

The outcome was that we discovered she had suffered a small stroke and needed blood pressure medication and an aspirin a day. She had no paralysis nor problem with speech or vision. She has minimal lasting effects from the stroke.

The reminder about how to do laundry was not the only thing I learned though. Since her mother had died of a stroke at age 46, we were both keenly aware of this danger. We're grateful for the wake up call, for the Lord's care, and for good doctors. We're grateful for your concern, too.

Thinking back about doing laundry led me to remember Grandma Davis' advice. "Be sure to rinse well," she told me as I was going back to college after a weekend at home. Isn't it strange how that one item remains in my mind?

George H. Davis

As I was growing up, we had a Maytag washer on the back porch. On wash day it would be rolled into place and two rinse tubs would join it. We'd put bluing into one of those tubs.

The part of wash day I remember best, aside from getting to start the gasoline engine, was cleaning the clothes lines. I would take a small rag, soak it in kerosene, and clean the lines before any clean clothes were hung there. On really cold days, the clothes would freeze on the line and have to be taken down and finish drying in the house.

The other thing I remember is a relative of Grandma's showing us how they rode in the German cavalry. Our horse decided to take him under the clothes line and he dismounted rather abruptly, but that's another story.

January 1996

The Arenas of Life

Christianity is not fleshed out in an arena with its crowds and excitement. Rallies and inspiration are useful to motivate some to faithful living. For others, however, the cheerleader atmosphere does little.

The real test of one's Christianity is not at Church or at a mass meeting but in the day to day routine of family and work. Someone has said, "It's not how high you jump but how straight you walk when you hit the ground."

The arena where we're expected to demonstrate God's presence is in our family, our work, and our play. The gritty business of getting along with another human who's as stubborn as we are tests our patience and persistence. Add to that the inevitable pressures of child rearing and you begin to know the meaning of being tested. Then mix in the challenge of maintaining your integrity at work and you begin to feel like you're trying to occupy all three rings of a three-ring circus. But, you're not done! How do you play in a way that honors God and your commitment to Him? These are the real arenas where one's Christianity is proved.

Elijah appeared to win a great victory before the crowd on Mount Carmel but when Jezebel threatened him, he ran. Finally, at a cave on Mount Horeb, the LORD spoke, "Go out and stand on the mountain before the LORD, for the LORD is about to pass by" (1 Kings 19:11a NRSV).

You'll remember that Elijah, who had called down fire on Mt. Carmel, now experienced God, not in the rock-splitting wind nor the earthquake or the fire, but in "a sound of sheer silence" (v. 12b). In the eerie silence Elijah went out to the mouth of the cave where God demanded to know why he was there.

Elijah gave his well-rehearsed complaint:

I have been very zealous for the LORD, the God of hosts; for the Israelites have forsaken your covenant, thrown down your altars, and killed your prophets with the sword. I alone am left, and they are seeking my life, to take it away (v. 14).

Maybe you'll also remember that God gave the self-pitying prophet more work than he would accomplish. He sent him to anoint new kings for Syria and Israel and his successor; when God tells you to choose your successor, you can be fairly sure your work is about over. Then God announced to Elijah that he was not alone—there were seven thousand who had not bowed to Baal nor kissed him.

How could a man like Elijah, who had seen God's great victory at Mt. Carmel, become so frightened and depressed that he asked God to kill him? While he often performed in the public arena, his own reassurance came in a solitary, inescapable silence.

The old auditorium at Ridgecrest Baptist Assembly in the Blue Ridge Mountains of North Carolina used to bear this inscription on its cornerstone:
From these mountain peaks of inspiration
   Southern Baptists would carry the Gospel
     to every valley of human need.

I'm reminded that it was when Jesus and his inner circle of disciples came down from the Mount of Transfiguration that they met the epileptic boy and his father.

We're often like Peter who wanted to pitch three tents and stay on the mountain—life isn't lived on the mountain. There's power in peak experiences of inspiration but the real test is whether our lives are transformed day by day.

February 1996

A Davis Invasion

Until 1993 I had understood that my Davis ancestors came from Tennessee and Kentucky. A cousin shared information that they came from Surry County, North Carolina.

Elijah Henry Davis moved his family to Jefferson County, Illinois in the mid to late 1830s. At least four of his brothers also moved from Surry County to Jefferson County. Elijah was my grandfather's grandfather. His grandfather, David Davis, emigrated from Wales to Virginia. He apparently was a seafarer. One source describes him as "the owner of a vessel which plied the Atlantic carrying people from the Old Country to the United States."

In about 1784 David moved from Goochland, Virginia to Surry County. Several of his sons were planters and large slave holders. However, when the Davis family moved to Illinois, "many of them took an active part in defending the Old Flag during the late war." I take that to mean they fought for the Union cause.

What does all this have to do with me today? Well, I'm going to be in Surry Baptist Association for a World Missions Conference March 24-31. I'm to speak in ten churches over the eight days but I'm hoping to have some time for digging into my family history, too. I notice that there's a Davis Street in Mount Airy, where we'll be staying. Oh, did I tell you that one of my brothers, John will be there too? He works with ministries and education in Madison Baptist Association in Huntsville, Alabama. I hope they can stand two Davises.

You may see this interest in family history as pre-occupation with the past but I see it as learning more about the present. I doubt that any of us escape the influence of our ancestry. We get not only our gene pool from them but also our attitudes and

George H. Davis

preferences. Of course we can change them but we have to change from something to something else. I think it may be helpful to know where we've come from.

I have some sense of going home as I plan for next week. I realize that David's descendants may only have lived in North Carolina for fifty-five to sixty-five years. I don't know if some stayed there or not; we may or may not find some relatives. I guess one of my hopes would be to find David's grave.

Yes, I remember John the Baptizer's warnings to those who boasted about their ancestry:

> don't think you can pull rank by claiming Abraham as "father." Being a child of Abraham is neither here nor there—children of Abraham are a dime a dozen. God can make children from stones if he wants (Luke 3:8 *The Message* by Eugene Peterson).

Davises may be a dime a dozen out there.

Anyway, pray for Director of Missions Wayne Trexler and the churches of Surry Association that they'll survive the Davis invasion.

March 1996

Why Did He Move?

One question I've mulled over as I've tried to put together my family history is why my branch of the Davis family left North Carolina for southern Illinois. I know Elijah Davis moved west in the mid- to late 1830's; I don't know why. I know that at least four of his brothers also settled in Illinois. I know that their father, Reece, joined them in 1849.

Could it be that they were opposed to slavery? That doesn't seem to fit though many of the family are reported to have fought with Union forces. Elijah's father and grandfather were slave owners in Carolina. I wonder what would have turned Elijah against slavery.

I've wondered if the promise of free or cheap land was involved in moving west. His grandfather bought 200 acres for "fifty shillings for every hundred acres" and another 200 for "thirty shillings for every hundred acres." I don't know exactly how much that is but I'd like to buy some central Illinois farmland for that price.

When we were in North Carolina, my brother John and I visited the historical museum in Mount Airy. One of the ladies there suggested that they may have worn the land out after a few generations and decided to move on. I'm not sure the land they moved to in Jefferson County, Illinois was much better than what they left. They came from the foothills of the Blue Ridge Mountains to settle east of Mt. Vernon, on relatively flat land. I don't know what they'd heard from the Lewis and Clark expedition early in the 1800's.

I found another possible reason while visiting the Surry County (NC) courthouse. We found a trust deed that Elijah's father, Reece, had made in 1838. He apparently owed a C. W. Williams $130; he put up four of his slaves as security. I don't know what the outcome of that venture was but I'm beginning to wonder if he followed his son west to avoid debt!

by George

I've been told that if you look up your family tree long enough, you'll find someone hanging there. Well, at least I have multiple choices now. Maybe it's "all of the above" or "none of the above."

Trying to speculate on the reasons other persons did what they did, especially in another time, is risky; there's so much information I don't have. It makes you wonder why anyone, in his or her right mind, would speculate, doesn't it?

I guess there's little harm can come as long as it's in my family and it's at least five generations removed. When it gets hairy is when I try to figure out your motives, without even talking to you! I have enough trouble figuring out why I act like I do, let alone worrying about you.

April 1996

"The Thrill of Victory; The Agony of Defeat"

You've heard of the thrill of victory and the agony of defeat. Well, I experienced both (with a twist) last month.

It began when a lady I didn't recognize showed up for one of our workshops; she wasn't from any of our churches. Then I remembered getting a call from a lady asking what time the workshop began. My mind began racing. She must, somehow, have gotten hold of a copy of our April newsletter and decided she was interested in that meeting. My only question was how she had seen the newsletter.

However, my bubble burst when I learned that the host pastor had placed an ad in the local paper and she had responded to it; she had called the Church for details. So, it wasn't our newsletter that drew her but the ad. It wasn't my victory but it was a victory. She had no connection to any church but showed an interest in becoming involved.

The other experience has not shown a bright side yet. I was told that the State Royal Ambassador/Challenger Track Meet had been canceled this year. The information came from the State Associational Planning/Briefing Meeting. I thought it was curious that I'd received nothing in writing but went ahead with the information I had.

After consulting with some of our RA leaders, we canceled our track meet and sent a note to pastors and Men's Ministries directors. We included a note in the newsletter. A day or two later we got a call from the State office telling us the meet had not been canceled.

I know you can't believe everything you see in print but it's agonizing to be the bearer of faulty information. It's not the first time I've made a mistake but this time it had potential for harm across the State. We mail our newsletter to the other associations and some might pick up incorrect information— if they read it!

I take some pride in our newsletter and try to keep it accurate and interesting. Sometimes I feel I'm at least moderately successful. I know that I find it hard to admit to mistakes—I'm more that a little stubborn. I guess I've received a needed reminder to be more careful and maybe a little less proud!

May 1996

George H. Davis

Too Much Pressure

What happens when families find that old ways of celebrating no longer work? They find new ways. We switched our larger family get together from Christmas to Memorial Day weekend. This year we had 51 at our family gathering.

Not everyone can make every reunion. What do we do? We don't sit around, wringing our hands and wishing everyone in our family felt more loyalty. We celebrate what we have and work to make it better. We recognize that every family is a blend of other families and every member decides on their own priorities. We learn to respect one another rather than suspect the worst.

Another experience this summer has reminded me of a lesson I learned several years ago. A pair of robins built a nest on our front porch lamp. It wasn't too much of a nuisance until the babies hatched and their parents began feeding them. Then they kept the side of the house and the porch littered with their droppings.

I washed the siding and the porch with a garden hose. It wasn't long until it was as messy as ever. So, after a few days I got out the hose again; this time I attached a nozzle. The force of the water must have startled the birds because they began bailing out of the nest.

They were not big enough to fly much. They managed to get down without injuring themselves but could not fly back. I caught those I could find and put them back into the nest, but they wouldn't stay.

The lesson—too much pressure scares birds…and people. The people part happened when I was in seminary and was pastor of a rural church near Louisville, Illinois. It was a one-room building with a basement.

We were reaching some young families and were expecting our first child. We had talked about how we could make a room for a nursery. Though it would not be ideal, we could fix a room in the basement; that seemed to be the best option.

One night during a business meeting, I suggested we talk about it. No one said anything. So, I turned the meeting over to a deacon and made a motion that we fix up a nursery room. Of course, it got seconded and it carried—how many motions can you think of that lost in a Baptist church?

Several days later, we were visiting with the Sunday School Superintendent. Jim asked me to come outside so we could talk.

"George," he began, "people don't like that way of doing things." They may not vote against it but "they don't intend to do anything about it."

I appreciated Jim's willingness to let me know what I had missed—people don't like to be forced. It doesn't take a fire hose to scare people off!

June 1996

You might be getting old if…

You might be getting old if…
- You enjoy a leisurely stroll through the cemetery.
- After a stroll through the cemetery, you realize you have more friends there

by George

- than in town.
- You, upon being introduced to someone, think, "I think I knew your father."
- You can remember when we sang only the "first, second, and last" stanzas of most hymns.
- You remember funeral visitation at home.
- You remember when your church called a pastor for a year at a time.
- You remember shaped-note hymnals.
- You remember pledging allegiance "to the flag of United States of America, one nation, indivisible, with liberty and justice for all" before "under God" was added.
- You attended revival services every night for two weeks (or more).
- You sang out of *Songs of Faith*.
- You were baptized in a creek or river.
- You remember Nursery, Beginners, Primaries, Juniors, Intermediates, Young People, and Adults.
- Your Sunday School class met in a room made by drawing curtains.
- You remember funeral home fans.
- You attended an associational annual meeting that lasted three days.
- You stayed in the home of strangers while attending an associational (or state) meeting.
- Your pastor preached at your church only on the first and third Sundays each month.
- You remember copies of the Revised Standard Version of the Bible being burned.

July 1996

East Central Prairie

There's no accounting for taste—I've heard that and I partly believe it. I'm no musician but, like many others, I like the music I grew up with. I remember sitting around the radio Saturday nights, listening to Your Hit Parade. Gisele MacKenzie and others would sing popular songs.

I don't remember the first time I heard Red River Valley but it still has an emotional impact on me; whenever I hear it, I get choked up. Of course, it doesn't take much to bring a lump to my throat or a tear to my eye. Maybe it's the music, especially if it's played on a harmonica. Maybe it's the thought of leaving; that's never been easy for me. So, on the occasion of the public announcement of my retirement, I've paraphrased Red River Valley.

According to *Reader's Digest Family Songbook* (1969), in 1896 James J. Kerrigan wrote a Tin Pan Alley song called In the Bright Mohawk Valley. "Pioneers heading Westward picked up the tune, simplified the melody, and changed the lamenting lover to a cowboy and the locale to the Texas panhandle" (p. 222). So, in honor of the centennial of the original version, here's my contribution.

George H. Davis

From this prairie I've said I am going;
You may miss my odd thoughts and wry smile,
For I've said I am taking my byline
That brightened your pathway awhile.

Chorus
Come and sit by my side if you love me;
Do not hasten to bid me adieu,
But remember the East Central prairie
And the guy who has written for you.

From this prairie I've said I am going;
When I go, my "by George" goes along.
Would I leave it alone unprotected,
Would I let someone else sing my song?

As I go to my home in the country,
May we never forget these good years,
That we spent on the East Central prairie
And the times we shared laughter and tears.

I can see you're a little choked up too, aren't you?

August 1996

New Set of Beaters

Maybe you don't need a new mixer; maybe all you really need is a new set of beaters. We've had a heavy duty kitchen mixer almost all our married life—now approaching forty-four years. We started with one from Leona's mother and later bought a replacement. I remember buying at least two sets of beaters for them— one in Evansville, Indiana and the last in Peoria.

Sometimes it's taken some detective work to find a small appliance repair shop that handles parts. Then you have to order the right beaters—that seldom happens the first time. It's a little inconvenient and not at all inexpensive, until you compare it to the price of a new mixer!

We live in a throw away culture. If something doesn't work like it's supposed to, we throw it away and get a new one. We do it with everything from the myriad of small appliances it takes to run a household these days to computers. We're used to junking the old to get something bigger and faster; we assume new is better.

I guess it's partly a generational thing. My wife and I belong to a generation born during the depression of the thirties. We were raised to make do with what we had.

We grew up with the saying, "Don't throw out the baby with the bath water." It makes little sense to the current generation. You have to explain that we used to bathe babies in a dish pan on the kitchen table.

by George

I think I know how stupid that sounds in the computer age. We're used to computers lasting maybe five years then needing to be upgraded. It's not that they're broken. They're just outmoded. They're too small and too slow. We now have new machines that can outperform the old ones.

That principle may not apply to every area of our lives though. Sometimes a cast iron skillet is exactly what you need. Sometimes it's hard to improve on an old, heavy duty kitchen mixer. The only catch is, you've got to find a new set of beaters about every fifteen years.

In many of our households, we have so much stuff it's pathetic. Leona and I have been trying to get ready to move. I've been cleaning out the garage and she's been working on the pantry—do I have to explain what a pantry is?

The other day she handed me a waffle iron to throw out. My immediate reaction was to ask, "Is it broken?" My concern wasn't that we'd be destitute without it—we still have two working waffle irons.

Again, I guess it's a generational thing. Our generation finds it hard to throw things away. We think, "Maybe it could be repaired" or "I may need this some day." The next generation might say, "Maybe we could sell this in our next garage sale." Isn't it interesting how we've discovered ways to recycle our once-essential, now-discarded stuff? One person's trash is another's treasure was never so true as on a summer weekend.

I wonder who invented garage sales. Was it our acquisitive generation or was it our kids, looking over all we've stashed away and asking, "What are we going to do with all this stuff?" Or, did it take the combined efforts of two generations?

September 1996

Music in Worship

Not only can't white men jump, they can't clap, either. That's the impression I got at the annual meeting of our State convention earlier this month. We were meeting at St. Mark's Baptist Church in Harvey.

The Church seemed to be made up primarily of African Americans. Choirs from two African American churches sang. Their music was—spirited; I don't know how else to describe it.

Sometimes they would ask the congregation to "put your hands together." They would begin clapping to the beat of their music. I watched as some tried to join them. Some were fairly proficient, many were off beat, others were uncomfortable.

I don't mean to buy into the stereotype that African Americans are born with a sense of rhythm. Neither do I believe that Anglos do not have music in their souls. The beat and the tunes may be different or we may join in a mixed chorus at times. We need to learn to respect each other's traditions.

Music in worship is one of the current battlefields in churches. Some would ignore hymnals and use choruses. Some favor music with a country flavor. Others want only the "old" songs. Generally, they mean those they grew up with—many were written in the late 19th and early 20th centuries; they're really not that old.

There's also controversy over the proper instruments to use in church. Of course, there's the noninstrumental Church of Christ. Some feel only an organ or perhaps an organ and a piano are appropriate; they sound "holy." Of course, a piano can be used for honky tonk music, so some would rule it out. Some would like to use guitars and drums; others think that would be sacrilegious.

It may not surprise you if I tell you I'm a rather sentimental person. Almost any time I hear a Burl Ives song, I notice a lump in my throat. I've been a fan of the Jasper County (Illinois) native for a long time. A few years ago, my wife and I got to hear him in person at Krannert Center for the Performing Arts on the campus of the University of Illinois.

I suspect many people are touched by some musician or some kind of music. How can we use this powerful instrument to tell of God's love? I doubt there's a more effective way to reach people.

We probably learn more theology (good and bad) from songs than from sermons. They have a way of staying with us—not many sermons are that poetic.

November 1996

Bye, George

It was September 1958 when I had my first contact with an East Central church. Dale Clemens was pastor at Farmer City. I had followed him in a student pastorate at Second Little Prairie, near Louisville, Illinois. He had booked me to preach a revival during our Seminary spring break. However, he had left Second Little Prairie before the revival. They wanted me to come ahead and they called me as pastor.

Dale invited me to preach a revival in Farmer City. Leona and I had moved to Altamont and had a year-old son. We spent the week with the Clemens. Curt and Ann Rau were married that week; I don't remember about any other results.

My second connection in East Central came when Larry Askew and Pat Davis asked me to marry them at Temple Baptist Church, Champaign. Larry had been music director at Second Baptist Church, Herrin, where I served as pastor. He had been a student at Southern Illinois University, Carbondale.

At that time Temple had not built their sanctuary; what is now their fellowship hall served. When I got to the Church, I noticed that their library was named in honor of George Turner. He had been a University of Illinois student who had died of cancer. I was his family's pastor at Louisville.

When I became director of missions here, one of my first visits was to Hillcrest Baptist Church, Tuscola. There I discovered people I had known in three previous locations. Morris and Joyce Weaver, who had been members at Herrin, Second were there. So was Jim Coatney; his family was members at Louisville, First while I served Second Little Prairie, north of town. One of our families lived across the street from the Coatneys, so I knew them well. Dick Stilley had grown up in Liberty Baptist Church near Macedonia, Illinois; that was one of my college pastorates. He and his wife also were at Hillcrest.

by George

One of my last duties in East Central was to attend William Hedges funeral. I had known his son, Bill. He was in school at the U of I when I was at SIU. We met through State Baptist Student Union functions. I also had met William.

It was only after he died that I discovered his significance in the beginning of the first Southern Baptist churches in this area. As he taught school in various locations, he served as pastor at a number of churches.

I also felt connected when I learned he was to be buried at Arrington Prairie Baptist Church, near Sims, Illinois. I had served the Association there before coming to East Central. I remembered the Church's nickname--Dickeyville. William's first wife had been a Dickey.

Ric Hardison suggested this modification of my usual signature.

bye, George

December 1996

Louisville Baptist Association Newsletter
Louisville Baptist Association
January 2001 – June 2005

Welcome to the New Millennium!

If you think it took a long time to elect a president, think about how long it took us to get into the new millennium. Some tried to jump start the process, thinking that 2000 was the first year of the new millennium; it was actually the last year of the 21st century and of the second millennium of the Christian era.

As a child, I remember wondering if I would live to see the new century. I thought I probably would but knew it was not guaranteed.

One of my favorite Biblical passages is from Psalm 90, titled A Prayer of Moses, the man of God: "So teach us to number our days, that we may apply *our* hearts unto wisdom" (v. 12).

Wisdom doesn't come just from living, it comes from learning from life. We all make mistakes; if we learn from them, we gain wisdom. If we don't learn, we are doomed to repeat them.

I've surely done my share of dumb things. I remember (as pastor at Second Little Prairie) explaining that Lazarus (who was raised from the dead) and Lazareth (of the rich man and Lazareth parable) were different and that even the spelling of their names was different.

Imagine my chagrin when I discovered that, although they were different men, their names were spelled the same; I thought I had heard people pronounce their names differently. I don't remember whether I confessed my error or not.

January 2001

Who's Got Poor Memory?

I'm amazed at the poor memory of recent generations. When I speak of pastors I have known or historical events I remember, they act like I was speaking in an unknown tongue. It puzzles me that they do not recall what is so fresh in my mind.

My recall sometimes plays tricks on me. I'm sometimes confused and often blank when I hit the rewind button; facts are missing and people don't always appear in the proper order. None the less, I'm left in the lurch when people a little younger than myself do not remember what is so clear to me.

I remember many of the pastors that have served our churches over the past fifty years. Clebert Weger, who served at Louisville, was a fishing buddy. We spent a few hours at Lake Sara. The Mathises, from Watson, still keep in touch with us.

I remember when Dr. Dobbs was at Effingham, First. And Carvin Bryant. I remember Ed Williams from Oak Street, Flora. And Ferdie Schimpf

I remember Clyde Sinclair and Charlie Allen. Charlie was from Iola and was associational clerk for several years. I remember F.M. Sparling from Watson.

by George

I remember when Kenneth Hall was our associational missionary. It was Brother Hall that gave me some of my first chances to serve on the associational level; he asked me to be part of the Vacation Bible School team.

February 2001

I Remember Charles

I remember when Charles Everitt became missionary for Louisville Baptist Association; I was pastor at Altamont. I was in my second year as moderator of the Association when he came in April of 1959.

Charles got me involved in teaching Seminary Extension classes. I taught for four years and served as registrar/treasurer for the Louisville/Westfield Center. He served both Associations and we spent some time together on the road.

I remember that one pastor was using his newsletter to attack Louisville Association and our missionary. At our annual meeting I made a motion that we seat the messengers except for those from that church.

Trying to overcome my brashness, Charles offered an amendment that a committee be appointed to confer with the messengers from the offending church. The Association saw the wisdom of that action. That's probably not the only time he bailed me out.

I still remember my surprise when he called in the summer of 1990 inviting me to preach at a homecoming Mullen Baptist Church was having. He was serving as their pastor ten years after he had officially retired.

I don't remember all his stories but I do remember his good humor and his willingness to work.

March 2001

Churches in Association

The Association is more than a meeting we go to, it's what we are. It's more than an organization we form, it's who we are. We are *in* association. We respect and care for each other. We encourage and pray for one another.

Association is our response to God's call. He has called us to follow Him and live as family. We serve in our churches as brothers and sisters. Across our churches, we make up the larger family as it gathers for reunions.

There are four First or First Southern Baptist Churches in Louisville Association. But it's not our name nor our size that interests the Lord. He's watching to see how closely we're following Him. Are we going after the people he cares about or do we want to do some screening first?

For most of us, we came to know Baptists outside our own churches when we met others at Associational meetings. The Association continues to exist after the meetings are adjourned. *That's* what Association is.

George H. Davis

As we set out to serve the Lord, we may have to do some organizing or reorganizing but the heart of who we are is association--families of believers working to make the family grow.

April 2001

What are You Planting?

It's probably too late this year, but I have a suggestion for your crop next year. Unless you already have specific needs, I'll offer this.

Have you noticed how many communication towers are sprouting up? I notice them most along Interstate highways but they're not limited to those areas. We have one near the intersection of Routes 50 and 51 in Sandoval.

I'm certainly not an expert on communication towers but I have observed some things. I'm not sure how close you can plant them but sometimes they seem to be within shouting distance of each other. I wonder if there is a string running between them with tin cans at each end?

I don't know what kind of yield to expect. If you believe those commercials for wireless phones, you'd better expect some static. At least many of them promise to do away with it. If it wasn't a problem, there surely would be less attention paid it.

One advantage I see is that you won't need any fertilizer; maybe just a little herbicide to keep the weeds down. So if you have some high ground, don't be surprised if someone offers you a deal.

May 2001

Trackin' up the Floor

We have two doors in our house; one goes into the kitchen where there is linoleum floor. The other is the front door which is seldom used. It goes into a carpeted entryway.

We have a problem with debris getting tracked onto our kitchen floor. If you're not familiar with "debris," it is dirt or grime or whatever tracks are made of. I've noticed this gets worse when two things happen: (1) the grass is wet and (2) there is foot traffic.

The grass gets wet when there is dew and when it rains. The foot traffic is a result of us going in and out or of company coming. I don't want to eliminate the moisture nor the company. Neither do I want us to be caged in or out. I guess we'll have to learn to live with the debris.

Churches have similar problems. People, unused to coming to church, sometimes track debris into our buildings. Not all the tracks are left on the floor. Sometimes people behave in ways we think inappropriate; sometimes they wear clothing that we deem out of place.

The question is, "Do we want to shut them out of our buildings? Or, should we be reaching out and welcoming these people?"

Can we quietly clean up after them and help them come to love the Church as we do? Or, will we insist that they clean themselves up and then welcome them?

June 2001

Don't Kill the Rooster!

Baptist preachers have a reputation for liking fried chicken. At least, they take a lot of kidding about it. I may be telling more about myself than I should, but I probably would not choose chicken as my favorite meat. As far as I'm concerned, a pork chop is hard to beat.

Some may wonder if the preachers' taste for chicken doesn't amount to a desire to get even with the rooster that woke Simon Peter to his failure. The problem with that kind of thinking is that it treats the rooster as the villain and not as the alarm. It was Peter who was guilty, not the rooster; he was God's gift to deliver a message to Peter.

Who said, "If you don't like the message, don't kill the messenger"? When God sends a rooster to make us aware of our distance from him, we should thank him, not seek to kill his messenger. Our proper response is to weep over sin and turn from it. The rooster is our friend; the sin is our enemy.

July 2001

Is it a Hill or a Valley?

If you happen to hear me talking about the road to our house, you may perk up when I mention a "hill." I put that in quotation marks because I'm using it in an unusual way.

As I was growing up we referred to the area on each side of a small creek as "the hill." Actually it's hardly a creek—more of a ditch. It's more properly called a valley than a hill. But we called it "the hill."

Since we've moved back home, I've realized that we probably misnamed it. But I've also discovered that we were not alone. There's a road a few miles east of us called Seven Hills Road. I've raised the question of why it's so named when actually the road crosses seven creeks, not hills.

You may say that you can't have a valley without a hill on each side. I suggest that when the surrounding terrain is relatively level and a creek runs through it, what you have is a valley, not two hills. About the nearest thing we have to a hill is Interstate overpasses.

It may sound a little like the argument whether a glass of water is half full or half empty. I don't intend to attribute negative or positive values to either hill or valley. Maybe we ought to talk about a change in elevation rather than try to decide on the norm.

August 2001

George H. Davis

Majority Rules?

One of the blessings of congregational government is that the majority rules. Baptists share with other evangelicals in emphasizing that earthly authority in churches should rest upon the congregation. Of course, ultimate authority belongs to God alone.

Ministers and lay persons may lead but they have authority only as it is given by the congregation. It is the body who finally decides its direction.

The curse of majority rule kicks in when the majority runs rough shod over the minority. The rights of every member should be honored. No one should be disregarded. Each one is a person and each one should be valued.

We should not forget that the majority has sometimes been wrong. Remember the report of the majority of spies who toured the Promised Land before Israel invaded? Ten of the twelve felt they should not attempt to take the Land. Israel followed their advice—to their life long regret. Two of the spies urged Israel to proceed but they were voted down. They lived to be proven right but that was little comfort during the forty years of aimless wandering.

Only as we value one another and are willing to submit our wills to one another can democracy work in our churches. If we insist on lording it over those who disagree with us, we may have purity but we'll surely lack fellowship.

September 2001

Brothers

I wasn't surprised to get an E-mail from my brother Don from New York City. He lives in Mt. Juliet, Tennessee, just east of Nashville. He is in NYC with Disaster Relief workers from Tennessee. They're preparing meals for police and firemen working at the site of the World Trade Center.

Don and his wife, Ann, are featured in the current issue of *Ventures* learner guide, a LifeWay Bible study quarterly for senior adults. In addition to Don's Disaster Relief work, they have made scores of mission trips overseas. He's retired from the former Baptist Sunday School Board.

Our next brother, John and his wife, Agnes, were with us recently. He was here for an On Mission Celebration in Kaskaskia Association. The event was cancelled because several of the missionaries could not get airline reservations. John had come early to help me with some remodeling to our upstairs bedrooms. I was glad for his help. He has recently retired as a Church and Community worker with the North American Mission Board.

I thought of my youngest brother when I discovered a homemade toboggan in our machine shed. I was cleaning up scrap metal when I noticed a piece of corrugated roofing with a thirty gallon barrel fastened to one end. It had runners attached to the bottom side and similar boards on the top edges. I didn't recognize it so I E-mailed my brothers asking if they knew anything about it. None did except Richard, who figured it was about fifty years old.

October 2001

by George

This World is not My Home

The Illinois Secretary of State's office is in the process of issuing new vehicle license plates; the old ones are about worn out. When you get new plates, you have the option to retain your old numbers and letters. If you choose to do so, you will be given a temporary plate to use while the new ones are being made.

They used to issue a paper tag to tape to your window; now it's a cardboard plate for the rear of your vehicle. I remember, during the War, when plates were made of soybeans.

We had better get used to temporary tags; that's all any of us can hope for. No permanent tags are available. No, I'm not talking about vehicle license; I'm talking about a license to live.

I was shocked to receive word of the death of a preacher friend, Jim Crask. I had known him since our days with Greater Wabash Association in Fairfield. He came as pastor at Samaria Baptist Church, near Albion, while I was pastor at Grayville, First. I went on to become director of missions there and worked with Jim on a number of projects. He went on to serve Emmanuel, Mt. Carmel; Zif; and Hutsonville. He was a big, but gentle man; I'll miss him.

Maybe it's my seventieth birthday that's got me facing my mortality. Anyway, I think it's a good thing to do.

November 2001

I Like What I Like

No one ever accused me of being a musician but that doesn't keep me from enjoying the music I like. I took a required music appreciation course in college but the range of music I like is still somewhat limited.

Recently I joined a congregation in singing a hymn not usually thought of as being a Christmas song but its message rang true:

My Father's house of light,
    My glory-circled throne;
I left, for earthly night,
    For wand'rings sad and lone;
I left, I left it all for thee,
    Hast thou left aught for Me?
....
And I have brought to thee,
    Down from My home above,
Salvation full and free,
    My pardon and My love;
I bring, I bring rich gifts to thee,
    What hast thou brought to Me?

George H. Davis

I like most traditional Christmas music but I also find the Christmas message in a number of other songs. Frances Havergal certainly captured it in I Gave My Life for Thee. What's your nomination for a surprising Christmas song?

December 2001

Why does Paul Write of "Silly Women"?

In what is probably his last letter, Paul warns about people
who make their way into households and captivate silly women, overwhelmed by their sins and swayed by all kinds of desires, who are always being instructed and can never arrive at a knowledge of the truth (2 Timothy 36-7 NRSV).

I wonder why Paul singled out women and did not mention men. Is it only women who act silly or do men have trouble arriving "at a knowledge of the truth", too?

Hosea writes
Ephraim has become like a dove,
    silly and without sense;
    they call upon Egypt, they go to Assyria.
As they go, I will cast my net over them;
    I will bring them down like birds of the air (7:11-12).

If you've ever watched doves fly, you'll remember now they dart first this way then that.

January 2002

Baptist Ground Hog Day

Don Sharp used to speak of Race Relations Sunday as "Baptist Ground Hog Day." He saw it as a time when we (white and black) stick our heads out of our holes and look around then retreat back into them.

I have learned a lot about myself and about black Baptists from Don and others in Chicago. I was surprised that some African Americans were as scared to journey into southern Illinois as some of us used to be going through East St. Louis.

I remember a gathering of pastors (black and white). After we'd spent some time in prayer, one black minister confessed, "This is the first time I've prayed with a white man."

February 2002

It's Unofficial

Going by the birds I've seen lately, there's no doubt it's unofficially spring. Don't pay too much attention to a temporary setback; what's a one-inch blizzard going to do that would discourage us?

I've observed robins, killdeer, and meadow lark. I know that robins can be around all winter but I hadn't seen any on our prairie until recently.

I know it can snow while spring is trying to take hold. I remember a March 1, forty-nine years ago, when it snowed about six or eight inches while we were in church Sunday morning. We had gotten married the night before and had driven from Coulterville to Pinckneyville the next morning. My bride was teaching in Coulterville. You've never heard of a honeymoon in Coulterville?

I've heard that it snowed thirty-six inches on February 28, 1900. That was my paternal grandparents wedding day. They were married in Patoka.

Not only do I see migratory birds coming back into our area, I hear of churches in revival or planning for revival. About the only surer seasonal sign is a fall revival.

Since fewer and fewer of us are tied to farming, August revivals are falling by the wayside. It used to be thought that the farmer had nothing to do in August so we'd plan a revival then. Actually, a farmer seldom lacks something to do.

March 2002

Learning to Drive

I guess I've been driving for at least fifty-five years and I'm still learning. Last fall we bought a pickup and I've discovered it doesn't drive like a front-wheel-drive car.

Yes, I remember driving rear-wheel-drive vehicles, but I have gotten so used to front-wheel-drives that it has taken some adjustment.

During the winter (and I use that word carelessly), I followed a salt truck across part of the Kinoka Road. There was just a skiff of snow, or so I thought, until the salt truck pulled off and I went on. It wasn't long before I was all over the road, fighting too hard to stay between the ditches. I learned I needed some weight in the back end of that pickup to keep some traction with the road.

Where am I going with this? Well, hopefully, not in the ditch. But I notice a lot of people are winding up in the ditch. What kept me out was not driving skill but the grace of God. And that's not only true of my driving, but also of my life.

Wasn't it Paul who said, "So if you *think* you are standing, watch out that you do not fall" (1 Corinthians 10:12 NRSV)?

When I get to thinking I'm an expert driver, I'm in trouble. When I get to thinking I'm an expert Christian, I'm in trouble.

Different situations call for new skills and new vehicles don't always operate like old ones did. I need to be on my toes and to recognize my need of God's constant grace.

April 2002

Near Visits with Friends

On a recent Saturday my wife and I set out to return Bible School material to the Book Store. We got as far as the Rend Lake rest stop and decided that sounded like a good idea.

George H. Davis

I was waiting for Leona in the reception area when I noticed a familiar face—Junie Noonan and his brother Jerry had been faithful at Second Baptist in Herrin. The familiar face was Junie's. I spoke to him and he asked where my wife was and went to get Jerry. We had a good visit.

We stopped in Fairfield on our way home to visit friends there. The ladies had an open house to attend and David and I visited and managed the antique shop.

It wasn't long before a lady from Albion stopped by with her sister from El Paso (Illinois). I asked if she knew the pastor at the Baptist Church there. "Cheri?" she responded and then proceeded to name the rest of the family. It was almost like a visit with the Grizzards.

On the way home, we stopped at Salem for supper. As we were being seated, Leona asked if that wasn't Bob Easter entering the restaurant. I went to check and it was. Bob teaches swine production at the University of Illinois. He and his family were active in Pennsylvania Avenue Baptist in Urbana when we went there. Remembering they lived in Mahomet, I asked about Ric Hardison, on staff at Grace Baptist Church there. Bob responded that he had performed the wedding of their daughter and her husband. Another near visit.

One of the blessings of years of service is that you can run into friends anywhere.

May 2002

Does God Like Family Reunions?

I used to think family reunions were boring; they were for old people. About the only redeeming thing about them was the opportunity to take a row boat out on the lake at the Mt. Vernon City Park. The rest of the time was spent listening to old people talk.

Oh, how I wish I could turn the calendar back! I'd like to hear what those "old people" were saying. One of them was my Grandpa Davis. His grandfather moved his family from Surry County (NC) to Jefferson County (IL). His father moved from Jefferson County to Marion County.

When I was a kid, I didn't think there was much an older person could teach me; now I realize how little I know. There are so many questions I have now and there's no one to answer them. Now I'm one of the "old people." Bob Hope was quoted on his ninety-ninth birthday as saying, "There's nobody around to call me 'kid.'"

Our generation gathers each Memorial Day Sunday. While our parents were living, we tried to meet at Christmas, but with grown kids and grandkids, we're finding Memorial Day works better.

Sometimes pastors see family reunions as their enemies—they take people away from church services. Sometimes I wonder which God is more interested in, church services or family reunions. I guess I'd better let him answer that.

June 2002

by George

Is the World Getting Worse All the Time?

My first memory of saying the pledge of allegiance does not include the words "under God". That does not mean I was raised as a heathen but that I grew up before the 1950's; it was in the fifties that these two words were added.

Since then we're not necessarily any more Christian than those who grew up earlier. It takes more than reciting a few liturgical words to gain God's notice.

A ruling by a court in California has surely unsettled some people. But some of these same people will say, "*I told you* the world is getting worse all the time. Doesn't the Bible say so?"

Well, I guess my answer would have to be, "No." I haven't found that teaching in the Bible. I think it comes from those who already have their minds made up and then interpret the Bible according to their predisposition.

Jesus spoke about some false signs of His return, "You will hear of wars and rumors of wars; see that you are not alarmed; for this must take place, but the end is not yet" (Matthew 24:6 NRSV). He also gave a true sign, "This good news of the kingdom will be proclaimed to throughout the world, as a testimony to all the nations; then the end will come" (Matthew 24:14). I suspect we ought to pay more attention to what Jesus said than we do to what others say.

July 2002

I'm Not a Housekeeper

For the past six weeks I've struggled with my duties as a housekeeper. I've had the theory for some time that everyone is out of his or her element at times. When that happens, we struggle.

It doesn't mean we are dumb; only that nobody is smart about everything. I may know a little about theology and ministry but that doesn't make me an expert in every other area. I may know a little about Baptists that doesn't qualify me to speak for all Christians. When I get outside my fields of training and experience, I may be as lost as a goose.

After my wife's surgery, I tried to care for her. I attempted to prepare meals but if it hadn't been for the gracious ladies at First Baptist, Patoka we would have had to choke down some pretty poor excuses for food. She's a trained home economist and a good cook but I take a lot of supervision to get through meal preparation. Even then, it doesn't always taste that good.

I even discovered that I don't know much about doing laundry. When I was in college I did my own laundry, at least when I wasn't coming home for the weekend or didn't mail it home. I'm not kidding; I had a box I used to mail my laundry back and forth. I still have it's successor but haven't used it lately. I hope I don't have to use it again soon or resume my training as a chef.

September 2002

George H. Davis

Is Man Bad or Good?

I struggle with this question. I hear man presented as completely twisted and distorted and getting worse all the time. But then I hear stories of heroism and unselfish giving. Which is true? Is man bad or good or is he/she somewhere in between?

In the Bible I read testimony on both sides. In one place I read that God is ready to give up on man and destroy him. In another place I read of God's redemptive love for man.

Whatever our conclusion about man's moral value, I think we have to make it jibe with our understanding of Jesus Christ. Theologians proclaim (and I agree) that Jesus is "fully God; fully man." If man is of no moral value, what does that say about Jesus?

Paul says that in Adam we die and in Christ we live. I take that to mean that as we follow in Adam's rebellion we incur exclusion from Eden. As we follow Christ we share in his Paradise. I don't see sin as being transmitted by sexual activity, nor do I see it being stopped by sexual inactivity. Sin is not only physical; it's also spiritual.

If man is evil, when did he get that way? When God made him, he proclaimed him "very good." I know that we put a lot of emphasis on a "fall." I'm not sure the Bible has that much to say about it. I think I'm ready to go back to some of the classic theologians; popular theology doesn't satisfy. I sometimes fail to recognize the man I'm hearing described.

November 2002

This Little Church Went to Market

Gary E. Gilley wrote a book with this title but I haven't been able to find it yet. I've wondered how he develops the idea. Here are some of *my* thoughts.

This little church went to market. They called a pastor who was into demographics and bought into a marketing philosophy. Their message was pitched toward the unchurched. Their services were a mix of entertainment and enlistment.

This little church stayed home. "Old Time Religion" was their theme. If it was good enough for Paul and Silas—actually, they more often patterned after their own grandfathers; they weren't into being too radical.

This little church had roast beef. "The best is none too good for us" was their motto. They built a larger, finer building. There was nothing wrong with their old building but it didn't project a very good image in the community. They didn't get too excited about missions. "After all," they reasoned, "If we don't take care of ourselves, who will take care of us?"

This little church had none. They took pride in being little. They had no bulletin, no budget, no calendar; if you just repeat what you've been doing, why would you need these things?

This little church cried, "Wee, wee, wee," all the way home. "What do they expect of us? We're just a little church," was their predictable response to every challenge. They felt they couldn't do anything and lived up to that expectation.

December 2002

by George

I Believe My Memory is Improving

I have recently discovered that my memory is improving. Well, perhaps I should qualify "improve." I don't mean to imply that the improvement has been across the board. What I've discovered is that I remember longer, that is, "farther back" than some do.

I'm not sure whether this is a byproduct of age or if there are other factors. I first noticed it when Bill Weedman and I were talking about the death of a former director of missions. He said, "You're probably the only active director of missions who remembers him." At first, I was stunned; then I realized he was probably right.

Since then I've noticed that it's not unusual for me to remember persons or events from the 1940's or 1950's. What scares me is that doesn't seem to be that long ago. I've also noticed that some people around me don't remember those things.

January 2003

One Hundred Year Old Letter Provides Clues

I recently received a copy of a letter written on February 25, 1900. But the really staggering thing was that it was written by my Grandpa Davis' sister. She writes to a cousin in Texas:

> I don't guess you kenw he [her brother, Willie] was dead am sorry I havent written sooner, he died the third of November. Our family seems to be breaking up very fast, But our heaven father knows what is best. There is just three of us in family Oscar came home from Idho about the twenty fifth of November. Oscar is not at home now he is in St. Lowis but is coming home tomorrow, and will be married Wensday, The girls name is Kate Wasem. They are going to live with us.

I knew several facts about my great-grandfather's family. He and Hester Richardson were married in 1869. Within less than twenty years they would lose a son and three daughters. Then, in 1899 Hester and the oldest son died. It's no wonder Rose (the letter writer) says "our family seems to be breaking up very fast." Ironically, she would die within three years.

Oscar and Kate did marry on February 28, 1900 and moved into that house—the house where I would spend my early years. In December 1900 Oscar bought land one-half mile east, where we now live. My grandparents would live there until 1938 when they moved into town and our family moved into this house.

March 2003

Dissent Observed

When a doctor was shot outside a medical clinic, a group of prolife and prochoice church leaders became concerned about the depth of feelings developing in their city.

George H. Davis

They agreed to meet and seek solutions but not to release findings until they could do so unanimously. They met for several years.

I was reminded of this by the dissent over the War in Iraq. Then I thought back to our doctrinal wars in the Southern Baptist Convention. Some would say the battles were more political than doctrinal. A pastor observes, "It's not what color the carpet will be; it's *who gets to say* what color the carpet will be."

When we start taking sides (whatever the issue) one of the first things we do is choose as bad a name as we can think of for the other side and as good a name we can think of for ourselves. Each side tries to get their story out to the media and tries to smear the other side.

What grabbed my attention about the church leaders meeting was that they agreed not to use names the other side found objectionable. That's so differently than we usually operate. We find it hard not to take sides and even harder not to let our prejudices sway our conclusions.

Few of us can remain pure observers; the fight draws us into the fray. Before we know it we have moved from questioning to shouting.

April 2003

I Hate It When This Happens

I hate it when everybody piles in at church at the same time. To begin with, someone got my parking place. Everybody knows that place belongs to me (I probably shouldn't have put my name on it). Our family has been going to church here since before the war—the Spanish American War, that is.

Then I got inside and tried to find my pew. Guess what? Somebody's got it. How could they not know that's my place? You don't suppose they just don't care, do you? I had to go clear down to the second row; talk about embarrassing.

To top it all off, they moved your Sunday School class. We'd met for years in our own class room. A while back someone decided we could meet in the kitchen and some of the kids could use our room. I thought the Bible taught you were supposed to respect your elders; but they just push us around when ever and where ever they want.

When I got ready to leave, I had to wait for ten minutes for people behind me to move. Talk about inconsiderate! Well, I can tell you one thing for sure. They won't have me to push around next week.

Have you ever had feelings like these?

May 2003

The Good Old Summer Time

Sprouting and growing is what summer is all about. Two of our most intensive activities take place then—Vacation Bible School and Camp. Both of them rank high in starting children and youth on their way in following Jesus.

Listen to Christians you respect and you'll hear them talk about more than one turning point in their life. For many of us, it's not "once for all" but "pressing on the upward way."

For me Camp was Royal Ambassador Camp at Lake Sallateeska. I still remember us singing Send the Light as a boat carried a light across the Lake. I made my first public decision for Christ there. Our pastor encouraged me to share that decision with our Church.

It was a few years later when I made another life changing decision. I realized I was only a nominal Christian and decided to take my vows to follow Christ more seriously. Paul Carleton, then pastor at First Baptist Church of Vandalia, spoke directly to me at a Baptist Student Union event in Carbondale.

It wasn't long before I felt God was calling me to preach. Though I sometimes faltered along that way, it became the road I would travel. Scores of people encouraged me and without them I'd have had a much more difficult time getting up and getting back on the path.

That's what our job is—planting seed and making it easier for it to grow. I hope we're not too busy for that.

June 2003

How Time and Distance Change

When I was growing up it took forty-five minutes to get to Salem. We knew that because the really important trips were to the Salem swimming pool and we knew how long it took to get there.

Now keep in mind, that was before we had the 55 mile per hour speed limit. Yes, I remember the 35 mile per hour limit during the War but I was not driving then.

Now we can get to Salem in about half an hour. How do we manage to clip 15 minutes off our driving time? Is the difference in our desire to get wet?

Our alternatives were the creek south of our house or a salt pit. We tried the salt pit once but nearly itched to death before we could get home and rinse off the salt. I learned only recently that the creek is called Louse Run. If my brothers and I had known that, we'd never have dipped a toe in it. I notice the Marion County Farm Bureau plat book inserts an "i" to clean it up a little. Louise does sound better than Louse, don't you think?

It's interesting how our perceptions change over the years. We didn't hesitate long to jump in the creek after we'd seen a snake there. Our theory was that they wouldn't bite underwater. Of course, we didn't stay under long to test our theory.

July 2003

The Least Generation

Tom Brokaw wrote about those involved in World War II in The Greatest Generation. Intending no disrespect to Mr. Brokaw nor to his focus generation, I want to highlight another group. Jesus said, "the least among all of you is the greatest" (Luke 9:48c NRSV).

Let me tell you about a group that meet these criteria: they attended college at Southern Illinois University, Carbondale in the 1940's and were involved in the Baptist Student Union. How many do you suppose could be found? Would it surprise you if I said eighty-eight made reservations for a recent reunion?

You don't need to be a genius to figure out that most of the attendees were in their seventies. Fourteen have been pastors; twelve have served as foreign missionaries. Most are lay members active in their churches.

Actually, I have to stretch just a little to get into this elite group. I enrolled in college as a freshman in the fall of 1949. But it was the spring of 1950 before I bumped into the BSU.

These two groups (Brokaw's and mine) are tied together by some common threads. Many of the college students of the 1940's were veterans of World War II. They came home with a call to serve God. Some battled with this call before answering.

They have made a tremendous impact on their communities and the world. One way they did this was by adopting John's motto: "He [Jesus] must increase, I must decrease" (John 3:30).

October 2003

Bringing in the Sheeps?

I remember hearing about a child emerging from church one Sunday morning singing lustily, Bringing in the sheeps, Bringing in the sheeps, We shall some rejoicing bringing in the sheeps.

I don't know whether you've noticed but "Bringing in the Sheaves" is not included in our most recent *Baptist Hymnal*. I don't know why, but it may be because sheaves is not a commonly used word. According to the *Merriam Webster's Collegiate Dictionary, Tenth Edition* "sheaves" is the plural of "sheaf." Sheaf is "a quantity of a cereal grass...bound together." A few of us are still around who have shocked wheat but most have no first hand experience with sheaves.

The song is a good one that balances sowing and reaping and many of us in this area know something about this:
Sowing in the morning, sowing seeds of kindness,
Sowing in the noontide, and the dewy eve;
Waiting for the harvest, and the time of reaping,
We shall come rejoicing, bringing in the sheaves.

Sowing in the sunshine, sowing in the shadows;
Fearing neither clouds nor winter's chilling breeze;
By and by the harvest, and the labor ended,
We shall come rejoicing, bringing in the sheaves.

by George

Going forth with weeping, sowing for the Master,
Tho' the loss sustained our spirit often grieves;
When our weeping's over, He will bid us welcome,
We shall come rejoicing, bringing in the sheaves.
Knowles Shaw (1834-1878)

November 2003

A Quiet Thanksgiving

As we left home for Thanksgiving with our children and grandchildren, I said goodbye to the rabbits and quail around the house; I wished them a quiet holiday.

One of our family traditions has been to go hunting on Thanksgiving afternoon. We might or might not carry a gun and we might or might not see any game; we had a good time.

It has been a while since we've indulged in that practice. My wife suggested that none of the game now living around the house remembered the hunts. It wasn't that we had killed so many but that we hadn't hunted them for several years. As I reviewed the years I didn't remember hearing any quail last year. Maybe the coyotes had gotten to them.

Then I remembered a Thanksgiving in Champaign when we got enough snow that we decided not to try going to Patoka. I don't remember much else about that day.

The first time I heard about shopping the Friday after Thanksgiving was when we lived in Grayville. A family there drove to Evansville, Indiana and spent the day shopping. That was in the early 1970's. Now you're almost considered unpatriotic if you don't spend the day shopping. I like eating leftovers better.

December 2003

Are We Missing Our Commission?

Have we misunderstood our commission? We seem to focus on getting people to make an initial decision for Christ but give little attention to their development as disciples. Our marching orders are to make disciples.

Should we be going back to see what's happening in the life of new converts a few months to a year after their initial decision? Can we assume that their growth will be automatic? I don't think so.

As a denomination we don't seem to have a program which helps Christians grow. For years we had Baptist Young People's Union, then Baptist Training Union, then Church Training. Now we seem to be floundering. There's little attention given to the development of disciples.

When it became apparent that our Sunday night programs were dying, some churches experimented with trying to do it all on Sunday morning. They'd start with Discipleship and follow with Bible Study, then worship.

George H. Davis

I remember being on the edge of a group of pastors who were asking the pastor of an experimental church what they did on Sunday night. "We stay home and watch Bonanza like God intended," was his reply.

January 2004

Can't Get Out of the Rut?

I remember when ruts were not thought of as our enemies. If you learned to drive on roads where the lanes were not marked, you'll remember taking the path that was the smoothest or surest. If several people took that path or if you took it often enough, ruts were cut in that road.

But ruts weren't always a bad thing; sometimes they helped guide us. If the roads were muddy we sometimes deliberately got into the ruts and followed them to our destination, or until we came to a better road. The ruts would help us steer. Without them we might be all over the road.

One of the problems we ran into was when the ground was frozen. Those ruts could give you quite a jolt as you bounced over them. Of course if the ruts got too deep we might get stuck and have to get pulled out.

If we met someone else using our ruts, we might be in trouble. I heard about two drivers like this. They managed to get stopped before any damage was done. They each got out and one hollered, "I never back up for a fool." Whereupon the other replied, "That's all right. I always do."

Now that most of our roads are improved, we've come full circle—we buy off-the-road vehicles. Can you beat that?

I've heard that ruts are graves with both ends knocked out. Now we're more apt to find the ruts in our minds.

February 2004

"Somebody said OK"

John and I were shopping; he's one of my brothers. Maybe I should tell you about our shopping practices. No, I guess that's not necessary. Suffice it to say that our wives usually release us from their supervision while we shop.

Anyway, we were wandering through a store. As I remember, there were a number of expensive toys there. I heard a child's voice quite distinctly; I didn't turn to identify him. I did allow my mind to wonder how he had gotten into trouble.

It didn't take much imagination to put him in a tight place. He had done something for which he had not received permission. He was inventive though, "Somebody said OK" was his alibi. He wasn't sure where the voice came from but he had clearly gotten approval.

Not having to name the source of your authority has certain advantages. You can say, "Everybody's doing it" or "My friends are doing it." But this youngster clearly had reached the pinnacle of permission—"Somebody said OK." He had taken it out of the realm of having to identify his source and could substantiate even an imaginary endorser. Gone was the burden of having to give chapter and verse.

I like the way this kid thinks; he may grow up to be a politician or a preacher some day. I can hear him promising, "*Somebody* said OK."

March 2004

A United Baptist Church?

When Patoka celebrated her sesquicentennial over Labor Day weekend, all four churches participated with floats in the parade and in having a community service Sunday morning. One thing that caught my eye was the names of the churches. Two had United in their names and two did not. The Methodist and the Pentecostal were named United Methodist and United Pentecostal. The Baptist and the Christian did not include this description in their names.

The more I thought about it, the more truth I saw in these names. Back in our history, some Baptist Churches were known as United Baptists but that has been some time ago. The thing that bothers me is not just the name but the fact that we are not united. I know it takes more than a name to make you united but I also thought about the years of division Southern Baptists have gone through. It hasn't taken much for us to fight over. Most recently we have disassociated ourselves with the Baptist World Alliance.

I know that some things are worth fighting over but, in my opinion, most of our recent fights are as much political as doctrinal. I'd like to see us recognize each other as brothers and sisters. I'd like to see us try to get along rather than try to put each other down.

September 2004

Building Blocks of My Life

As I took back over my life, I think of institutions that have been building blocks. I'll start with Baptist Training Union (BTU). Training Union was basically a Sunday evening program which focused on growing as a Christian. It differed from Sunday School in that it began with an area of Christian living rather than a scripture passage. We might see what light the Bible had to shed, but we always started with a topic and tried to develop it.

The main difference was that group members rather than a teacher presented various parts. Yes, sometimes we *read* them, but we were learning to speak before a group.

The next life builder was 4-H Club. It was an organization for youth, especially in rural and small town areas. It had a broad focus: head, heart, hands, and health. Though it was not specifically a Christian group, we found remarkable matches in Jesus' growth: He "increased in wisdom [head] and stature [health] and in favor with God [heart] and man [hands]" (Luke 2:52).

George H. Davis

We learned to care for animals, machinery, and ourselves. We also learned to present our project to the club.

A third builder was Baptist Student Union, now called Baptist Campus Ministries. They attempted to provide a link between the college student and the church. It was definitely a Christian organization.

There was a wide emphasis starting with evangelism, continuing with Christian growth and development. There were also opportunities for ministry.

Baptist associations have offered me opportunities to develop and grow. Fellowship between churches and skill development were spotlighted. One of the basic procedures was to train someone in a particular area and give them the opportunity to share their area of expertise. Leaders were developed and given recognition.

October 2004

Ask Van about the Cheer He Got

I was visiting First Baptist Church in Louisville Sunday morning, October 17. It happened that they had chosen that day to show their pastor, Van McQueen, how much they appreciate him. He was in the dark about their plans but noticed that some were bringing food and remarked that no one had told him there was to be a meal. He also knew that someone has named October as Pastor Appreciation month.

So, things proceeded rather normally. I sat in on the men's Sunday School class and then went into the sanctuary for worship. Still, not much out of the ordinary. Van preached a strong sermon from Revelation 13 (it was rather extraordinary).

After the invitation, the chairman of deacons stepped forward and presented the pastor with a card. Then he asked a young lady to continue. She had selected and rehearsed 12 to 15 youth and children. Under her leadership they gave the pastor a hearty cheer. They were wearing sports and school clothing and sounded like they were at a basketball game.

Their enthusiasm and energy were delightful; their genuineness was refreshing. We all enjoyed it. The next time you see Van, ask him about the cheer he got. He'll be glad to share it with you.

November 2004

What Do I Owe You?

I took my car to the Chevrolet dealer in St. Elmo. All the mechanics were busy but the shop manager offered to look at it. He soon had it running smoothly. When I asked him how much I owed him, he replied, "You probably can't pay me what I'm worth."

I grew up in the country. It was not unusual for people to walk to our house after becoming stuck on one of the roads around us. For a long time we had a mile of dirt road to get to a gravel road.

I remember Dad getting the team out, or later, starting the tractor. He'd make sure he had sufficient log chain.

Some people had little idea how to drive on a mud road. Others overestimated their driving ability.

Almost without fail, once they were back on solid ground, people would ask, "How much do I owe you?" Just as predictable, Dad's reply was, "Nothing." He would be upset if a person made a habit of getting stuck and depending on us to get them out. But he would get insulted if a person insisted on paying. He intended to be a good neighbor. He would not take advantage of anyone.

The truth was there might be a time when we needed help and he wouldn't hesitate to ask. Some of his children have benefited from his brand of neighborliness.

December 2004

Stay by the Stuff

I used 1 Samuel 30:24 as the text for a sermon. The story goes like this: David and his men had been out fighting and when they came home, they discovered that the Amalekites had captured their wives and children; Israel was about to stone David.

David gathered 400 of his troops and pursued the enemy. 200 of his men had been too exhausted to join in the battle. The enemy was captured but when David returned home this time he faced another problem. Those who had gone into battle didn't want to share their spoil with those who had "stayed by the stuff" as the King James version puts it.

David proclaimed a new law: As his share is who goes into the battle, so shall his share be who stays by the stuff; they shall share alike.

Some friends who heard the sermon found a refrigerator magnet with a saying by George Carlin: "Home is where you keep your stuff while you go out and buy other stuff." We still laugh about that.

I was reminded of that recently. I finally got around to telling my wife what I wanted for Christmas. "What I really need," I said, "is a pair of insulated coveralls; not Carhartts, because I couldn't live up to them."

Then she asked where my boots were and I began chasing down ideas. Then I remembered to look in a winter bag I carry with me in the truck; maybe they were in there. No luck, but guess what I found? Yes, I found a pair of coveralls I had bought last year and not yet worn. My problem is remembering where the stuff is!

January 2005

Old Friends

Many African societies divide humans into three categories: the still alive, the living dead, and the dead.

George H. Davis

The recently departed whose time on earth overlapped with people still here are the living dead. They are not wholly dead, for they still live in the memories of the living, who can call them to mind and bring them to life in anecdote. When the last person to know an ancestor dies, that person leaves the living dead to join the dead. The dead are not forgotten but revered (James W. Loewen, *Lies My Teacher Taught Me*, Simon & Schuster, 1995, page 239).

The opportunity to attend visitations and/or funerals for people I have known have made these concepts ring true for me. Lloyd Sinclair's funeral set me to remembering his dad—Clyde. I remember him well but I recognize that the herd of those who knew him is vanishing.

He pastored Meacham and at Greenland in the 1950's, at Wabash in the late sixties into the seventies. Then he served Second Little Prairie in 1975.

The forty years since our times of close fellowship make me glad there's another category—the alive again. By God's grace He will raise us up to enjoy that fellowship throughout eternity.

February 2005

Happy Father's Day

My idea of shopping is to know what I want and go get it. There's no need to browse or wander. There are a couple of exceptions. One is for tools and the other is for books.

We were on our way home from a trip to the doctor when Leona (without warning) said, "I want to stop here." She gave a general indication of which side of the street she was headed for.

Since I was driving, she was dependent on my good grace. Fortunately, I was in a tolerable mood. Of course, I stayed in the car while she squandered our time.

After a while she reappeared with a package. "Happy Father's Day," she cheered. I never claimed to be the sharpest tool in the shed, but neither was that my finest hour. Within a week of Father's Day I was pouting instead of smiling.

When we got home, Leona was patient while I tried to assemble whatever it was. What it was was three fans made of ribbon, turning opposite directions.

I realize how hard this is to conceptualize, but believe me, I've learned a lesson. We'll see how long it lasts.

June 2005

by George

Printed in the United States
152775LV00004B/8/P